HOSTAGE

Paul Chandler is a Cambridge-educated civil engineer and Rachel Chandler is a former government economist. Both have a passion for sailing and travelling, and honed their seamanship skills over some 30 years in the waters around the UK and the Mediterranean. The couple have enjoyed a part-time sailing lifestyle since retiring from full-time employment in 2005 and recently renewed their cruising adventures after restoring *Lynn Rival* in Dartmouth, Devon.

Sarah Edworthy is an experienced journalist who spent 16 years at the *Daily Telegraph* and currently writes for a variety of national publications and websites.

HOSTAGE

A Year at Gunpoint with
SOMALI GANGSTERS

Paul and Rachel Chandler

with Sarah Edworthy

MAINSTREAM
PUBLISHING

EDINBURGH AND LONDON

This edition, 2012

First published in Great Britain in 2011 by
MAINSTREAM PUBLISHING COMPANY
(EDINBURGH) LTD
7 Albany Street
Edinburgh EH1 3UG

ISBN 9781780575926

A catalogue record for this book is available
from the British Library

Printed in Great Britain by
CPI Group (UK) Ltd, Croydon, CR0 4YY

1 3 5 7 9 10 8 6 4 2

To the hundreds of seafarers held hostage by Somali pirates
– and their families. You are not forgotten.

Contents

Contents.

Glossary

Transliterations of Somali words as recorded in our diaries.

abbay – father
adan – white
af – tongue
alen – 'tea' leaves
ambi – mango
aniga – I/me
ari – goat
ashok – supper
athiga – you

baholi – bowl
banjo – fat
barballe – bottle
baree – tomorrow
basto – spaghetti
behr – liver
bes-bes – chilli
bilod – months, moons
bim – the sound of a gunshot
biu – water
bocol – 100
briis – rice
brr – bread
budde – small boat

cabadi – later, after

cadu – lunch
chad – narcotic green plant
contun – 50
courrah – breakfast
cun – 1,000

dabagaale – squirrel-like animal
daqika – minute
deri – tall
digir – beans
doxi – fly

ell – well

fadlun – please

ghodarr – vegetable sauce
gil – camel
guri – house

habeen – evening
hadha – now
hal – 1
halkan – outside
halkas – inside

9

haram – forbidden
hilip – meat
ho – here!

kam – how many?
ken – give me
kiss kiss – step by step
kitab – book
kursi – chair

lin – lime
lin bombelmo – grapefruit
lobaten – 20
lobo – 2

ma'awiis – skirt worn by Somali men
maga'a – name
magas – scissors
mahatsenit – thank you
mahwille – leader
maia – no
malmod – days
mante – today
midi – knife
mort – killed

nag(ti) – (my) woman

nin – man

pochuko – barbecue

Riija – Rachel

sadambe – day after tomorrow
sadden – 30
sadeh – 3
sagara – small deer
sahibki – friend
sano – year
segashen – 90
sheh – 'tea'
shun – 5
sideeten – 80
son – fast (not eating)
sooker – sugar
tadobaad – week
tadobo – 7
toban – 10
trrup – playing cards
tuk – thief

wahir – small
wain – big

yr – and

Prologue

Early December 2009

Shrouded in white tarpaulin, with her name heavily taped over, a 38-foot yacht arrives by road at Bucklers Hard, near Lymington in Hampshire. Without ceremony, the anonymous boat is propped up on sturdy timbers to wait for her owners to claim her. The boatyard is almost full to capacity now that the last few haul-outs are done. Owners come and go, 'winterising' their vessels – draining engine oil, topping up anti-freeze, removing berth cushions and other items prone to mildew. Repairs are carried out at slow tempo in nearby sheds. Boats are given one last look over, then securely covered. It's a time for reflection. The end of one sailing season is the cue to dream about the next.

Shrewd winter winds play on the tarpaulins, then abate and blow more freshly as if keen to fill sails. In early spring, owners return to check their boats, discuss estimates for works and prepare for launch. The yard once again bustles with workers carrying out maintenance, installing new equipment, moving boats in and out of the repair sheds while sailing folk in cheery fleeces and Puffa jackets share chatter about proposed cruises and the latest gizmos.

In this busy, convivial world of cleaning, mending, painting and anti-fouling, the mystery boat remains untended, unremarked upon. No one knows her provenance. No one imagines her extraordinary story. No one guesses that here, under a tarpaulin beside the Solent – in a boatyard famed for its construction of Nelson's favourite ship, the 64-gun HMS *Agamemnon* – is a notorious international crime scene, preserved as if it were a time capsule of six days of claustrophobic trauma. The barnacles encrusted around her scuppers are from the Indian Ocean. The scratches and scrape marks hidden from view on her duck-egg blue fibreglass hull are scars inflicted by pirates slamming attack skiffs up against her sides. A teak grab rail has been smashed by the blunt metal of a gun; hatch stays are bent and hinges shorn where her hatch cover has been ripped off. A clean entry-and-exit hole on the boom marks the spot where a Kalashnikov bullet whistled through.

Below deck, disarray indicates a brutal ransacking and rushed departure. The orderly wood-panelled saloon that has provided homeliness for three decades of cruising has been violated by 'pirates' who lolled insolently on the bunks, nervily toted guns and turned out every carefully packed shelf, drawer and locker in their single-minded bid for money. A cuddly gorilla, the boat's mascot, lies on the floor, toppled from its chart-table perch, next to a dagger wrapped in an ikat-dyed *ma'awiis*, a traditional Somali sarong-style men's skirt. A single leather sandal, adorned in favoured pirate style with 'Good-Time Charlie' gold buckles, lies discarded in a corner of the for'ard cabin. Mould grows where rice and flour supplies have spilled; cooking oil from a container labelled 'The Gift of Ireland via the World Food Programme' coats the galley floor.

This is *Lynn Rival*. Just weeks before her arrival in Bucklers Hard she had been attacked while cruising in the Seychelles archipelago, boarded by a gang of kidnappers and extortionists, and set on a course towards Somalia. After 6 days, and 500 nautical miles, she had been cut adrift as her owners, Paul and Rachel Chandler, were forced on board a 184-metre container ship, the Singapore-flagged MV *Kota Wajar,* also under control of pirates. They were transferred ashore, held hostage in the Somali bush and left to grieve for the loss of the vessel that was their life, their sense of purpose, the 'third person in the relationship'.

To all who had sailed in her, *Lynn Rival* was the purveyor of a no-nonsense, go-anywhere, blue-water cruising lifestyle.

She had borne her owners on many happy holidays with family and friends around the Mediterranean, and latterly on more adventurous, painstakingly planned voyages across the Aegean and into the Red Sea, from Oman to Mumbai, down the Indian coast to Cochin, to the Maldives and on to the Seychelles. 'A little bit of Britain in the Indian Ocean', she enabled her owners to fulfil an elemental urge to explore the world. She had hosted scenes of conviviality among kindred-spirited cruising couples as the Chandlers exchanged anecdotes, books, local knowledge and the odd clink of a glass in harbourside camaraderie. Bulletins of her travels were appreciated by extended family via a cruising blog and the satphone that Paul's 98-year-old father – who had relished the *Lynn Rival* enterprise – had given as a present.

Who would have thought that this would be *Lynn Rival*'s fate? Having begun life in the back garden of the Old Rectory in Norfolk, proudly built by Michael Morris, a surgeon at King's Lynn Hospital, for his retirement in the 1980s, she is now the first British sailing yacht to fall victim to 'piracy' on the increasingly unruly waters of the Indian Ocean.

By late April 2010 the yard has all but emptied of seaworthy boats except for *Lynn Rival* and a few other sad, neglected yachts standing on props, waiting for skippers and action. Disguised by her insurers from the media and from bounty hunters, she remains under wraps, 'under the radar' as it were, through that spring of 2010, and throughout the summer and autumn of that year. Friday, 29 October passes, a year to the day when she was left, bobbing and battered, in the ocean off Somalia. Will she end up like the slowly rotting hulk standing on props next to her, neither sailed nor sold? Or will she be spruced up magnificently, like the yacht on her other side, ready for another joyous cruising season? Her fate depends on that of Paul and Rachel, who are still held captive more than 4,000 miles away in Somalia . . .

Would they ever return to her? If they did, would they ever contemplate sailing again? And, if so, could they ever banish the ghosts of what happened on board their beloved boat?

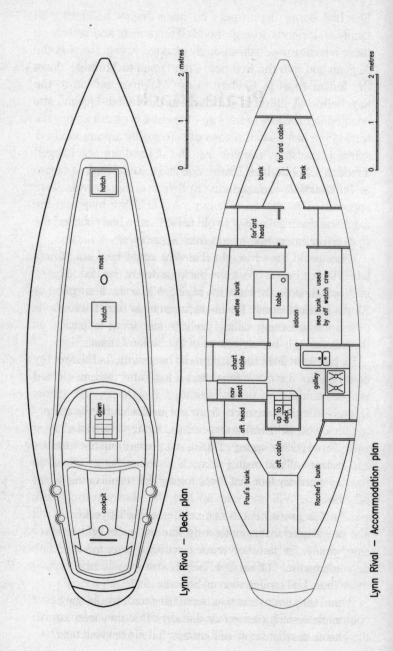

hatch

hatch

down

cockpit

mast

Lynn Rival – Deck plan

for'ard cabin

bunk

bunk

for'ard head

settee bunk

soloon

table

sea bunk – used by off watch crew

chart table

galley

nav seat

aft head

up to deck

aft cabin

Paul's bunk

Rachel's bunk

Lynn Rival – Accommodation plan

Pirate attack

The night is murky, with neither moon nor starry constellations to lighten the dark expanses of sea and sky around us. As we motor-sail onward, only the occasional whirring of the electric autopilot interrupts the all-encompassing drone of the engine. My head is fuzzy and I'm feeling queasy. I sit on deck next to the wheel, trying not to look at my watch. Time is passing slowly tonight. I go through the motions: keeping a look out, monitoring the instruments, allowing myself to doze in the knowledge that my alarm will buzz every 11 minutes to keep me alert.

Today has been a classic case of me thinking, 'Why am I doing this?' The first three days of a long sail are tough. Once I get my sea legs, I'm fine. We prepare ourselves by eating well and resting as much as we can, but it's often not until day four that I stop feeling sick. Paul is usually OK.

When we left Port Victoria in the Seychelles yesterday for Tanzania, the winds were forecast to be light and variable. In fact, they have been against us from the south-west. The swell is coming from the south-east. There isn't enough wind to drive us comfortably through the 'uppy-downy' sea, and we've been forced to sail on a more westerly course than intended. The conditions are nauseating. I am low and grumpy, but determined to do

15

my full watch because Paul needs his sleep. Two hours in, I'm telling myself that I'll get a lie-down soon, that at least it's warm, and in forty-eight hours I will feel fine.

The wind is dropping and the sails are no longer filling. I should take them down and change course back to the direct route for the Amirante Islands. It is almost 0230. There's a strange noise, a new hum noticeable above the familiar throb of our engine. It sounds like something approaching from astern. I glance over my shoulder and discern through the darkness an unlit narrow open boat accelerating towards us. Who can this be? There are fishermen in the area – we saw one at around 2100 – but they usually keep their distance. To be homed in on by a vessel at night is unusual. I fear the worst – a hostile attack – but I hope there is another explanation. After all, we are in the Seychelles archipelago, less than a day's sailing from the main island of Mahé.

I grab a torch and direct it at the boat. A skiff packed with shadowy figures is now almost upon us. Two shots ring out, making me drop the torch in fright. A jumble of arms get ready to grab hold of our guard wires, men jostling to clamber on board, guns clattering. The 16-foot, flat-bottomed skiff slams into our side.

Without thinking, I put up my hands and shout, 'No guns, no guns!' I want them to know we are unarmed. A second skiff appears within seconds on the other side to complete the entrapment. My mind races. Who are these people and what do they want? But I have no time to think. They are hostile, and I must concentrate on staying alive.

There is a tremendous kerfuffle as eight black men, mostly young and gangly, scramble over the rails, stumbling and struggling to find room to stand on the narrow deck while keeping hold of their guns. At least five rifles point menacingly at me. The men shout at each other in an incomprehensible language. A few have small torches. Narrow rays of light rake the air, randomly highlighting whites of eyes in nervous faces. Some wrestle to tie on their skiffs, while others seek to establish some authority over us. They bark commands at me in basic English.

'Stop engine!'

'Lights!'

I'm frozen to my spot behind the wheel, with my hands up, but realise I must do as they say. I shift the gear lever to put the engine into neutral and switch on the deck light. We slow down and start wallowing in the ocean swell with the boom swinging from side to side. The men are jumpy, still shouting at one another, gesticulating with their guns.

'Crew? Number?'

'Two. Me. And man,' I shout, indicating below.

'Crew, up, up!'

One attacker keeps shouting for lights, but we already have all our lights on. We don't have the capacity to light up like a Christmas tree! They are waiting for something, nervously scanning the surrounding sea, fighting to hold on with the movement of the boat, hindered by the boom swinging back and forth. I realise they want more lights so that others, following behind, can locate them. They seem as confused as me as to what happens next.

I'm slowly beginning to think. Our attackers must be Somali pirates. How did they get here, so far from Somalia, so close to the Seychelles? Why are the warships not stopping them? What is the Seychelles coastguard doing with all the new resources they are supposed to be deploying? Why weren't we warned when we left Port Victoria? Surely these groups of pirates must be easy to spot.

'Paul! Please come up,' I call out tensely, horrified by what is happening to us.

Paul sleeps naked and uncovered on the starboard bunk in the saloon. It's the most comfortable berth in the tropical heat and humidity.

I'd become conscious of an increase in engine speed, then the crack of gunshots brings me to full wakefulness. I hear Rachel scream, 'No guns! No guns!', and sit up in shock, frozen. There is a lot of noise from above, thumps to the side of the hull, shouting in a strange language and slamming of hatches on deck. I wrestle with the choice – Y-fronts or contact lenses? Or should I hide in the forecabin? Instead, I press the big red button on the EPIRB (Emergency Position Indicating Radio Beacon) and warily climb up the steep steps to the deck.

The cockpit is full of dark men standing on the seats with guns aimed at Rachel and now at me. The overcast sky prevents all but the occasional light from the moon. The man questioning Rachel looks at me.

I indicate my nakedness and point below: 'Clothes?'

The man gestures OK, so I drop back to the saloon and grab T-shirt, pants and shorts. I'm keen to get back on deck and keep their attention away from the EPIRB, its light flashing as it sends out a distress signal. I know if it is only on for a short time we can't rely on its signal being received.

Back in the cockpit, I exchange glances with Rachel. Our attackers make it clear we must keep quiet. And apart. They keep asking, 'Men? Crew?' They expect us to have more crew on board. We repeat, 'Only two.' Men go below to check.

Another looks closely at Rachel: 'You, man? Woman?'

With her short hair, dressed in polo top and leggings, they're not sure.

We wait for their next move. What do these thugs want from us? At least they have not realised that the EPIRB is transmitting. I wish it didn't have such an obvious flashing light giving away its activation . . .

Once activated, the EPIRB sends a signal every 50 seconds or so, via satellite, to the UK Maritime and Coastguard Agency. If it's doing its stuff, Falmouth will soon be forwarding data to the Seychelles coastguard, who should launch a search-and-rescue operation. A search by aircraft and coastguard vessels will easily find us come dawn. We have to be patient and sit out the next few hours as calmly as possible.

Another boat slams into our stern; more men clamber aboard. More guns. One of the new arrivals takes charge. He stares at us, then grunts instructions to the others. More clambering about, weapons being passed around; then, with much banging on deck, two rocket launchers and a bag of rocket-propelled grenades (RPG) are taken from the skiffs up to *Lynn Rival*'s foredeck.

The new boat is a larger open vessel, like an old-fashioned ship's lifeboat. This must be their mother boat, laden with barrels of supplies. Two men tie her on to the stern of *Lynn Rival*. The alpha male tells us his name is Buggas – he's strong and heavily built, about 5 ft 9 in., and looks to be in his early 30s. Buggas demands to know our nationality.

'You French?'

'No, British,' we say, indicating our red ensign, which is hanging limp on the flagstaff in the calm.

He points to our drooping Seychelles courtesy flag at the spreaders and insists, 'France! France!'

Is he worried or keen that we might be French?

'No, British,' we repeat.

Buggas doesn't seem happy. He breaks off to go below and look around. He notices the EPIRB flashing and angrily gestures at it, shouting for Paul to go below and switch it off.

I turn off the EPIRB and, surprisingly, Buggas leaves it sitting on the chart table.

Is this a nightmare? Attacked by pirates less than 60 miles west of the main island of Mahé, where 17 hours earlier we completed our departure formalities at the capital, Port Victoria. We're still well within the Seychelles

19

archipelago. About 70 miles west lie the northernmost islands of the Amirantes, one of the outer groups of islands much loved by couples seeking a quiet romantic getaway. And roughly 80 miles south in that island chain is Desroches, the largest of the Amirantes, where we had planned to anchor for a few hours before finally waving goodbye to the paradise that is the Seychelles.

Buggas comes back on deck and confers with the man who questioned us about crew. We think he must be second-in-command and mutter to each other the nickname, '2IC'.

Buggas demands money: 'Give me dollar!'

While cruising, I look after our cash flow, so I glance at Paul and volunteer to respond. Tentatively, I step forward. 2IC gestures with his gun for me to go below, then follows. I find the small canvas holdall that serves as my handbag and give him my purse with credit cards, US dollars and Euros, about £130 worth in total. We have a stash of $1,500 hidden away, but I don't want to give them that. 2IC grabs my handbag, empties out the contents and hands it to one of the youngsters. He counts the money in my purse and says, 'Small.' I explain we have no need for money at sea; we will get what we need from a bank in Tanzania, using plastic cards. 2IC is incredulous and sends me back on deck.

As I go up to the cockpit, I get a brief glimpse of others searching the boat, going through the lockers one by one. Now it's Paul's turn. Buggas takes him down below while I sit, closely guarded, anxious about what will happen next.

'Where money? Have money? Search money! Search gold!'

I don't know what Rachel has revealed, but I now know there are ten ruthless and jumpy men aboard *Lynn Rival*, each with an AK-47 automatic assault rifle, as well as rocket propelled grenade launchers. It is probably not a good idea to say 'No'. I open the drawer in the aft cabin and give him my money – about £25 and a few Seychelles rupees – as well as my diving watch.

'Money! Search money . . . Give 20,000 dollar – you go.'

'Small boat, small money.'

'You lie! Money? Search money.'

I am beginning to understand the one-track mind of the Somali pirate. I reach under Rachel's bunk, into the 'hidey hole' and pull out our cash reserve, about $1,500. I don't want to risk being caught out in a lie. I'm resigned to losing everything of value but hope they will soon realise the poverty of their target, rob us and move on.

Over the years, we've heard about armed attacks on yachts in various places around the world, including the Gulf of Aden, the Caribbean, South America, the Malacca Straits and even in the Mediterranean. We've often discussed what our tactics would be in the event of an attack. Our conclusion is always that it's best to comply when dealing with irrational people. The aim must be survival. As experienced sailors, we have a basic resilience; we trust each other not to jeopardise a situation by doing anything other than keeping our heads down and staying calm. So, though we are frightened and confused, we have confidence in each other and are able to function.

When Buggas orders Paul to motor towards Somalia with few words but much emphatic swinging and gesturing of an AK-47, he duly follows orders.

I put the engine in gear and set the course as directed. 2IC checks with a handheld GPS (Global Positioning System). He shows me: 325 degrees. I'm allowed to look at the handset and see it's hacked and hardwired to show only the direction back to their base in Somalia. Buggas shouts, 'Run, run!' – meaning full speed ahead! This is crazy, as poor *Lynn Rival*'s auxiliary engine will be severely overloaded towing their three boats.

Buggas keeps pressing us for money and valuables: 'Give me gold!' He follows me below to find it: my treasured wedding ring, watch, earrings. He secretes them away, saying dismissively, 'Small, no good.'

'Where dollar? Give me 20,000 dollar!'

I say we don't have 20,000 dollars.

'Man speak you 20,000 dollar.'

He's trying to trick me, and I register he is more manipulative than a plain thug. I repeat, 'We don't have 20,000 dollars.'

He hits back: 'No 20,000 dollar – bad things – you Somalia.'

I say I can do nothing. Frustrated, he shouts 'Up!' – a sign for me to go on deck, where he snarls, 'You liar!' and 'Shut up!', as if he's suddenly remembered these phrases. He sits and broods, then barks at members of the gang. Some continue to search the boat; others position themselves on deck, two with their guns trained on us. I sit, numb, with a sinking feeling that these men will not give up easily, trying not to be frightened of the guns.

The men have been on board for an hour or so now, still on edge and alert to our every move. Buggas is extraordinarily suspicious of anything that makes a noise or flashes. And when he is jumpy, his men are scared witless. They don't use the safety catches on their AK-47s; they don't care where they are pointed. So, no sudden movements. Submission and cooperation are the order of the day. They see Rachel's seasickness relief band and demand she throw it overboard. They take our Man Overboard wrist tags, smash them and chuck them away. They make us remove our life jackets and take out the gas cylinders that inflate them.

I sit and watch in despair. Our home, our life, all our hard

22

work and planning is being destroyed by these mindless, greedy thugs. Why can't they see that we're small beer? They're wasting their time. Why don't they take what they can and go looking for a ship? Perhaps dawn will bring a new light. Perhaps our EPIRB signal will have been picked up. Will anyone know we're in distress? Will anyone send help?

Just before dawn, Buggas turns his attention to communications.

'Phones! Satphone! Search!'

Off we go again. I hand over two old but treasured Nokia 6310i, each with a Seychelles SIM card, and the satphone – a Thuraya with a dual GSM/satellite SIM card.

Buggas knows about Thuraya. His face lights up and he switches it on.

I laugh. 'No good,' I say. Neither Rachel nor I expect it to work; we've been unable to get a signal anywhere near the Seychelles and don't expect to get reception until we are close to Africa. After a short delay, it works. A signal! The luck of the bad guys!

Buggas dials and begins shouting to someone he calls 'Arbou', presumably a pirate mate. We can't understand a word. We pick up 'British'. The odd glance from Buggas confirms that he's talking about us.

Dawn. *Lynn Rival* is heading north-west on autopilot, engine straining at full throttle. Three men on deck surround us – their assault rifles aimed carelessly at us – then shepherd us below.

'Down! No speak!'

Two of them follow us down into the saloon, where they keep their AK-47s trained on us. They gesticulate with their guns, saying, 'Sleep,' so we sit down on the starboard bunk next to each other. We're exhausted but not at all sleepy. One young guard sits, fidgeting nervously – barely three feet away, pointing his gun at us – and gestures that we should look down. It is sticky down below. The weather is calm, with no cooling wind. They have shut the door between the saloon and for'ard heads, so there's no through ventilation.

Buggas comes down to supervise, demanding, 'A/C?'

We don't know whether to laugh or cry. Laughing would lead to hysteria, so Paul shrugs and points to the one little twelve-volt fan we have in the saloon.

Buggas looks bemused and irritated. Can we hope he's beginning to accept how puny a prize we are?

He and 2IC are now standing at the navigation table, rifling through its contents. He calls over to us and points at the navigation computer.

'Computers? Search!'

I get out the personal and backup computers – all second-hand vintage laptops. There's no point in taking expensive gear into the environment of a small cruising yacht. Buggas's face is a picture of disparagement. He shakes his head.

Pointing at the navigation computer and the open chart, I say, 'I must navigate, keep log.'

'No,' growls Buggas, and pushes me away. But soon, 'OK, how far Somalia?'

I click on the range-and-bearing tool, zoom in on the coastline and pan along it. Buggas spots the town of Hobyo.

'Hobyo, how far? Mogadishu, how far?'

I show him – .we are about 680 nautical miles (780 statute miles) from Hobyo.

'Many days, maybe ten days,' I say. 'In one day, diesel finish.'

'Have diesel,' he responds triumphantly.

2IC demands a 'shower'. I show him the cramped toilet/shower cubicle in the aft cabin. He surveys the facilities in disgust.

Buggas demands 'Shampoo. Original!' He refuses my offer of a bar of soap. Suspecting he wants shower gel, I give him the first thing that comes to hand – Cif, abrasive household cleaner. I am blowed if I'm going to be helpful! I'm sent back up to the cockpit. Soon a naked Buggas appears, covered in Cif, apparently complaining that it isn't lathering! His men laugh at him and I have to restrain myself. I go below and hand him the washing-up liquid instead. One by one, the rest of gang have showers until we hear the unmistakable whine of the water pump running dry. They have used up our entire supply of fresh water.

I switch off the churning pump. Suddenly an alarm sounds. The engine is overheating. 'WHAT?' yells Buggas. That's the limit of his intelligence, never mind his English. I'm taken up to the cockpit. Rachel has stopped the engine. I check the instruments and show Buggas the gauge.

'Problem. Small engine. Wait five minutes,' I say, pointing at the three vessels tied behind us in a daisy chain.

Five minutes pass. Rachel re-starts the engine. So begins a cycle that would normally be so frustrating but in the circumstances is a welcome diversion.

After a few minutes, one of the pirates opens the throttle. Ten minutes later, the alarm goes off, we cut to idle, spend ten minutes cooling, and so on. They refuse to understand that we can only keep up 2700 rpm, giving a speed of about 2 knots, without overheating. Buggas scoffs at our slow progress, unable to accept the fact that we have an engine that is inadequate to meet his demand to run at full revs towing three boats! I tell them to motor their mother boat in parallel, towing one of the skiffs. I say then we could make about 4 knots (a fast walk), but I'm ignored.

Buggas wants more water. I explain, 'Small boat, small water, water finish.'

'You lie! Too much water.' He is sure we have another tank.

'No,' I say. 'Water finish. Only jerries.' I point to the aft cabin, show him our reserve: four full jerrycans under Rachel's bunk. I'm damned if I'll tell him we have an emergency desalinator. He concedes and indicates that we should keep the jerries. He wants *us* to have that water, not let his men shower it away. He knows he has to keep his hostages alive.

The pirates continue rummaging through our belongings. They came on board in long raggedy pants and vests, looking as if they'd not washed for days. They find Rachel's clothes and now appear on deck, freshly showered, wearing her tops and trousers. They may look fetching, but their casual disrespect for our personal things adds to our misery.

Buggas is keen for us to eat, but I don't feel hungry. It's not so much a question of feeling queasy – we're motoring in reasonably flat seas – simply the shock of what's happened. The boat is full of fresh food, but I can't face anything other than a cup of tea.

The gang have already helped themselves to our entire store of biscuits and what fresh fruit they can find. Buggas demands food, '*Briis* [rice], spaghetti!', and I show him our rice stocks. We have plenty more hidden away, but I don't see why I should be helpful. Bizarrely, they have yet to check any lockers that are hard to get at, such as under the berths. And they've not touched the fridge. Perhaps Buggas realises we don't have enough to feed them for long and is concerned that we have enough for ourselves? He has probably been told by his advisers on the end of the satphone that he must keep us alive.

They clamber into their mother boat to fetch spaghetti, then demand a cooking pot. One of the gang – a 6 ft 3 in. athletic-looking youngster with a shy smile – strives to cook something. He's obviously not used to working in a cramped galley, and my biggest pot is far too small for ten man-sized portions of pasta.

We are still not allowed to talk to one another, but we desperately need to establish some order to survive – to keep *Lynn Rival* functioning despite these crazy people on board. One of us needs to be alert, and we need somewhere to sleep. My berth is still relatively untouched so, at 1100, I tell Buggas I must sleep, and I manage to convey to Paul my intention to relieve him in four hours.

They want to keep us both below deck, while the boat steers herself, but with the engine overheating they need us to manage the situation. Regardless of our predicament, it is important that we keep *Lynn Rival* afloat and on course to keep us alive.

Alarm sounds! Engine overheating again. 'WHAT?' shouts Buggas. We rush up.

'Problem,' I say. 'Small engine – too much boats,' pointing at the flotilla astern. The pirates keep increasing the engine revs when we're not looking. They just don't understand that our engine can't cope with towing their three boats.

Buggas continues to use the satphone. Much shouting. Many calls. The SIM card is on a contract, direct debit from my bank account. I wonder whether anyone at Vodafone will notice the sudden volume of satellite calls to an 0025 number – Somalia. Surely they will? I'm worried about the bill I'll face when we get back to the UK. I assume we'll be released when the pirates realise the poverty of their catch.

In the afternoon it rains and the pirates take all our waterproofs. Buggas puts on a full set of oilskins and causes great amusement by coming on deck to show off his new look. The dungarees are a bit tight around his bum, but otherwise the fit is good. Our attackers are a bit more relaxed with us, and we with them, but both parties are mutually suspicious.

At all times, three men are armed and on guard while others keep watch on the foredeck or sleep down below. On watch, I'm allowed to sit at the wheel, keeping an eye on the course and engine instruments. Buggas or 2IC sits in the cockpit close to me, and at least one other guard perches beside the companionway with his AK-47 pointed at me. At one point, Buggas realises how terrified I am sitting directly in the firing line. He tells the guard to aim his gun elsewhere.

We are beginning to settle into a grisly routine, Buggas determined to take us to Somalia, us not knowing what is going to happen next. We are still close to the Seychelles. Dare we hope for help?

For their evening meal, they retrieve some of their own cooking pots and more provisions, including sacks of rice and flour. The pots are far too big for *Lynn Rival*'s cooker and sink. The galley is becoming a greasy mess, littered with debris and discarded cooking implements. Somali pirates may be clean in their personal hygiene – as long as there is water – but have no idea of keeping shipshape.

The gang accepts our regime. We manage to whisper a few words at each changeover, 1500, 1900, 2300, 0300 . . . but any more communication prompts a shout of 'No speak! Sleep!' and much signalling with an AK-47. They keep an eye on both of us: from the cockpit through the small porthole above the bunk, and by posting one young pirate permanently in the aft cabin.

Surely they must have realised by now that we are not a big catch. Why don't they take what they've got and go after something bigger? I hope the lack of supplies will encourage them to leave us, but, alas, they have water supplies on their boat – tasting of water treatment, which Buggas calls 'Silcom' – and plenty of diesel.

Saturday, 24 October

I sleep fitfully then wake to the sounds of dough-making and the overpowering, stomach-churning smell of chapatis deep-frying in oil. Paul manages to eat one.

I come on watch at 0700 and drink sweet tea. They call it *sheh*. It's warm, wet and brown, but really just sugar solution.

The galley is even worse, with flour, rice and oil spills everywhere. The young cook – who we learn is called Afieri – has no inclination to wash up. I slip on the debris-strewn floor so clean up as best I can. Then I check the for'ard heads. The pirates are using the toilets but not pumping them properly. I don't want to have a blocked toilet pump to deal with when this lot are gone.

Up on deck, the sky is overcast. It looks like we're in for a day of squalls and rain showers. Buggas and 2IC keep nagging about lack of speed. I ignore them or say, 'Small engine' or 'Little boat, no big ship'. The motor is coping at no more than 2600 rpm. We have little wind to help us and are only managing about 2 knots, so it's still a long way to Somalia – if that truly is their intent.

Buggas tells me, 'Look big ship. Somali men go. You free.'

I can't help but wish for a big ship to come along, preferably a warship. But does anyone know we've been attacked?

Sitting at the wheel, we are protected from the sun by the bimini awning, but when it rains I get wet through. I complain to Buggas because the men have taken our waterproof jackets. He makes one of the guards give me back a jacket, which Paul and I can share.

Down below, the off-watch gangsters go through our lockers again, discovering things to mess around with, playing CDs loudly, even complaining about our taste in music! Buggas sits in the cockpit, often on the phone. At one point he asks me, 'Boat; name?'

I say '*Lynn Rival*,' and he repeats it for his colleague on the phone.

Later he pretends to be civil and asks me about 'family' and 'home'. I tell him we have no children and our boat is our home. I ask if he has family and gather he has a wife and two children. At one point he goes down below and picks up the EPIRB from the chart table. He asks me what it is and manages to read a word written on the side, but his English is very poor. I don't think he understands much of what I say. He gestures throwing the EPIRB overboard. My heart beats faster, and I try to look nonchalant. I shrug, in the hope that he will sling it out – in the water, the EPIRB will be activated. He grins and puts it back on the table.

Off-watch in the daytime, I'm feeling distraught. The heat of the engine makes the cabin a stifling misery. The small fan provides little ventilation. I lie there sweating, finding it difficult to concentrate or distract myself by daydreaming. I don't want to read a novel. I'm not eating. My blood-sugar levels are low. I can't think straight. I'm just too worried about what's happening to us and what will happen next. There's no sign of anyone searching for us. Perhaps no one knows. What can we do? How long will this last? I cry to get things out of my system and feel slightly better.

Midday on Saturday, I am back on watch and Buggas is cross. We have so little money, only two mobile phones, three vintage computers, no air conditioning and 'Why slow?'

Words don't work, so I show him the engine, via the hatch in the aft cabin, and repeat slowly, 'Small engine.' I try to explain that we can motor-sail and go twice as fast. In light winds, the combination of sail and engine can double our speed. But we are heading almost directly into the wind, so we would need to bear away – to alter course perhaps 15 degrees from our desired heading – so that the sails could contribute.

One of the pirates understands; he must have some sailing experience, perhaps as a fisherman. He has a distinctive Roman nose, so we give him a nickname 'Nero'.

But do we *want* to go faster? Would it be better to extend the time at sea, limping towards their base? Then there would be more scope for a rescue attempt. Might the pirates even get so fed up they would leave us?

It doesn't matter – we cannot convince them to let us deviate even a few degrees from the course. Every few minutes one pirate checks the GPS to make sure we are pointing in the right direction.

We keep the mainsail up, sheeted hard in, so that it helps a little, both with stability and progress. Whenever the wind allows, we unfurl our foresails, genoa and/or staysail. It's hard work, as there is only ever one of us working, but the mental and physical distraction is good and there is a little satisfaction in disturbing the men on the foredeck, who are careless of what sheets (sail control lines) they are lying on.

One man, rummaging through the mess of our possessions and gear, comes up with the dead-man's handle for our dinghy outboard motor. It is actually a short lanyard that kills the motor if the operator falls out of the dinghy. He recognises it and asks, 'Small boat where?'

I point out the inflatable dinghy in its bag on deck. 2IC asks, 'Outboard? How many?'

I guess he means how powerful, so I indicate the outboard, affectionately known as an egg whisk, on our pushpit. It is completely covered in a red bag, so they haven't spotted it.

'Two horse,' I say, and hold up two fingers.

Cue much hilarity. All three armed men in the cockpit understand but do not believe.

'Two hundred?'

I've already noticed they have quite a good command

of English numbers – no doubt used when counting ransom.

'No. Two.'

Disbelief. I open the bag and show them the 'egg whisk'. They laugh. Surely, surely, they are beginning to realise what small fish they have caught?

In the afternoon I'm allowed to refuel from our jerrycans on deck. *Lynn Rival* can motor for ninety hours on a tank of fuel at a speed of about 5 knots, but towing three boats means we are using fuel at a horrendous rate. They watch but don't help.

After another flurry of sign language with Buggas, the mother boat is pulled alongside *Lynn Rival* – more scraping of the hull, damage to the guarding and toe rails – and I transfer our empty jerrycans to the mother boat and fill them from their diesel drums. I hoist them onto our deck, securing them into position properly. It's exhausting work in the tropical humidity, but another distraction.

Buggas is always on the satphone, calling his mates in Somalia. This prompts more of the same old questions:

'French?'

'No – British.'

Buggas is changing his tune. Our Britishness is of sudden interest. I get the sinking feeling that he has been told by his mates ashore that we are valuable prizes in our own right, never mind the small value of *Lynn Rival*. He now makes serious attempts to get us to eat. I know we should try to keep our energy levels up, but it's hard to get down to any cooking. The pirate cook has commandeered our small galley, and the mess is unimaginable. When I come off watch, later in the afternoon, I manage to make a bacon omelette. Some of the pirates recognise the smell of pork and affect disgust.

Below decks is now chaotic. The for'ard cabin is out of bounds, requisitioned by the pirates for storing arms and their rice, flour and other provisions. The off-watch gang has taken over the saloon as well – there are bodies all over the place, sleeping two or three to a bunk. Scrabble tiles, playing cards, papers and charts are strewn everywhere. It's like having a gang of delinquent teenagers squatting in your home. We're not particularly house-proud, but it's essential to keep shipshape when going on passage. Conditions change and anything rolling around the cabin is a safety hazard. At night, it's especially important to be able to find things where you expect them to be and to have essentials close to hand. In spite of these people, we still need to run the boat. Our familiar boat-management routine is something we must cling on to as best we can. At least when they give up on us we'll be able to limp back to Port Victoria.

Buggas is nagging me to eat. No doubt he wants to keep us healthy, to preserve our value. We have plenty of fresh food – meat, cheese, butter and milk – to consume. They've not touched the contents of the fridge. We normally have bacon and egg for breakfast, so have plentiful supplies of both. I manage to eat a little of Paul's bacon omelette, but by the evening the lack of food is taking its toll on my stamina and resilience.

I long to have a proper wash before going to sleep, but it's impossible. I'm deeply uncomfortable about the lack of privacy. When I go to the toilet, a guard sits outside the flimsy, barely fitting shower curtain, just inches away, his gun pointed towards me. There is little water left and nowhere to dry off. I'm used to emerging from the sweltering head and towelling myself in the cabin space, but I'm not doing that with an audience. I hide under my sheet and make do with wet wipes all over, telling myself it can't get any worse. And, it won't be for long.

Thirty-six hours have passed since the attack. There is absolutely no sight or sound of any search. Buggas and his thugs relax a bit. We lose hope of a rescue. The EPIRB signal must have failed. If it had worked, the authorities would know our position to within three miles. They would be able to check that *Lynn Rival* was indeed in the area, that our plan was to head for Tanzania, via Desroches. They would know the area is full of marine hazards, unlit islets, rocks and shoals, that it was on the fringe of pirate activity. So they would not assume it was a false alarm . . . Or would they? The Seychelles is well served by light aircraft and helicopters. As well as their coastguard service there is usually a naval vessel close to Mahé, often with a helicopter on board. So there should be no difficulty finding us . . . if anyone has tried.

But perhaps they are more clever. They do know where we are. They are watching from over the horizon. Help will come. Of course it will. The navies of over 20 countries are abroad. We *do* hope.

On watch in the early hours, I'm struggling to keep awake – drifting off into a nervous, exhausted dream world – then I jerk awake suddenly. Where am I? I'm on watch! Automatically I stand up to check the horizon. Oops, we've got company. I mustn't spook them by sudden movements. Soon my consciousness catches up with reality: anxiety, fear and despair re-emerge.

Sunday, 25 October

Excitement at 0630. Buggas calls me to the foredeck.

'Look. Big ship?'

One of the men thinks he's seen a ship and stands at the bow pointing. I find our monocular and scan the horizon but detect nothing. A few others join us looking, searching desperately. It's in all our interests that they find a more rewarding prey. Our hopes are raised, but there is nothing there.

It turns out to be a hot, sunny and calm day. Our progress is still painfully slow. We fill up again with diesel from their big drums.

Buggas sits next to me in the cockpit. He tells me there are no schools in Somalia and his men are illiterate. I've noticed that they show little respect for him and often challenge his commands. He has to shout and threaten to get them to do what he wants. They often have pow-wows that evolve into big arguments. Their moods go up and down. They are bored, listless and searching for things to do. They complain we don't have any Somali music, no TV, videos or DVDs. Our cigarettes are stale, our clothes uninteresting. They desperately try to find some entertainment on our pocket shortwave radio.

Later 2IC sits down next to me: 'You British, big money, four million dollar.'

'You're joking.'

'Somali men hungry. No fish. Government give money, poor people. British government, big money, no problem.'

My heart sinks. I say, 'British government, no money for criminals,' but know they won't understand. They are so confident, so cocky. They have nothing to lose. With their guns, they feel invincible.

As I go off watch, I notice the EPIRB is still sitting, tantalisingly, on the chart table. Should I risk taking it and switching it on again? We're closely watched. There are always at least two sets of eyes trained on me and a matching number of AKs. I decide it's too risky.

Strangely, I feel better. We've been at sea for three days, I've got my sea legs and I'm eating again. I even manage to read a bit of a David Baldacci novel, *Simple Genius*, but find it hard-going.

By now our situation has become a question of survival. When we change over watches, Paul and I speak briefly to check how the other is coping. I am frantically hoping that something will happen to make the pirates give up and leave us before we land in Somalia – a fate I dread the thought of. Our overriding aim must be to stay alive. We are like zombies on overdrive, concentrating on keeping the boat going and complying with our captors, avoiding antagonism.

Mental numbness has set in. My mind doesn't want to think beyond immediate decision-making. Future? What future? Our home is wrecked. Our dream has become a nightmare. I stay composed by taking pleasure in small achievements: the establishment of routines, even reading while in the cockpit, trying to guard the throttle against their ever-present desire to open it up. In other circumstances, this would be an idyllic afternoon at sea.

I persuade Buggas to put a man in his mother boat and motor independently. Our speed increases to 4 knots. Two of the pirates, 'Nero' and one who appears to be the mechanic (charged with keeping their all-important outboards working), manage to keep station about ten metres away from *Lynn Rival*. But the others are less competent. *Lynn Rival*'s hull is constantly battered, gouged and scraped as the boats surge together. Fuel transfer is traumatic. When the mother boat comes alongside, the men swing clumsily on our guardrails and on the lightweight, stainless-steel framing of our bimini and the arch supporting our wind turbine and solar panels. It pains me to survey *Lynn Rival*. All I see is bent steel, chafed cables, smashed teak toe rails, broken flagstaff, while the mother boat keeps pounding into *Lynn Rival*'s stern, banging and shuddering against the mechanism of our wind-vane steering gear.

Paul seems to be bearing up. Buggas enquires how we are – does he expect a polite response? – and checks we are eating. I cook risotto for supper with Seychelles smoked tuna. Nero is suspicious, accusing me of using 'ham'. Otherwise the men seem relaxed and often smile.

The mother boat frequently comes alongside for changes of crew or simply to exchange words, crashing into the side of poor *Lynn Rival* without a care. I notice it has SABIR BOAT SGC169 2001 marked in six-inch-high black lettering on the side and wonder where it came from. I must not worry about what is beyond our control. Exhausted resignation sets in.

At night, the wind picks up during a rainstorm. We heel over under too much sail. The pirates are frantic in panic. I try to take control – to reduce sail – but they get in the way. Poor Paul is expected to get out of bed to help!

Wind! Rain! Consternation! I don't bat an eyelid, hidden away down below. In the barely remembered normal times, it would have to be far, far worse weather for Rachel to need to disturb me. But now the noise, the shouting of ten frightened men, and Buggas peering down at me demands instant action: 'UP! UP!'

Never mind contact lenses or clothes. I go up in underpants. A quick scan around – Rachel OK, *Lynn Rival* OK. I examine the anemometer from about 6 inches (no contact lenses) – 28 knots, steady wind: a nice Force 7, almost *Lynn Rival*'s favourite. But there's chaos on deck as the lee rail goes under – if I increase the angle of heel, could the pirates be thrown off deck? Tempting, but no. Let's just furl the genoa.

At least one or two are willing to help, but it's mostly hindrance because they don't know what they're doing. Ten too many crew! We settle down under full main and staysail, making about 6 knots, despite the tow. Ideally we'd have a reef in the main, but hey, who cares? I enjoy the sailing, enjoy the rain. For a few blissful moments, I forget our ten resident thugs with their AK-47s.

After midnight, it's my watch, still in heavy rain. I wonder if there's any shampoo left? Yes! Clothes off, shower and scrub up in the cockpit. The baddies watch in disbelief. They are nervous and not at all comfortable on a heeling yacht, but they don't stop me. I have gained a little freedom of movement in the storm. Then Buggas asks for the shampoo. He and I are showering together, naked in the cockpit – you couldn't make it up!

Monday, 26 October

I wake again to the sounds and stench of bread-making. Lying in my bunk, I rummage around to find clothes for going on deck. I sleep in a sleeveless T-shirt and knickers under a sheet for modesty. The heat is stifling, and I worry about developing prickly-heat rash. Lucky Paul can lie naked without a sheet, but I'm too shy.

I dress under the sheet, changing into tropical sailing gear: three-quarter-length shorts and short-sleeved loose shirt. My bunk is wide, so there's room for storing bedding and clothing at the sides. I safeguard whatever essentials we've managed to hang on to there, away from the big thieves aboard, plus bottles of drinking water that we replenish from our jerrycan stocks. In these conditions, avoiding dehydration is more important than eating.

I stuff my diary and book between the mattress and hull, then take what I need from the few personal items I keep on a small shelf above my bunk: watch, sunglasses, sunblock and sunhat. I brush my teeth and put my contact lenses in, ready to go up and relieve Paul. We exchange a few brief words about the weather, course and engine. Afieri gives me some deep-fried chapati and sweet tea (tasting of steriliser).

2IC accosts Paul as he goes down below, pointing to his lower back, saying, 'Problem, give medicine!' It seems he has lumbago. Paul calls me to help, and I get our first-aid box from the saloon. It is mostly still intact, although on the first day 2IC helped himself to all the paracetamol. I give him some pain-relief gel. Buggas queries the procedure, 'No injection?', and looks incredulous when I tell him I don't know how to give injections.

Another pirate has itchy skin on his arms, scratching

and grimacing to demonstrate. It's probably a heat rash, but I find it hard to diagnose on black skin, not being able to detect any redness and feeling reluctant to touch him. I give him some itch-relief cream.

Yet another has stomach pains. By gesture, I manage to establish that he's not been going to the toilet, so it's probably constipation. I tell him to drink plenty of water and give him fruit juice. Despite these minor ailments, and their life on bare rations at sea, the pirates look healthy. Most are thin but not emaciated. They are strong, with good teeth. Sometimes they complain of sore eyes, but that's a fact of life for all of us in a windy, salty environment. Quite a few are heavy smokers, getting through the stocks we keep for trading with fishermen in no time.

It's another hot day with little wind. I sit at the wheel feeling listless, watching the comings and goings of the guards. Sometimes Buggas sits in the cockpit making phone calls or brooding. Baby Face – as we call a shy, nervy teenager – sits by the companionway, going up to the foredeck and back from time to time, struggling to move about with his gun at the ready. I try not to think about the possibility of an accidental shot in my direction, but several times I find myself wishing to be killed outright and not have to suffer a lingering death.

I concentrate on running the boat: hoping for a distraction. Is it time to run the bilge pump yet? When motoring, we have to run it every few hours to keep the boat dry. The cook comes up to complain the gas is out. It's time to switch to another cylinder. Then I notice some of the damage they are inflicting on *Lynn Rival* and feel heartbroken. I struggle not to cry when I see yet another incident. The rope towing their boats is tied on over the solar panel wiring. It's chafed through, so we won't have that source of power if the engine fails. I remind myself there's no sense in worrying about things we can't change.

Monday is a sombre day of inactivity as we struggle to come to terms with our new reality. The pirates relax more as each hour passes with no sign of pursuit or rescue, and the coast of their lawless homeland draws nearer. Buggas makes frequent calls to his pals. Clearly he can't wait to reunite with them.

'Hobyo how far?' – every few hours the same question.

'Go quick! Quick!'

Cue for a pirate to grab the throttle, and we repeat the engine overheating/cooling palaver. I try to read. My mind isn't ready to escape into a novel, but I make myself concentrate on John Gribben's Science: A History, a wonderful canter through the development of modern science since the 'dark ages', told with an emphasis on the scientists rather than their work. I don't feel like cooking, but whenever the pirates do, they give me portions of rice, pasta and chapatis.

The weather continues to be changeable, the wind usually close to dead ahead. So with sail changes and fuel transfers, the time passes. We are allowed to sit together in the cockpit for short periods, but whenever we speak, we are reprimanded sharply: 'No speak! Down!'

We exist; we hope.

In the afternoon, another hammer blow. Our Radar Target Enhancer (RTE) controller is spotted by 2IC. He notices its little green light and shouts, 'Signal? Finish!' The active unit is at the top of the mast and it uses very little power. When a ship's radar hits us, the RTE sends back an enhanced signal. It makes us appear like a small trawler on a ship's radar, so that a good (for example, military) radar operator could pick us up at more than 40 miles. Otherwise our echo would only be noticed at four or five miles, and then only by an alert operator. I still dream of rescue, and with the RTE on there was much more hope that we would be found.

Crack!

A gunshot on the foredeck. Shouts. Then silence. I look at Buggas and shrug my shoulders as if to say 'What?'

He looks at me, puts his finger to his head and moves it in that universal signal indicating madness. This is the second accidental discharge since the attack. We are clearly at greater risk from these than of deliberate shooting, but I don't care any more – how quickly one becomes blasé about gunfire and the careless pointing of weapons. The one thing the movies don't prepare you for is the sheer shock and violence of the noise of AK-47 and light machine-gun fire.

The pirates eat well: fried bread for breakfast, spaghetti at lunchtime, rice for supper. When off watch, they like to muck around, laughing and joking. I am getting to know their personalities. Nero and Afieri are particularly active and noisy, annoyingly confident 'Good-Time Charlies'. When the mother boat comes closer alongside, they shout to each other until it recedes out of earshot again. They smoke, fiddle with the radio and act like bored children, but they also show signs of familiarity with technology, perhaps learned from being aboard pirated ships. 2IC seems to understand aspects of navigation and he can work out how to turn an MP3 player on and off, though he is fooled by the 'hold' function. They're definitely not archetypal villains, more like Robin Hood and his merry men. They crave a better life. I try to understand why they're acting so inhumanely towards us, apparently without a care.

The hours pass. Despite the lack of water, the pirates wash their hands, feet and faces frequently, but I see no sign of praying. Before dark, I psyche myself up to make supper. The galley is filthy. I have yet to persuade Afieri to rinse out with salt water, let alone use washing-up liquid or kitchen roll. I clean up what I can and manage to make a Spanish omelette.

The night is dark, at first overcast, then clear. The stars are magnificent and being able to see them is always inspiring. Later, we have more cloud and heavy rain. Some of the gangsters wash their hair. The lack of fresh water is taking its toll – the smell is quite high in the saloon – and everyone's borrowed gear is getting dirty and scruffy. Do they care? No doubt they are looking forward to getting back to base. Who knows what Buggas has promised them.

2IC is in a particularly jumpy mood. When Paul goes down below at watch change, I say to him, 'Sleep well.'

2IC pipes up, 'Sig-nal? Sig-nal?'

'No,' I say. '*Sleep. Well.*'

He insists 'Sig-nal' and takes me down below to show me the word 'signal' written on the Radar Target Enhancer. Perhaps he thought he'd rumbled a plot to switch it back on.

Tuesday, 27 October

I take over the watch to find a bright day, but the brightness is of course only in the skies. We are inching inexorably closer to Somalia. There is sufficient fuel, water and food. The pirates are relaxed, no longer worried about possible military intervention, and buoyed by their misplaced belief in our value. Are the chances of rescue passing?

No sailing today, but we keep the mainsail up for stability and perhaps a little help for our poor abused Bukh diesel engine. It is becoming very slow to pick up after a cooling stop, so I persuade Buggas to let me change the filters. This is never an easy process. The smell of the spilled diesel and the uneasy motion (because of lack of wind) in uncomfortable positions induces queasiness. Doing it at gunpoint doesn't help. The filters are dirty but not 'plugged'. With new ones installed, the engine runs better but won't rev above 2400 rpm.

More fried bread and sweet tea for breakfast. As ever, Buggas is complaining about the lack of speed. I decide to wash my hair in the cockpit using salt water. The guards stay out of my way as I haul in a bucket of seawater from over the side. Re-energised by clean hair, I tackle the galley floor – once again smeared in grease and debris – with another bucket of seawater. I persuade the guards to let me go forward to get mangoes and other food stocks from under the bow cabin berths. I have to clamber over their sacks of rice and flour, and push aside a bag of RPGs. We have mango and cookies and proper tea for lunch.

Buggas has his usual high-decibel phone calls. Then he tells me, 'You go on land in Somalia. Pack your personal possessions.' He also mentions a translator. I realise the plan is to take us ashore once we get to Somalia and that there are people in the pirate organisation who speak English. It's hard to think straight. I'm still hoping that they'll leave us for a big ship, or we'll encounter a warship and be rescued, but I'm losing hope. Clearly they're determined to try to get a ransom for us. But what will happen to *Lynn Rival*?

I try to ask him how many bags we can pack, but he doesn't understand. He's learned the phrase 'Pack your personal possessions' and that is all he'll say. We are still some way from Somalia and there's no room below for packing, so I don't do anything about it. Maybe, just maybe, it won't be necessary. I'm not going to give up hope until I have to.

At about 1400 one of the foredeck gang sights a big ship. Buggas goes to the bow. There is much excitement and shouting. They call over the mother boat and the off-watch men gather their guns and dress for action. Buggas comes to the stern and ties on the mother boat. Men board the two skiffs and start the motors, one 60 hp, the other 40 hp. 2IC shouts at me to stop our engine. We slow down and drift off course. The autopilot alarm goes off. Nero shouts at me, assuming I'm doing something to hinder them. Little does he know how excited I am by this turn of events. I switch off the autopilot and try to stay calm. Some of the men zoom off in the two skiffs. Buggas tells me to speed up again. Those skiffs can travel at more than 25 knots, so they soon disappear over the horizon. We keep looking. I expect they will return soon, as they've no lights or navigation equipment . . .

Rachel was on watch in the early afternoon when I became aware of frenetic activity on deck and below. I managed to ignore it and stayed cocooned in 'our' bunk, our haven, hiding with my back to everything, mentally as well as physically. When I get up at 1500, the boat seems empty – what has happened? I poke my head up through the hatch and emerge cautiously into the cockpit. Rachel is OK, sitting behind the wheel. Buggas is standing on one of the seats, peering towards the horizon, ahead on the port side. Two other pirates stand on deck, one with his rifle pointed at me. He gestures with it – 'Down!' – and indicates I should sit in the cockpit, but not close to Rachel. We are towing the mother boat again, and both the attack skiffs have gone. There seem to be only three pirates on board.

Buggas says, 'Ship! Look!', and points towards the west. He wants me to look to see if there is any sign of anything. Seven of the pirates, including 2IC, have gone in the skiffs to attack a ship. If they are successful, might they now leave us for the greater prize? Or have they been convinced by their mates ashore that we are worth more than a ship crewed by non-Europeans? It doesn't matter. Time passes and there is no sign of anything.

Buggas, Afieri and Baby Face guard us closely. The dynamic has changed: just three of them and two of us. We are now towing the heavier mother boat, so progress is slow, especially as the engine problem gets worse.

Buggas agrees I should change the filters again. More spilled diesel; new filters; the old ones again not that bad. Has bad fuel got through to the injection pump? My mind isn't functioning – I should be able to diagnose the problem, but conditions aren't exactly normal.

With this new phase, my mind starts to relax, and think without constraints . . . Would a breakdown be helpful? It would be easy to 'forget' to turn the fuel back on, so the engine would only run for a few moments after restarting. They would never know – they would just assume it has died. Again I wonder. Would it help? Just three bad guys. A calm sea. The navies must know where we are. Will they try something? Could they, if we gave them more time? But . . . maybe we would be taken into the mother boat, then we would have several days in an open boat with no shade, no facilities – no, that isn't an attractive option, especially for Rachel. So, fuel switched on . . .

I finish the job, all fantasies of sabotage, delay and escape gone. I re-start the engine. It is running better but still struggling.

As we all are. They're nervous. We're scared. The atmosphere is tense. The two boats haven't returned. Just before dusk I am on watch when we hear a noise – a helicopter! The sound comes from south-west of us, but not far away. Buggas pulls out a knife and cuts through the tow rope, letting the mother boat go free (complete with their diesel, water and food stocks). He barks, 'DOWN! DOWN!' Afieri waves his gun. He is too young to have a beard, too young to be pointing an assault rifle at me. He is nervous, untrained, armed and frightened. His terror is contagious.

I hurry below, followed by Afieri. He turns into the aft cabin and prods Rachel awake in her bunk and tells her by hand signal to come into the saloon and lie down on the starboard bunk. I am on the port bunk. Two men with AK-47s pointing at us scream, 'DOWN! No speak!' We know by now what demeanour is required. We are to sleep in the saloon amongst the stale bedding and debris left by the gang.

Buggas comes down, eyes bulging, clearly terrified. The centre hatch above and door to the bow cabin are closed. We can still hear the chopper but don't see it. It must have been military – there aren't any civilian flights out this way.

Someone knows we're here! The helicopter must have seen us and realise we've been hijacked. All three are again on the deck, one watching us through the hatch. At one point, I hear them singing, trying to stay awake. I doze fitfully, wondering about the helicopter. With only three of them on board, now would be a good time for a rescue attempt. I have hope again.

'Up! Up!' Every hour or so I'm summoned to the cockpit.

'Quick! Go quick!'

What can I do? Even without the drag from towing the mother boat and skiffs we are only making about 3 knots, with white smoke coming from the exhaust and little if any help from the sails. With the seven men gone, there is an air of . . . what? Raw fear . . . nameless dread . . . expectation of something awful . . .

Then comes the wind. A blessed relief. This is *our* element. *They* don't understand. They're clumsy. They get in the way. They're suspicious and frightened. They are more terrified by the howling gale, the driving rain, the angle of heel, the noisy rigging and flogging sails than by the chance of attack. I look around: speed 7 knots, wind steady at 30 knots (Force 7), more in the gusts. Aries vane gear working well. *Lynn Rival* is flying. I'm thinking: empty the mind, enjoy the moment. Ignore these bastards. I grin, looking at Buggas, who is not a happy bunny.

'WHAT?' he shouts.

'What?' I respond, looking enquiringly. After all, *he* is in command.

He shouts in Somali. I guess he means 'DO
SOMETHING!' OK, never mind the safety harness, never
mind the life jacket. This is *Lynn Rival*; she will look after
me. I know every inch of her decks, every line by feel. It's
very wet. Ropes are all over the place, untidy, but working.
Nothing's broken. Our Hood sails can take it. So can I. So
can *we*. Two reefs in the main. Genoa furled away. Storm
jib out. We're still making over 6 knots.

'Down! Down!'

Wet and exhausted, all I can do is peer at Rachel in the
dark. She won't be worried about the boat. I can only
imagine what she is thinking. How long can this go on?
No sleep. Just sitting, waiting, wondering, hoping.

Wednesday, 28 October

More rain at dawn. Can't sleep, just lying on the saloon
bunks, waiting. Paul is called up on deck yet again. Next
minute he's sent back down. The throttle is wide open,
but the engine is struggling. All he can do is try another
change of the fuel filters. I'm not allowed to move. Afieri
sits at the chart table with his gun on his lap while Paul
works in the aft cabin. Buggas is on deck, shouting on the
satphone. CRACK! Afieri's AK-47 goes off. The noise is
ear-splitting. 'Fucking hell!' shouts Paul. His head was
only inches from the thin plywood bulkhead separating
him from Afieri's gun. Buggas is furious, shouting and
screaming at Afieri, occasionally breaking off, almost
comically, to say, 'No problem' to us. Paul fears his
eardrum is perforated. It reminds us how fragile our
situation is, how easily we could be killed or maimed
through incompetence or carelessness.

Buggas comes down: 'Speak! Warship!' – gesturing at
the VHF radio, then pointing his gun at me. 'Tell turn
away or kill you!'

I haven't seen the ship. I turn on the VHF, tuned
automatically to channel 16, the international distress

channel. I listen for a moment; the airwaves are silent; then I follow the well-rehearsed standard procedure:

Paul: *US Warship, US Warship, US Warship, this is sailing yacht Lynn Rival, Lynn Rival, Lynn Rival, over.*
Warship: *Lynn Rival, this is EU warship F212.*
Paul: *EU warship, we are two British, one male and one female, have been kidnapped. We are both well and unharmed. Please turn away or we will be killed.*
Warship: *Lynn Rival. Understood. We are turning away now. Confirm one male, one female, unharmed. Are you being threatened?*
Repeated shouting from Buggas: 'Tell turn away – or kill you.'
Paul: *Correct. Not directly threatened at present.*
What the hell did I mean by that?
Warship: *Did you cut free the mother boat?*
Paul: *Yes. Our captors did.*

Then I am told to switch off, by an emphatic chopping of Buggas's hand. 'Down! Sleep!'

Afterwards Buggas is more relaxed and enquires after my well-being. Apparently a ship, possibly a fishing vessel, is coming from the shore to collect us.

Gloom! I wonder what has happened to the warship. So close, but will it do anything? What can it do? I'm not allowed on deck but ask to go into the aft cabin. Paul is allowed to make tea, which he brings to me with some cookies – a brief chance to exchange news. I stay in my bunk until the afternoon, dreading what might be coming next.

The engine is no better. It's an overcast day – calm and no help from the wind. I start worrying about packing our bags and draw up a list. If a boat is coming to collect us, it won't be long before we arrive in Somalia and they take us on land. Or is rescue still possible?

Rachel is allowed to go to her bunk in the aft cabin. I stay, sitting in the saloon, my mind racing but exhausted. After a couple of hours, 'UP! UP!' Wearily, I climb up.

Buggas gesticulates at the speed indicator, 'Go quick!'

The throttle is fully open, white smoke from the exhaust, but the engine only making a fast idle. I shrug, 'You want me look engine?'

Buggas shrugs as well, 'No!'

There is no wind. I point at the uselessly flapping sails, 'Sails away?'

'OK.'

I go on deck and put all the sails away. All we can do is motor, at about 1.5 knots, and hope the engine will not give up altogether.

'Down!'

I sit in the saloon again. One of the other two men is always watching, between me and where Rachel's bunk is, gun at the ready. No way we can communicate.

'Up! Up! Speak other captain.'

Buggas hands me the satphone. I take it and endure a poorly understood conversation with a man. I think he is coming in a small trawler from Somalia to tow us. I give him our position. He says he can make 17 knots and will reach us by midnight.

Later, Rachel comes up. No one seems inclined to prevent her, and we sit together behind the wheel. It's the first time we've had contact for a while. We share a few precious moments, but I'm restless. I say to Buggas, 'Other captain – tow?'

'Yes.'

'Get ready? Ropes?' I ask, indicating that we should get heavy towing warps out to make up a bridle on deck. He agrees.

Rachel and I work together, getting the big, heavy ropes from the locker. After laying them out, we secure them to all the strong fixtures, such as the big winches, to distribute the forces in preparation for a tow.

Buggas says, 'You go ship. Pack bags.'

I assume he means for the tow and that we will be returned to *Lynn Rival* when we reach shallow water. He says that is right, so I search out some bags and start choosing what to take, just for a short time. He stares at me and wants to see everything I pack. A few T-shirts, shorts and pants: those that haven't been trashed by the pirates. My camera: 'No problem'; a handful of books, two pads of paper, documents, passports and ship's papers: he doesn't seem concerned. Then I go up and Rachel goes down.

I grab what clothes I can find, our medicine chest and stocks of toiletries. Miraculously, I find the crib board and playing cards amongst all the debris in the saloon. I pack my diary, passport, crossword and yoga books. The situation is heartbreaking and chaotic, but I push myself to think clearly and do my best. Our existence is reduced to the contents of five small bags.

While Buggas is bellowing down the phone, I brew tea but can't face making anything else. We are all waiting for the arrival of the boat coming to collect us. I sense we are counting down to a traumatic event. At dusk, we're sent down below – me to my bunk, Paul to sit in the saloon. Baby Face keeps a close eye on us, sitting with his rifle pointed in our direction, alert to any move we make.

Buggas spends all his time shouting on the satphone and at the other two. His behaviour becomes manic. He comes down below and starts calling on the VHF, 'Arbou! Arbou! Arbou!', whistling and blocking Channel 16 with all manner of silly noises in an attempt to attract attention. Then he goes up on deck to use the satphone again, shouting endlessly. He is up and down the companionway steps like a yo-yo.

The engine is gamely running but only just making steerage way. Then, at about 2300, we have another VHF exchange with a warship. Buggas is frightened again and beside himself with anger.

'Radio! Speak warship! Speak – back off. No back off – kill you,' he shouts, as he aims his gun deliberately at me and gestures towards the VHF.

I switch on and immediately the calm, measured tones of a professional naval radio operator fill the boat.

Warship: Kota Wajar, this is Alpha 389. You are in my security zone. Alter course to north, please.

Warship: Kota Wajar, this is Alpha 389. You are threatening my security. Alter course to north. Please acknowledge.

I assume Alpha 389 is the warship. She must be calling another ship – the *Kota Wajar* – but I hear no response. I wait, allowing time for the *Kota Wajar* to reply. Buggas shouts, 'What he speak? Speak back off! No back off – kill you!'

Paul: EU Warship, EU Warship, this is sailing yacht Lynn Rival, Lynn Rival, over.

Warship: Kota Wajar, you are within my security radius. Alter course towards north immediately or I may take action.

Warship: Lynn Rival, I am under attack from a previously pirated ship. I will come back to you.

Warship: Kota Wajar, you are within my security radius. Alter course towards north immediately or I may take action.

Paul: Alpha 389, this is Lynn Rival. We are very frightened. We have been told we will be killed if you do not stand off.

Warship: Lynn Rival, I am under attack from a previously pirated ship. I will come back to you.

Warship: Kota Wajar, you are threatening my security. Alter course towards north immediately or I may take action, which will include the use of lethal force.

Warship: *Kota Wajar, alter course towards north immediately or I may take action, which will include the use of lethal force.*

Buggas looks ferocious: 'Speak back off. NO BACK OFF – KILL YOU!' There is no doubt he means it. He looks ready to start shooting.

Paul: *Alpha 389 this is Lynn Rival. Our captors say they will kill us if you do not stand off. We are terrified.*

Buggas screams, 'FINISH!'

Lethal force? Impressive. But only to an English speaker! Still, there is comfort in the professional manner of a navy at work.

The engine is now running on one cylinder, poor thing. I don't think it likes Somali fuel. I am called up, sent down, called up, sent down, like a jack out of the box; all the time three guns pointed at me. Always the same command: 'Quick! Quick!'; and always the same response from me: a shrug. Buggas makes me keep my head down. I have no idea whether the warship is within sight. I am exhausted, praying for a military intervention. They know we are here. Why don't they attack? Kill the bastards. Never mind us – we've had a good life. They've had six days to find us and stage a rescue or exercise 'law enforcement'. Soon it will be too late.

Buggas is ranting, behaving like a lunatic. I stay down below, hiding as best I can. There is nothing I can do. I just long to be rescued. The guards keep an eye on me, shining a torch through the porthole above. It's close to midnight, and Paul is called on deck again.

'UP! UP!' Here we go again. Oh! I can see a ship; no, two ships. There is a bright waxing moon, coming up to full, and the scene is one I'll never forget. No more than 200 metres away, ahead and slightly to port, a ship –

quite clearly the black silhouette of a warship, ready for action. And even closer, to starboard, the looming bulk of a commercial ship – a container ship, of perhaps 20,000 tonnes, heading directly away from us but not appearing to be making much speed.

'GO! GO!' Buggas pushes me towards the wheel, points at the container ship and indicates with his gun that I should 'ram' her.

I stand up on the seats to see better. 'DOWN!' he cries, with more violent movement of his AK-47. I head directly at the side of the ship, only a few metres away. We are still under power but only making about 1 knot. The ship has very little way on. Suddenly, there is a bang as we hit her. I see faces on the cable tier – the partly open lower deck where the mooring warps are handled. Men with guns – are any firing? I don't know. There's a lot of shouting, arms reaching out towards our rigging, then screeching as the ship slowly moves past. I think *Lynn Rival* screams as the rusty rivets tear into her hull, as the spreaders, holding the main rigging wires away from the mast, scrape along the side of the ship, setting my teeth on edge.

I look the other way; the warship is even closer, moving slowly and turning sharply to port. Certainly her skipper is courageous, manoeuvring so close to the container ship. Suddenly the warship lights us up with a searchlight. Is the navy – whose navy, I can't tell – going to take action? Please! Please! Then I hear gunfire from the container ship. The light goes out as we slip free of the ship. Buggas looks angrily at me – pointing with his rifle towards the container ship – wanting me to go into her stern. We have just enough power to nose into the centre of her stern. Again our rigging is grabbed, *Lynn Rival* is held close in, now almost out of sight of the warship, shielded by the bulk of the container ship.

'Engine finish!' commands Buggas. 'Light finish!'

I don't remember how, but the VHF is still on. The

DSC (digital selective calling) alarm suddenly wails with an incoming call. It's unlikely there are other ships nearby, so it must be coming from the warship. No time to respond – anyway, I won't be allowed near it! A rough rope ladder is thrown over the stern of the container ship, from the cable tier about 15 feet above. Buggas gesticulates: 'Up! Up!'

As I make for the ladder, one of the pirates ties a rope around my waist and pushes me up. I clamber over the rail onto the deck. I am pulled towards a bollard, some way from the rail, with another command: 'Sit!' Many pirates are about, all with AK-47s, all shouting. But most vividly I notice a pair of goats, tethered to the rail on the starboard side, away from all the excitement. Where is Rachel?

I'm lying on my bunk with no idea of what's going on. I dare not move. I just hope Paul is OK. I can't hear much over the engine, but Buggas keeps shouting (hoarsely by now) and they are all clambering around on deck. Suddenly, there's an almighty crash. Poor *Lynn Rival*! Poor us! What have we done to deserve this? A short pause. Then another mighty crash. I've had enough. I'm so exhausted and miserable. Do I care? The engine stops, but I still can't hear much. There's much background noise, shouting and confusion. The rocking of the boat is less. I hear some footsteps on deck above. A screeching noise erupts from the cabin: our VHF DSC alarm. Who set that off, and why? Then I hear Buggas shouting through the porthole above my bunk: 'UP! UP!'

Already dressed, I get out of my bunk. I can't find my shoes – most have been taken by the gang – so go up on deck barefooted. I see that we're alongside a big ship. There is one pirate in our cockpit and another on the foredeck. No sign of Paul. A gun directs me to the starboard side deck. Reluctantly, I go.

I am about to abandon *Lynn Rival*. This is the end.
There is a rope ladder for me to climb up the side of the
ship, five metres to the chain deck. Although the sea is
calm, there is inevitable churn from the ship's
propellers. *Lynn Rival* is crashing back and fore against
the side of the ship, so I can't easily grab the ladder.
They tie a rope around my waist. I manage to get onto
the ladder and climb aboard. As I reach the top, I see
the warship, standing by about 100 metres away, clear
in the moonlight, menacing but useless.

Disorientated and full of despair, I step on board,
looking for Paul. Immediately, I'm greeted by a softly
spoken man. 'Don't worry. You're safe now,' he has the
effrontery to say. He must be one of the pirates'
translators.

I'm furious. My life, my home, my everything has
been taken by these thugs. How dare they say such
things. The smug bastards. Safe? Now we're in the
clutches of the Somali pirate hierarchy? Now that *Lynn
Rival* is gone?

Paul is behind me, sitting forlornly on the deck
amongst the grime. We try to console each other. I
have no shoes. One of the gang is told to give me the
flip-flops he has stolen from Paul. Our bags! We ask the
translator where our packed bags are and he looks
bemused. We say we have bags ready on board. He
shouts to some others and one of the gangsters goes
back on board *Lynn Rival* to get them. One by one, our
bags are brought to us. Relief! Paul put a plastic bag of
books ready on the saloon table. Can we have those?
Someone is sent back again to get them.

A second man introduces himself as Omar and says
he has spoken to Sarah, my sister. My heart sinks at the
mention of our family and the thought of what they
must be going through. Before we are led to the door to
the accommodation decks, I take one last, lingering
look at poor *Lynn Rival*. Her rigging is suffering. One

of the spreaders breaks off. What will happen to her, our home, our life and our guardian? She is now abandoned, never to be seen again. The warship is slowly moving away, looking sinister but defeated.

Aboard *Kota Wajar*

Thursday, 29 October
0200

It's hard to take stock of our situation. The lighting is poor. We are aboard a long, low-sided commercial ship laden with metal containers and armed men everywhere. After six days at gunpoint on *Lynn Rival*, we are now in a pirate stronghold. Some pick up our bags and we follow them across the deck; others come up behind. The rest just stare.

They shepherd us through a door into the ship's accommodation block and upstairs, one, two, three, maybe four metal flights of stairs. Hustled along the side of the ship, we enter the bridge, where men in uniform, ship's officers, look tired but curious. Some say hello, but I don't know what to say. I'm upset and angry, so fearful of what is happening to us, and utterly disconsolate over the loss of *Lynn Rival*.

'Welcome. We are in the same boat.'

These are the first words of Captain Zaidi, master of the MV *Kota Wajar*, whose guests we have suddenly become. I like his sense of humour, although I don't think it is deliberate. We certainly appreciate his welcome hugs and friendly smile, and I apologise for 'ramming' his ship.

Captain Zaidi is effusive, welcoming and apologetic all at once. It's such a relief to meet a civilised person again. After hugging, exchanging names and shaking hands, he offers us the use of his cabin and instructs the steward to take us there.

The pirates seem to melt away – a relief, after six days of having at least one never more than two feet from us – but I notice several on the bridge, with light machine guns and RPG launchers at each side as well as the ever present AK-47s. Some of the ship's officers are lying on mattresses on the bridge.

We are led down a flight to the captain's day cabin, a large room with windows on the ship's starboard side and ahead, with easy chairs and an 'office' area with a desk and communications equipment. Buggas sits smugly in one chair. He ignores us. A better-dressed pirate in the other easy chair introduces himself, 'I am Commander. No problem. You home soon.'

Captain Zaidi bustles in and shows us through to his cabin. 'You must stay here – they make me sleep on the bridge, so I cannot use it,' he explains. He shows us the large bed, properly made up with clean linen, and the en-suite bathroom with bath, shower and toilet. There is also a desk and a window with the view forward obscured by containers stacked five high on the deck. 'You must lock the door when inside,' he warns. 'Don't let them in.'

He tells the steward to get the floor cleaned. 'The pirates have been using it – they make it filthy!'

One of the seamen arrives with our bags, another cleans up. Captain Zaidi himself helps Rachel to mop the floor. A pirate shoves by them to use the bathroom, but Rachel shoos him away. The captain tells us we will be anchoring at about 1100 off the coast of Somalia. And then? He's not sure. He asks the steward to bring us tea, fruit, whatever we want. Then he returns to the bridge – if we need anything we are to call him on the ship's phone. We shower – wonderful – and 'sleep' until 0600. Sleep? My mind is racing. What will happen? Will we be allowed to stay on the ship? There are so many needling questions about the future and such deep grief for *Lynn Rival*. But we are clean, we have a fresh bed, the air conditioning hums and the door is locked. We can rest more comfortably than we have for six days.

I'm looking forward to a proper wash and the chance to talk to Paul without being overheard. The captain told us they were hijacked 14 days ago, about 300 miles north of the Seychelles, then forced to head towards Somalia, to anchor about a mile offshore, some 30 miles south-west of the port of Hobyo. The officers and crew had their cabins ransacked and personal possessions stolen, just like us. Recently, they had been forced to motor to another hijacked ship and provide bunker fuel so that the Ukrainian crew could run their power systems. Then they had been forced to meet us some 180 miles from the coast. The officers have been made to sleep on the bridge. Captain Zaidi urged us to keep a close eye on our belongings: 'The only way to keep hold of anything is to have it on your person.' Nevertheless, he tried to reassure us. He hopes the pirates will keep us on board the *Kota Wajar*, and he says he will do his best to help us get out of this situation. Such a kind man! He has enough problems of his own without worrying about us.

We are brought tea, toasted sandwiches and other snacks. We wash and snuggle up in bed, enjoying the air-conditioned comfort. The captain's office is often full of shouting pirates, reminding us of where we are. No doubt our captors are happy to be amongst friends (fellow thieves!) again. We sleep fitfully, taking advantage of what is likely to be a short respite.

0630. The steward knocks: 'Breakfast.'

How civilised! The polite young Indian steward suggests we come down to the canteen one at a time, so the other can lock the door and guard our new 'haven'. I go down to enjoy omelette, salad, fish and tea, and sit with some of the ship's officers and crew, who are subdued but friendly and hospitable. The steward fusses over me, bringing hot water for tea, cold water and fruit.

I wake to the noise of pirates shouting, then doze till 0900. I get dressed, then sit up in bed and start writing. It's time to catch up on my diary and take stock while Paul is at breakfast. He returns with toast, omelette and tea for me. He's found out that there are 17 crew on board, of different nationalities, all kind and friendly. He also met the captain of another hijacked vessel in the anchorage, a Spanish trawler, who was visiting our ship for some reason. We try to relax, making the most of the comforts of the captain's cabin. It's good to be able to talk. We go over the attack. Does anyone know that it happened in the Seychelles? People should know that the authorities – warships and coastguard – are failing to stop the pirates getting into Seychelles waters. We were far from the high-risk area for piracy.

As a distraction we check our insurance documents and make a list of things stolen. We think about the things we want to try to tell our family, like cancelling the satphone account. We return to discussing the attack. Could we have foreseen it? Were we seduced by the presence of warships in the Seychelles and the publicity about increased coastguard activity? We checked all available sources of information. Did we miss anything we could have acted on? We spoke to fellow yachtsmen who had experience in the area, including one who left on the same route the day before us. They would have said something if they had known. We carried out normal exit procedures and the authorities said nothing.

Soon the captain's steward is back to tell us it's lunchtime. Paul goes to the mess and comes back telling me I should meet some of the crew. I go down, followed by a guard who sits and watches while I eat. A few of the officers and I talk freely. Everyone is sympathetic, telling me to be happy I am alive and not to worry about *Lynn*

Rival, but I end up crying. My emotions just overflow. I can't help thinking that our lives are ruined. We chose to opt out of the rat race and go cruising for as long as our health and savings would allow. For ten years we worked towards this dream – saving as much as we could, preparing ourselves and *Lynn Rival* for the challenges of ocean passages and self-sufficiency. The focus was *Lynn Rival*. Now she's gone – our home, our life, our sense of purpose – and whatever savings and assets we have will go on a ransom if we are to resume life as free people. How, at our age, will we ever start from scratch again? The shock that stunned me during the trauma of the attack and six-day occupation has subsided. I feel very, very depressed.

I return to the captain's cabin followed by my guard, who joins the others already hanging around in the captain's office. Buggas, Afieri and Baby Face are still loitering, no doubt keen to keep an eye on their prize.

We spend the afternoon reading and writing, trying to restore strength and emotional equilibrium. Mid afternoon brings another bang on the door: 'Come to bridge. Speak to family.'

It's Omar, a taller, better dressed, more refined Somali. I learn he is a 'translator' and he will be negotiating for our release. I leave Rachel in the cabin and follow him up to the bridge. Omar tells me to wait just inside the enclosed bridge while he heads out to the open wing on the port side. It's a chance for me to assess the pirate strength. I count one light machine gun, one RPG launcher and about three or four men with AK-47s. The same on the starboard side. The central area is left to the officers and crew. The pirates are relaxed, drinking tea from water bottles and passing around bunches of *chad*, the green narcotic plant. They offer me both. I politely accept the 'tea'. My nose says it is whisky! So I decline, shaking my head. I accept a few shoots of *chad* and follow their example, discarding the leaves and chewing the stems. It's bitter; no more agreeable than when I first tried it, years ago, in Aden, where it's known as *qat*. Strangely I remember that in Yemen it was normal to chew the leaves and discard the stalks.

Omar spends some time trying to make the call, then leans in – 'Come' – and hands me his mobile phone. It's a new model, colour screen, but the reception is poor. Omar does not say who is at the other end. He simply tells me to speak 'about your welfare, your situation'.

I say hello and ask who is there . . . It is someone called Angus, with Stephen, Rachel's brother.

Angus: *I have a message from Stephen – everyone here is fine. We are all thinking of you and hope you are both well. We can't wait to speak to you and see you.*
Paul: *Well, that's awfully nice. [Laughs.]*
Angus: *Paul, can you describe how you are being held?*
Paul: *We are in the captain's cabin of the container ship Kota Wajar.*
Angus: *Have you been rescued or have you been kidnapped?*
Paul: *We are hostage together with the crew of this ship.*
Angus: *Can you describe how you were taken hostage?*
Paul: *We were 57 miles from the north point of Mahé in the Seychelles . . . I was off watch – I was asleep and men with guns came aboard. It was Friday last week at 0230 local time.*
Angus: *What happened then?*
Paul: *We were forced to sail on motor towards Somalia . . .*
Angus: *How far are you off the Somali coast, do you think?*
Paul: *One mile. We are at anchor.*
Angus: *Do you know what the nearest town is?*
Paul: *Where is the nearest town? Hang on a minute . . . Hobyo – north-east from Mogadishu – about 200 miles.*
Angus: *Have your hostage takers demanded any ransom?*

Paul: *Not officially – they keep asking for money and took everything of value on the boat.*

Angus: *Do you know what nationality of ship you are being held on?*

Paul: *Yes – Kota Wajar is a Singapore ship – I think PIL is the line.*

Angus: *How are you being treated?*

Omar grabs the phone, one of the nearby pirates is shouting at him. The pirate is angry, threatening me with his gun. I guess he's nervous that I have said where we are. But surely they realise that the navies have been shadowing the ship? Omar says they will reconnect the call, but despite trying many times we don't speak again, and I am taken back to the cabin. I start to write up my diary notes, recording as much as I can of the past six days.

We are feeling more and more frustrated as well as confused. We've no idea who's who and what's going on. Paul is despondent about the difficulty of communicating with anyone outside. We are totally in the gang's control, dependent on their whim. We gird our emotions and try to stay calm. Paul goes down to the mess for supper at 1730 and I go down after, accompanied by a guard, and meet more of the crew. We talk guardedly about the situation we are all in. I ask how they are coping. They are trying to keep busy, following their normal routines, undertaking maintenance work and so on, but they are running out of things to do. Some of them have now been allowed to speak to their families and though glad to have this opportunity they are worried about the impact this situation is having on them. We talk about the pirates and agree that their behaviour is inhuman.

Back in the captain's cabin we lock ourselves in and try to ignore the noise from the office. We soon have another visitor. It's Moses, one of the ship's technicians. The pirates have put all the confiscated personal laptops in one of the drawers in the captain's cabin. Moses has been allowed access to them. He tells us there have been a number of people calling today on the ship's telephone, asking for us. A little later, the captain's steward comes to visit. He has my purse and credit cards. Apparently our pirates had asked if they were worth anything and he persuaded them they were no good. It is some comfort to get them back, even though I don't anticipate using them again. I hope my sister has already cancelled my cards.

I hear some Arabic spoken outside, another mystery. I start to undress for bed when I hear another knock on the door. A pirate summons us both to the bridge for a telephone interview with the BBC World Service.

It is dark: a dry, clear night. We are led to the starboard side of the bridge, out onto the wing, where we look out over the windswept ocean, wishing we were out there, where we are supposed to be, en route to Tanzania, far away from this evil place.

Omar makes the call, passes the phone to Paul and says, 'Speak about health. Say you are well. No speak of location.'

Briefly I hear a man speaking heavily accented English. He must be a Somali. We exchange hellos. Another man comes on. He doesn't sound like a natural English speaker. I can understand him, but the line is poor. He says he is with the BBC World Service and asks if we are OK. 'Yes,' I say. 'We are both well and unharmed. I cannot talk about anything else.' I have played my part, and Omar takes the phone. We are taken back down to the cabin and left in peace for the night and the following morning.

Friday, 30 October

The Captain's steward keeps us supplied with snacks while we wonder when the next shock will come. 'Our' pirates – Buggas, Afieri and Baby Face – seem to have disappeared. Paul goes down to the mess for breakfast and brings back some for me. The captain comes in to warn us to be careful what we say to the crew in case it gets passed on to our captors. I accompany him back up to the bridge. He shows me around and tells me about the rendezvous with *Lynn Rival*. Like us, he needs to offload. He describes how he was forced to ignore the VHF calls from the warship telling him to alter course. The pirates were hitting him on the head with a bottle of water, insisting he maintain course. It conjures a surreal picture, but I empathise with the horror he must have felt at hearing the warship's threats.

I go down for lunch at 1130 and enjoy fried fish and a fresh orange while I chat with some more of the crew. After lunch, Paul goes up to the bridge while I stay in the cabin. There's a knock at the door. I open it to a couple of pirates. One says, in rehearsed English, 'You go boat. You go ashore. Soon fly home!'

I say we must pack our bags. I must get Paul. They repeat, 'Go boat,' gesticulating that I should follow them. I start shoving things back in our bags. I'm terrified about leaving our last worldly possessions unattended but decide to go up to the bridge to find Paul.

Captain Zaidi had asked me to pop up to the bridge for a chat, so after lunch I make my way up, unchallenged, and learn about the ship and her equipment. The MV *Kota Wajar* is a typical medium-sized container ship of 17,000 GRT (Gross Registered Tonnage) and 185m long. She carries about 950 containers, stacked high on deck, with a cruising speed of a little less than 20 knots. As one seafarer to another, we are lost in discussions about the business of navigating at sea – the differing perspectives from a ship's bridge as opposed to a yacht's deck; the two big radar consoles – when Rachel's head appears around the door.

'Paul, we have to go – I've started packing the bags.'

My heart falls into a churning stomach. I'd forgotten for

a few hours that we have been kidnapped, that we have lost our home and that we have no idea what the future may hold. I see the fear on Rachel's face and I think, 'We have each other – we'll be OK.'

We descend the steps into the cabin, Captain Zaidi behind us. It's last-minute panic. We hurl everything into the bags, the steward helping with water bottles. Captain Zaidi thrusts fruit, tea bags, toilet rolls into our hands. Then towels (we'd only remembered to bring one from *Lynn Rival*), one large and one small. And a bag each of walnuts and chickpea snacks. By now two pirates are seizing our bags and we are hustled towards the stairs again. As we pass through the day cabin, another English-speaking Somali, presumably a translator, comments, 'Negotiations going well – you go home soon.' We are led down to the cable deck, suddenly isolated and alone again. Captain Zaidi has been taken back to the bridge. More ordnance – here are many men with machine guns and AK-47s, and the goats, complete with a bunch of hay.

'Wait!' An AK-47 is aimed at my stomach for emphasis while Rachel is led to the rail and disappears down the rope ladder.

I clamber down the ladder into a waiting skiff, helped by two men already on board. Three or four other pirates join us, but no bags, no Paul! We set off for the shore, a wet, bumpy ride. I struggle to hold on. Where can Paul be? Please don't say I am to go ashore alone. Halfway towards land, we encounter the hijacked Spanish trawler and draw up alongside. There's much shouting to and fro. A full midday sun shines and I have no sunhat. I keep my head down but can't resist one quick glance up, when I register some of the ship's crew staring at me. What must they be thinking?

Eventually someone throws a life jacket on board. It's given to me and I put it on. We proceed to the shore and they drive the skiff right up the beach. I'm helped out and taken across the sand to a waiting Toyota Land Cruiser. This is a carefully orchestrated operation. The door is opened and I climb onto one of the back seats. Air-conditioning! A bottle of chilled water! I'm numb with fear and ask desperately for Paul.

'Paul is coming,' says a well-spoken man in the driver's seat, who I think must be one of the translators. I look around and see a fleet of skiffs on the beach. Some men are working with angle grinders and welders on engine mountings, others carrying and fetching. There's great activity. This must be a hub of pirate operations . . . I see Paul coming ashore in another skiff.

I watch Rachel go, then have to wait. Soon, our bags are lowered over the rail. Then I hear, 'Down! Now!' I climb over the rail and down the ladder into a skiff. Buggas! He is sitting in the stern next to a pirate I haven't seen before who operates the 60 hp outboard motor. One more pirate drops into the skiff and we're off. Rachel must be in another boat. It's a fast, wet, helter-skelter ride to shore. It is sunny but windy. As we reach shallower water, the seas build up. Buggas throws me an oilskin, pulls a tarpaulin over me and another one over our bags. We swerve as the driver slaloms a passage through the waves. Buggas bids me to hold on tight. We approach the shore at over 25 knots, drive straight up the sandy beach and lurch to a halt.

'Out! Run! Run!'

I climb over the gunwale and stagger up the beach about a hundred metres to a high point where two Toyota Land Cruisers wait, black with tinted windows, bad man's wheels! One door is held open – I climb in and it's slammed shut. Thank God, Rachel is already in the car. Welcome to Somalia.

I'm so happy to see Paul – and our bags. Paul gets into the car next to me and we wait, noticing at least one other

Toyota and two old Land Rovers nearby. Buggas comes up to our vehicle and I remark ironically to Paul, 'He's wearing your watch.' This is Paul's treasured Rolex, which he has owned for more than 30 years, acquired when he worked in Saudi Arabia and for the first time in his life had more money than he needed. Our driver, the translator, then says something sharp to Buggas in Somali. He must be fairly senior in the pirate organisation because Buggas, cowed, points to the old watch Paul is now wearing. Our driver intervenes again in Somali. Paul offers the old one to Buggas and, miraculously, gets his trusty old Rolex back.

Sitting in the back of the car, holding hands with Rachel, I reflect on our situation. Our 36-hour interlude on the *Kota Wajar* has been a godsend. The hospitality of Captain Zaidi, his officers and crew has been wonderful. They're not in a good situation themselves, but they selflessly welcomed us and did more than we had any right to expect to make us comfortable. We have been given a chance to tuck our recent experience away in a deep part of our minds. The trauma of the attack, the seizure of *Lynn Rival* and our passage across the ocean at gunpoint will not be forgotten, but we can face the uncertain future clean, rested and reassured that for now we are together.

I guess we are ready for anything. We are going to have to adjust from being in charge to being prisoners. Rachel and I have always been equal skippers on *Lynn Rival*, taking alternate watch responsibilities. We are planners, managers and doers. Now we have to adjust to passive roles as hostages. As sailors we cope with discomfort and living with the bare minimum, but we do so knowing there'll be an end to a passage. We just have to hold on. In this situation, we don't have an end that we can see on a chart or a map. Worrying about what will happen next is a new and debilitating emotion.

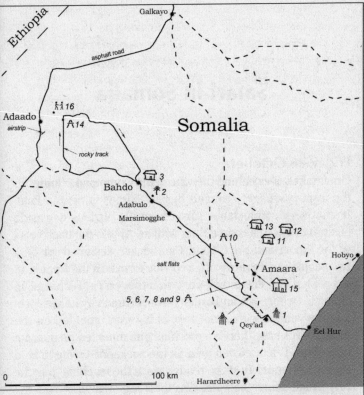

Ethiopia

Galkayo

asphalt road

Adaado
airstrip

鬥16

A14

rocky track

Somalia

🛖3

Bahdo 🌴2

Adabulo

Marsimogghe

🏠13 🛖12

A10 🏠11

Hobyo

salt flats

Amaara

🏠15

5, 6, 7, 8 and 9 A

🛖4 Qey'ad

Eel Hur

0 ——— 100 km

Harardheere

Legend	
🌴	day camp
A	tarpaulin shelter
🛖	African hut
🛖	village house
🏠	big home
鬥	rendezvous
---	main tracks
—	our routes

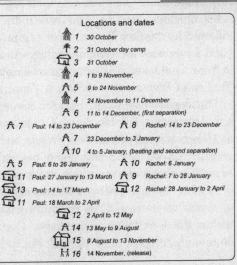

Locations and dates

🛖 1   *30 October*

🌴 2   *31 October day camp*

🛖 3   *31 October*

🛖 4   *1 to 9 November,*

A 5   *9 to 24 November*

🛖 4   *24 November to 11 December*

A 6   *11 to 14 December, (first separation)*

A 7   *Paul: 14 to 23 December*   A 8   *Rachel: 14 to 23 December*

A 7   *23 December to 3 January*

A 10   *4 to 5 January, (beating and second separation)*

A 5   *Paul: 6 to 26 January*   A 10   *Rachel: 6 January*

🛖 11   *Paul: 27 January to 13 March*   A 9   *Rachel: 7 to 28 January*

🛖 13   *Paul: 14 to 17 March*   🛖 12   *Rachel: 28 January to 2 April*

🛖 11   *Paul: 18 March to 2 April*

🛖 12   *2 April to 12 May*

A 14   *13 May to 9 August*

🏠 15   *9 August to 13 November*

鬥 16   *14 November, (release)*

Safari in Somalia

Friday, 30 October

Omar takes over behind the wheel, the Commander jumps in the front passenger seat and Buggas climbs in next to Paul. It's not very comfortable. Apart from the obvious downside of sitting next to a coarse thug with an AK-47, the back seats of the 'Sport and Surf' Land Cruiser are designed for only two people. As we move off, a convoy forms. At the front is an old white Land Rover pick-up – what they call a 'Technical' in countries where law and order is conspicuous by its absence: a utility vehicle with some sort of big gun mounted on the back. In this case there's a machine gun mounted on the roof of the cab. Ten or eleven men fill the back, one trying to hold the rocket launcher at the ready, one at the machine gun, the rest brandishing their AK-47s, their legs hanging over the sides, flip-flops dangling. And three in the cab. Then our car, followed by another Toyota. Bringing up the rear is a khaki Land Rover with the same manning arrangement as the one in front. Quite some security escort for a tourist couple from Tunbridge Wells!

The convoy formation induces something of a holiday atmosphere among the Somali contingent, while we are apprehensive, full of nameless dreads, our minds unwilling to accept that we are being taken beyond reach of rescue. Armed robbery has morphed into kidnapping. By common definition, we have not been victims of 'piracy', as at the time of attack we were not 'on the high seas'. We were sailing within the Seychelles archipelago. Our attackers may be commonly referred to as 'pirates', but we see them plainly as criminal gangsters – they are kidnappers and extortionists.

We have no idea where they are taking us, or how far. As we drive inland, Omar goes into tour-guide mode, assuming a lecturing tone, pointing out the wildlife: *sagara* (small deer), donkeys, *ari* (goat), the occasional *gil* (camel) and a variety of birds. Laughing, he points out a 'Somali house' – a nomad hut roughly constructed of scrap wood and plastic – and asks the name of the small deer in English. We have no idea but suggest they make good eating, which makes him and the others guffaw.

The sandy track through sparse coastal grassland allows fairly fast progress. In a little over an hour we have covered about 30 km. We skirt a small village, which Omar says is called Qey'ad, and turn off the main track into thick bush, with trees large enough to hide the cars. Here, we stop and are taken a short distance on foot to an abandoned wooden hut in a small clearing. The men are all around, establishing a camp, clearing places on the ground to put down their mats and setting up the machine-gun stations. Our bags are brought to us.

The hut is our first experience of Somali construction. About eighteen feet in diameter, with low walls, it has four internal poles supporting a conical roof. Both the roof and walls are formed of stout cut and trimmed branches, covered and woven with smaller branches. This one has seen better days and the thatch is decidedly thin. There's certainly plenty of ventilation, so the inside is comfortable although obviously not waterproof. When is the rainy season? We haven't done any research for Somalia, so we wonder how much the climate differs from the coastal areas of Tanzania, for which we have prepared.

Omar's English is confusing, so we have to concentrate hard to understand him explaining that we'll be living in camps for a few days, fending for ourselves. He wants a list of our requirements so he can get them from the town. We are bemused, but Paul gets out a pen and paper. Where do we begin? How do we know what is available? Paul writes down:

mattresses, sheets, blankets, torches, Primus stove, fuel, lighter, kettle, cooking pot, water, tea, sugar, rice, flour, fruit, vegetables and meat. We ask if it gets cold at night and decide to add jackets just in case. Paul thinks of chairs. Squatting, as the locals do, doesn't come naturally to us.

Omar disappears with our wish list. Another man who speaks English tells us 'these people' have not decided how much money to ask for: 'You will speak to your family now. Tell them you are well. Do not tell them your location.' Buggas and some of the gangsters gather round, interested in what is going on, even though none seems to speak more than a few words of English.

Paul is handed the phone. It's Stephen but there's a long delay on the line, which makes communication difficult. After an exchange of hellos, Rachel takes over.

> *Rachel: Hello, Stephen?*
>
> *Stephen: Hello, Rachel, how are you?*
>
> *Rachel: I'm bearing up.*
>
> *Stephen: Good.*
>
> *Rachel: Thank you for everything you're doing.*
>
> *Stephen: We're working hard for you, I can assure you.*
>
> *Rachel: Thank you very much. Please give everyone our love, especially Paul's father.*
>
> *Stephen: We think of you all the time.*
>
> *Rachel: I'm sure you do. Please try not to worry about us. Tell everybody to try.*
>
> *Stephen: We're speaking to everybody to try to get your release.*
>
> *Rachel: Yes, I realise and please don't worry about us – we're managing.*
>
> *Stephen: Can you tell me anything about where you are – no, I'm sorry – are you on land?*
>
> *Rachel: Yes.*
>
> *Stephen: We're trying to persuade them that you're blameless tourists and hopefully they will realise that releasing you will show them in a good light. Can you tell*

us about the conditions you're held in?

Rachel: *They tell us that we're safe and we shouldn't worry and that if we want anything they will provide it in terms of food and water and everything like that, you know, they are very hospitable people so don't worry . . . Physically we're fine, physically we're healthy.*

Stephen: *I've spoken to the prime minister, the Somali PM, and he tells me they don't mean you any harm. Are you in a house?*

Rachel: *Yes. I can't say.*

Stephen: *No, no, don't worry.*

Rachel: *I'm sorry for all the trouble I've been causing you.*

Stephen: *No, no, don't be sorry for anything.*

Rachel: *So I mean the only thing is we're devastated at losing* Lynn Rival – *we're so upset.*

Stephen: *It's still afloat and . . . the navy have got her. We're working to persuade the people that releasing you will make them be seen in a very positive light, and we're appealing to their compassionate nature.*

Rachel: *Good.*

Angus: *Rachel, it's Angus Walker here from ITV News. I'm sitting next to Steve – do the hostage takers have any message for anyone?*

Rachel: *I think, they think I ought to stop now.*

Stephen: *We love you.*

Rachel: *Thank you, thank you, and we really appreciate what everyone is trying to do for us. Thank you. Goodbye.*

Once the call is over our mystery helper leaves us, ominously reciting the sickening mantra: 'Don't worry. You're safe. All they want is money.'

I know that Stephen will do his best for us. He's a retired farmer, not a professional negotiator, but we have no one else. I trust he's getting good advice from the government and police. When Stephen mentions that the navy has *Lynn Rival*, I'm wary. It's probably better our captors think *Lynn Rival* – our home – is gone. I don't dare suggest to Stephen that it's no good appealing to the gangsters' compassionate nature. I fear that they have none. When Angus of ITN intervened, I realised our conversation is likely to be broadcast on TV. How humiliating is that? How awful that every detail of our plight will be public knowledge! I worry about the impact our capture will have on family and friends.

I wonder how many calls they will allow us. We have to assume there may be no more. They haven't told us to ask for money – they seem to be content that our families know we are at the mercy of a gang of thugs and beyond the reach of law enforcement. I begin to realise how difficult it's going to be to get any message across. Do they have proper telephones here? Are we to be taken to a town, where the translators might have an office? I am concerned that the media may portray our attack as having occurred on the high seas, near the Somali coast, rather than in the Seychelles, almost 800 miles away. I tried to make that clear in yesterday's call from the *Kota Wajar*, but I make a mental note to try to get it over again. It's important to me that we aren't seen as negligent.

Left alone, we discuss our growing unease about the problem of communication. The mobile phone connections are poor. They tell us what to say and listen in to our every word. Who knows what they understand or make of what we say? They cut us off when we go 'off message'. We have no control. We have to stay calm and keep hoping that something will be resolved.

The gangsters who had been listening in to the call have long since dispersed. Buggas and the Commander are around but keep their distance. We emerge from the hut, where what seems to be dozens of men watch us, standing or sitting with AK-47s to hand. It is an intimidating group to approach to ask if we can go to the toilet and wash. Buggas leads us a short distance away, behind some bushes, and brings a 20-litre plastic container of well water plus a much smaller, used oil container to decant it into, complete with globules of emulsified oil in the bottom.

After washing, we sit and wait in the decrepit hut for Omar to come with our supplies. At dusk, we notice some of the guards praying. So some of them are religious! Is that a good sign? Omar returns with the all-important torches. At least we can see what he's brought us: a mat, two thin foam mattresses, sheets, blankets, pillows and pillowcases; plates, bowls, forks and spoons; glass mugs and a Thermos flask; biscuits, tea bags and two polyester tracksuits. He has also brought back some cooked spaghetti in an insulated container but realises he's forgotten the fish. We wait for him to go back into town to get it, with high hopes of some nice fried fish like we've tasted when cruising along the coast of Yemen. It turns out to be tinned tuna, which we tip over the spaghetti and eat with the forks thoughtfully bought for us! The gangsters eat by squatting around a cooking pot, taking turns to scoop out the spaghetti with their right hands, then shovelling it into their mouths.

Omar shows us where to put our mat and mattresses on the ground outside the hut. There's nothing else to do, so we organise our bedding, undress and try to sleep. Guards sit or lie down all around us; some are noisy, making mobile phone calls. We doze, exhausted by the constant anxiety.

Our trip ashore has been a journey into the unknown. I'm edgy and fearful about what will happen next, but the adventurer inside me is also fascinated to see what Somalia is like. I clutch on to the hope of rescue or release, determined not to let my anger and anxiety get the better of me. The situation is so surreal; it's difficult to function and be a 'good hostage', like when we were asked to write a list of things we need. I was so cross and indignant, I wanted to tell them how ridiculous they are. What do we need? Well, everything: our life, our home, our boat!

At 10.30 p.m. the gangsters start getting up and moving around, shouting to one another. A few are using torches to see what they are doing. Then we hear that horribly familiar command: 'Up! Up!' – and realise we must be moving on. It's not as if we were really comfortable, so it's easy to get up, dress again and pack our things. Omar brings our Toyota closer, forcing it through the bush making that painful screech of paintwork being scratched. Our bags are first in, then our newly acquired bedding and household items. We get in our familiar seats and move on by 11.30 p.m.

We're given two bottles of mineral water; Omar says he has plenty in the back. The policy of maintaining the value of the assets may be coming from him. The convoy forms as before and off we go . . . and on we go . . . and on, and on. We are heading inland again, our speed between 10 and 40 kph, going mostly west-north-west for the first few hours. The road is poor, only a track twisting and turning between low bushes, sometimes sandy, making for more comfort and a little speed, but with frequent stony outcrops, taken very slowly, following ever-increasing detours around the worst patches, trying to find a better route. Most of the time either Buggas or the Commander is shouting into a mobile phone against a backdrop of Somali music on the radio.

> It's uncomfortable sitting between a shouting Buggas and Rachel, but at least I can see better through the windscreen. I can't see much through the heavily tinted side windows, just the eerie white outlines of bush and scrub either side in the headlights. We climb gently, about 300 m in 20 km, until we join a more worn track that seems to follow the route of a wadi up an escarpment. Often the wadi sides are six feet high, giving the impression of being in a tunnel. But always the twisting and tilting, trying to hold on – no grab handles within reach – trying not to crush Rachel or fall against Buggas's gun. At least there's no other traffic. After we reach the plateau, the track improves and we head north. The

vehicles halt frequently without anyone getting out, just yelled discussions between the drivers. They navigate their way across the desolate terrain though there are neither signposts nor village names.

Saturday, 31 October

As dawn breaks, we pass through an area of open scrubland and come upon a 'checkpoint', manned by a few Somalis with AK-47s hiding behind some oil drums. There's a mobile-phone mast in the distance and a few buildings, maybe a village. Omar hangs back while the lead Land Rover stops and the occupants engage in gangster chat, with much waving of guns. Both the Commander and Buggas point their guns aggressively out of the windows, and we drive on as fast as the road allows. We see a big drilling rig not far away, presumably boring wells. Within a few miles we pass extensive salt pans. The road meanders around them and settles into a long, fairly straight, flattish stretch. Traffic! An ancient truck approaches us, loaded with empty salt sacks, belching thick black smoke. Omar sensibly pulls off the road. He tells us that the truck will take a full load back to Mogadishu – this being the main road.

'Service station,' Omar announces, referring to a cluster of bushes where we are allowed out for a quick stretch, toilet break and dawn prayers for some. A few of the gangsters come to look at us. A machine gunner is wearing one of our sailing jackets from *Lynn Rival*! Another – a fat man – introduces himself as Mohamed. Then onwards again. Our backs are stiff and sore from the jolting when, at about 7.30 a.m., we enter a large village and stop outside a stone building, single storey with no doors or windows, just a shell.

'Go inside, we stay here,' says Omar, getting two plastic chairs out of the back and handing them to us, without a hint about how long we are to stay. We pace the room then sit down and wait while Omar goes off. Our bags remain in the car, so we dig out the cards and start a game of cribbage, going through the motions, but very tired. The gangsters are milling around, watching us but not bothered what we do. Tea arrives – a misnomer; Somali *sheh* is hot sugar solution with a little brown dye, at a concentration that even our experience in Arab countries has failed to prepare us for. There's also some flat bread, nicely baked not fried. We appreciate the energy boost from the sweet tea and study the not very interesting scenery. A few local people wander by, including children, but they're shy and don't bother us. After another ten minutes, the men become jumpy, signalling with their guns that it's time for us to get back into 'our' car. Omar says, 'No breakfast here. We – um – go on.'

We clamber wearily back into the Toyota and wait as the convoy assembles. Omar points out a cart pulled along by an ass, wooden wheels squeaking at each turn. He says these are people who 'move from place to place'. We teach him the word 'nomad'. A small child sits on the cart, packed in amongst the family belongings, looking vulnerable with an untreated harelip – a reminder of the children so often shown in newspaper appeals for aid.

In the daylight, there is plenty to see: signs of cultivation – fields marked out by thorny brushwood fences that act as goat barriers – and a landscape dotted with herds of goats and strange-looking black-headed sheep. As we tick off the miles, we spot camel trains, donkeys, long-necked birds and much more. The track is often straight for long stretches, but, with no other traffic, it doesn't feel like the main road Omar claims it is.

A mobile-phone mast indicates that we are approaching the next settlement. At the village, Omar stops briefly to talk to a few local men, apparently asking directions, and then drives off track and across the scrub until we reach a more bushy area with tall trees.

Omar declares he needs a rest from driving. The gangsters secure a boundary while Omar gets out our mats and tells us to sleep under the shade of a tree. He warns us to be careful of the thorns, and we soon discover how insidious they are, scratching our bodies and lodging painfully under the skin of our hands, our feet and even our heads. Omar asks if we like goat meat and promises we'll have some later. The rest of the gang, 25 to 30 men, spread out under adjoining trees. It's only 8.30 a.m., but it's already getting warm.

Watchful, bored, we sit and listen to the wildlife in the semi-desert landscape. As well as the grazing animals we are becoming aware of the huge variety of beetles and birds. One bird is particularly mesmerising – it behaves like a grouse but has the long legs and neck of a wader. I try to give my mind a rest and watch the new world go by while my muscles relax from the tensions of the drive. Just after noon, Omar brings us a late breakfast: '*Behr* – goat liver. You like?'

'Yes, thank you very much.'

Liver and onion. Is this a special treat? It's delicious. We are appreciative, though conscious that we don't owe them any thanks, but it goes against the grain not to be polite. We won't lower ourselves to their level.

Our temporary camp is visited by goats and goatherds, and we're surprised that our captors are apparently welcomed by locals and relaxed about us being seen. They seem to be on good terms with everyone they meet passing through these villages. Surely ordinary, hard-working Somali people don't tolerate these villains?

I fidget and doze until mid-afternoon, trying to catch up on my sleep. The shade is not good, and I'm feeling hot and bothered. Our guards keep their distance. From time to time we hear Paul's mobile phone ringing, unsettling because we realise that Buggas is now using Paul's handset. At 3 p.m., we are given a container of water for washing, but there's nowhere for me to hide, so I just wash my hands. Not for the first time am I conscious of being the only woman in a large group of strange men.

Later in the day we are given some pieces of stewed goat, which we chew with relish. Rice follows, with a few bits of flavouring, probably onions. It's now almost dark.

Omar's whining soft voice and laboured English – increasingly irritating – announces another journey: 'We go – um – not far. To special house. The main road and airport are not far. You will – um – have no more long journey.' Taking him at his word, we force our muscles into cramp position and off we go. Same convoy again.

In little more than an hour we reach a small town, a more substantial settlement than the villages we have seen. Many of the buildings are of concrete blockwork with 'crinkly tin' roofs. Speeding through, we catch glimpses of a few shops, then suddenly stop and turn sharp right, through a gateway barely wide enough for the car, and into a small walled yard. Steel gates slam shut behind. There is a palpable sense of arrival.

It's dark, so we can't see well, but our 'special house' is in fact a small yard, surrounded by an eight-foot-high rendered wall, with a terrace of three single-roomed 'houses' on one side. The furthest seems to be occupied by a family. Buggas, the Commander and Omar disappear into the middle room. Our bags and bedding are dumped in the next. A smaller room near the end contains drums of well water. Finally there's a small hole-in-the-floor privy with a door but no roof. All the construction is of concrete blockwork, with fresh cement render in the privy. Has it been prepared specially for us?

The men mill around the small yard, in and out of the gate and back again, seemingly checking out this latest 'position'. Buggas barks a few orders from time to time. They settle in groups, some inside, some out, chatting and arguing. At the far end of the yard, there's a rough, brushwood hut containing a bleating goat that adds to the noise level. We see glimpses of the family in the end house, but they keep their distance. How do they feel about this sudden invasion?

I'm disturbed by the close proximity of our guards and their guns. They're extremely noisy. I feel intensely claustrophobic. I ask Omar about the water situation and use of the toilet. Knowing that water is scarce in Somalia, I wonder if we'll be rationed. Omar gives me an old oil container and tells me to ask for water when I need it. On his instructions, one of the gangsters fills up my container from the drums. Then I ask Omar to show me the toilet, and he demonstrates how to squat over it! I'm still left wondering how much water I can use, and we have no proper washing bowl. I make-do using a flannel and one of our newly acquired stainless-steel food bowls.

Omar confirms we will be here for a while, so we unpack by torchlight. The room is about 12 foot by 10, with a small window, which like the door has a rough curtain nailed over it. We put our mat and bedding on the floor, and arrange our bags. There's nothing else to do, so we lie down but can't sleep. We have to put up with gangster chatter, mobile calls and also bleating goats, but thankfully no mosquitoes.

My mind is going over and over the prospect of living in this place for days, let alone months on end, cooped up like animals in an airless room with little light, surrounded by armed, hostile men. How can we possibly survive?

Omar is the only one who speaks any English, but he's difficult to understand. He seems to talk in code, using English words, but I don't follow what he means. He says we have driven inland and are fairly close to an airport. Surely he can't mean Mogadishu airport? My knowledge of Somalia and its geography, let alone its culture, is almost non-existent.

I sink to a new low. This, for me, is the darkest point yet in our ordeal. In the frenetic safari activity of the past days, my mind has been able to put aside the reality, perhaps even experience it as if it were a dream. How could it be happening? Now it hits me. We have been kidnapped by a bunch of violent thugs, boys with assault rifles. We have been taken to the heart of the most lawless country on earth. We are far from the coast, 150 km I reckon. How wide is Somalia? I think maybe 300 km. So we are just as far from the border with Ethiopia. There is no law enforcement. Fanatical religious terrorists, sub-groups of al-Qaeda, are at large. Gangs of armed boys and men roam at will. How can we survive? How can 'our' gang protect us? How can they let us go, even supposing some deal can be done? As we go to lie down, I am almost in tears. I mustn't let Rachel know how I feel.

I merely say, 'I don't think I'm going to like it here.'

Sunday, 1 November

I wake at dawn to the sounds of the town coming to life: goats bleating, cockerels crowing and children – or is it women? – chattering in high-pitched voices as they pass nearby. I'm restless and want to get up, but Paul is still sleeping. There's no point in getting up. The yard is full of men, and I don't want to sit outside on my own. Eventually I rise, dress and go to the toilet, keeping my head down. I need water to wash my face and flush the loo, so muster the courage to ask for some. Omar is not around and none of the men look at all friendly. When I say, 'I want water' – what else can I say? – they look away and obviously don't want to help me. I'm not allowed to siphon it off myself, not that I want to, as the tube doesn't look at all hygienic! I stand there pathetically until someone points me to another small container. It's half full – enough, until the next time.

A goat wanders in and bleats. Rachel shoos it out. A gangster has made an open fire in the yard, and he brings hot water in a flask to make tea. They give us a few handfuls of sugar, wrapped in a bit of torn-off black plastic bag. There's still no sign of Omar. When Paul gets up, we sit outside in the shade of our Toyota, drinking tea and awaiting developments. Once the sun is up, the heat and direct sunlight are intolerable. The yard offers no shade, so we move back inside, though there's no through ventilation and the tin roof generates a micro-climate of high humidity. Using the table for our newly acquired household goods, we try to create some order out of chaos by organising our things, including a big tin of dried milk. We tie back the window curtain to allow in more light and improve the air flow. One of the guards notices and shouts, 'No,' then gesticulates aggressively. They are watching our every move.

After spaghetti and goat stew for brunch, we try to do some exercises to relieve our stiff backs, but it's impossible to relax. Reading is difficult with so little light. Paul has a siesta! By midday, the compound is quiet. Most of the gangsters have disappeared. We feel almost abandoned. Where have they gone? Are they having a meeting to decide how much money to ask for?

At 2.30 p.m. Omar rushes into our room. 'We go. Al-Qaeda come. They will kill you.'

Hurriedly shoving everything into the car, we jump in. The gates open and Omar starts to back out. 'Wait!' Paul shouts. 'The chairs – don't leave the chairs!' We roar off out of town with the other vehicles. Buggas, the Commander and Omar are all shouting wildly on their mobile phones. An arm is sticking out of the other Toyota, clutching our precious chairs. They won't be with us for long! We follow the khaki Land Rover. Omar says al-Qaeda are only 10 km down the road. 'They will kill you,' he repeats, with glee.

We circle around town to retrace our route. After about an hour, the khaki Land Rover stops, dropping engine oil. An older gangster we nickname 'Land Rover Man' looks under the bonnet and shrugs. Buggas and the Commander start screaming into mobile phones again, without getting out of the car. Half an hour passes; another Toyota arrives. Summoned up from where? From whom? Men pile in and we set off again, one extra body in our car – now four in the back. The white Land Rover takes over in the lead. Omar puts his foot down; we get used to the bodily contact, playing sardines with gangsters. Our backs are soon in agony from the twisting, and there's no chance of changing position.

Are we heading back to where we came from? We retrace yesterday's route, although we don't pass the salt pans. We have one brief stop for a stretch, the toilet bush and a few prayers.

At dusk, Omar passes his mobile to me. 'Speak to this man.'

I try to hold the phone to my ear, despite the jolting. A voice says something, but I can't understand. I've got Buggas's AK-47 sticking into my right knee and I'm trying not to crush Rachel on my left, while Omar twirls the wheel to avoid the rockiest bits. Finally, I make something out:

Man: *I am Somali man with the British Embassy in Nairobi. How are you? Can I help you?'*
What can I say? Where to begin? A helicopter and a lot of firepower would be a start.
Paul: *We have been kidnapped. We have lost our home, lost everything. Other than that we are fine.*
Thanks to my father for my sense of humour.
Man: *Give me contact in London.*
Paul: *Sarah Collett. The authorities will know her number.*

Contact lost. I am suspicious, but maybe his question had been designed to prove he was speaking to the right person.

Soon afterwards, we stop in the unlit outskirts of a village. From the shadows, a man emerges holding the ubiquitous AK-47. He climbs awkwardly into the front of the car, sharing the front seat with the Commander. Perhaps he's a guide? We lurch slowly onward, looking for something, the Land Rover and the other Toyotas behind us. Stop. Discussion. Move on. Argument. Stop.

Shouting between the drivers. Phone calls. Turn back. Goodness knows how they have any idea where we are. Eventually, we pull off the track and drive through the bush, twisting and turning to find a clear path. Yes, we have reached our destination. Over there – an African hut in a brushwood-fenced compound is caught in the headlights.

It is now 8.30 p.m. We've endured another six-hour drive. We have no sense of where we are or whether each day will be like this. The car door opens. 'Out!'

We emerge wearily and walk into the compound. Buggas is shouting at the men as they set up camp in the dark. The mood is a mixture of excitement and confusion. Our bags are put in the hut, but Omar shows us a place to sleep outside. We put down the mat and organise our bedding. No tea, no hot food, just cold, congealed spaghetti and a tin of tuna for supper. Our backs are hurting so much that all we want to do is lie down, too exhausted to think or dwell on our situation. Omar and some of the gang sleep next to us in the compound. Others station themselves self-importantly outside the thorn barrier. They are happily chewing *chad* and shouting, but we're far too tired to be bothered by them.

Life in the bush

Monday, 2 November

Splat. A drop of rain wakes me. It is still dark, an hour before dawn. A few more drops fall on my face. Rachel and I get up, grab our mattresses and move into the hut. I wonder if it's time to settle down, or will we soon hear the cry 'Up! Up!' and have to get into that damned car again?

Bags of rice and flour are thrust in through our doorway as the heavens open. The rain's not that heavy, not like the tropical storms we're used to at sea, but enough to galvanise the gangsters into action. Buggas appears and shuffles into the hut. We sit on our mattresses, folding them into as small a heap as possible, clear of the drips that are starting to come through. The tarp only covers part of the roof. Soon it's light, and within an hour five or six men are inside, standing near the doorway, not concerned for us but wary of intruding more on our space. Damp, wretched and despairing, we huddle on our pile. The rain goes on. No one says much. No one moves.

By about ten, I've had enough – waste not, want not. Checking my pants are in place, I grab the shampoo and head out for a freshwater shower. It's good to wash off the sweaty grime that has built up on my skin. Buggas follows suit, demanding shampoo. The gangsters peer out and laugh, not too much, because they're scared of offending their boss. The rain eases off, so I go back in and dress.

Our new home is in better condition than the first hut, though only about 12 feet in diameter and with no internal structure. A bright orange tarpaulin is incorporated into the roof construction. The thorn tree branches that form a palisade around the compound are robust enough to keep the goats out, or perhaps in. There is a large tree in one corner, opposite the hut doorway. Some of the gangsters throw a mat down under it; they must be our daytime 'close guard', having a machine gun and RPG launcher to hand as well as their AK-47s. They look straight into the hut.

The cooks get the fire going, and at about eleven we have 'hostage special breakfast' – hot water for tea, chapati cooked in oil and a bowl of fried goat liver with onion.

'Where toilet?' we ask. Buggas points eastward, so we go exploring. Out of the hut, turn left then through the gap in the goat barrier, sharp right and around the outside of the compound, past the cook's fire, past the white Land Rover tucked partly under a tree, then away towards the east, away from the thugs with guns. How far dare we go? Fifty yards? A hundred? The gangsters don't seem concerned, so we go on until we find a group of dense bushes, giving some semblance of all-round concealment.

For mid-afternoon lunch we are brought goat stew with potatoes, onions and rice. It doesn't look as if we'll starve, but there's no sign of any greens. After lunch, it's still overcast, so we venture out past the thorn barrier and mime a walking action, repeating, 'Exercise, exercise' to the two nearest guards. After a quick shouting exchange with Buggas, they give the OK.

> So off we go. I wear my Henri Lloyd sailing sandals. They have a wonderful grip on deck; let's see how they perform in the scrub. Rachel has only my spare Tribord flip-flops, so power-walking is out of the question.

Heading west, we manage to explore our immediate surroundings; two men with AK-47s follow ten paces behind.

We see two groups of men sitting under trees; we don't go near. Perhaps these are defensive outposts. We follow a trodden path through the low scrub until we reach a water catchment – an area of about 200 square yards cleared of scrub, protected by a thorn barrier. There is an underground reservoir at the low point. A few gangsters are there. One beckons: 'Look.'

The tank is a hole in the ground, lined with plastic sheeting, with a covering of branches, more plastic and soil. There is a small opening, from which water is obtained by dropping in cut-off oil or jerrycans on a line. It looks shallow, and the water is sandy after the morning's rain. It must be serving the nomad families as they eke out a subsistence life with their herd of goats, and perhaps a few camels, and the local family who struggle to grow beans in a field south of our hut. What will they make of this invasion? How long will this meagre resource supply 30 men? Will the locals be compensated by the gang? Maybe there'll be a fight over it if we stay too long!

We move on. 'Stop!' One of the gang is waving at us – mobile phone in one hand, AK-47 in the other. He wants to take a photo of us. Then he wants his mate to take a picture of us with him. Our first taste of celebrity?

We decide to walk around the bean field to stretch our legs. The field is clear of scrub and surrounded by a substantial thorn barrier. At the far side, our guards come closer and gesticulate with their guns – we must head back. 'OK. OK. We go this way.' We are determined to complete the circuit rather than retrace our steps. There's little they can do; will they shoot us?

We make our way back through the cook's area, passing jerrycans of water, the embers of the morning's fire, scattered pots and a knife lying in the sand.

Back in the hut, back down on the floor. As expected, the chairs didn't make it. There's no sign of Buggas, or anyone who understands English, so I look for objects that can

double up as stools. A small plastic barrel looks spare. I
squirrel it away in the hut. We'll be able to take turns.

By early evening we're wondering if we'll be based here. Two
or three cars appear. Omar, the Commander and several
other men get out. The new arrivals sit under the tree outside
our hut and stare at us. They are not obviously gang members,
some being better dressed, Western style, others wearing
smart headscarves. The gangsters mostly wear T-shirts and
ma'awiis, the traditional Somali men's skirt.

We discuss the visitors quietly between ourselves. Paul
calls them 'spectators' and suggests they are paying to come
to see us. Or perhaps they are the locals, coming to collect
payment for disruption, for water, for their secrecy? Buggas
cheerfully struts around like a peacock in natty Western
clothes, proper shoes and socks. We are being shown off as
his prize, his passport to millions.

Rachel has the runs and declines supper. Consternation!
Buggas is summoned. 'Eat!'

We explain, mime, gesticulate: 'No problem. Tomorrow
OK. One day no food.' We are used to bouts of traveller's
diarrhoea and have faith in the 24-hour starvation remedy.

More machine guns turn up and are positioned in close
defence for the night. One of them is set up alongside our
hut, its field of fire covering the entrance; the other is mounted
outside the compound, covering the approach to the hut. A
'killing zone' right outside our doorway. Four or five gangsters
squat outside the hut, alongside the machine guns, and talk
for several hours. Three or four others put a mat under the
tree opposite; they lie down, cocooned in their blankets. We
manage to drift into some form of sleep.

Tuesday, 3 November

Another day, another hot water flask – at dawn. Rachel
misses out on a goat-liver-and-chapati breakfast and goat
stew for lunch but starts drinking rehydrating salts from
Lynn Rival's medical stocks.

It's still overcast, with occasional showers. We lie
restlessly. The ammo stocks are left in our care. Eight tins
of 7.62 mm cartridges, one opened with a crude can
opener and only half full. Do they leave them with us for
safety?

We've spent four days on land living with gangsters. The
baffling thing is the sheer number – up to thirty men. We're
confused about who might be in charge. Surely not the bully
Buggas? The better educated and friendly Omar must be part
of a bigger organisation? And then there are the visitors. One
in particular looked more worldly, standing aloof, wearing
glasses and taking photos of us on his mobile phone. Surely
sense will prevail and they will understand that we're just a
couple of middle-aged tourists who don't deserve this
treatment?

Omar is obviously concerned about our welfare. He brings
us a washing bowl, detergent, pegs and toilet tissue. He talks
of us being 'on safari', which Buggas and the Commander
find hilarious. We have to get used to pirate humour.

The Commander is a mysterious figure. He hangs around
and is obviously senior but surprisingly quiet compared to
Buggas. None of the rest of the gang seems to be much more
than a hand hired to cook, drive or point an AK-47. The
gangsters, although criminals, are not complete savages.
They're particular about personal hygiene but not so careful
with their guns. As on *Lynn Rival*, we worry more about an
accidental shot in our direction than a deliberate one.

This region of Somalia is very harsh, but people survive
here so why shouldn't we? We're used to testing conditions.
You have to be self-sufficient to cross oceans in a small yacht,
and adaptable enough to deal with problems. Being frugal
with power and fresh water comes naturally to us. We can
manage with few material items, but can we cope with our
captors and life at gunpoint?

Omar tells us, 'These people are ready to negotiate for
solution.' He says nothing about money. He tells us the local

al-Qaeda cell want to swap us for Guantanamo detainees! It's hard to take this seriously, so we focus on what comes next. 'These people are poor – um – they have no jobs and need your help . . . hurry and ask your family to do their best.' He wants a contact number for the person who will negotiate for us. We have no one except Stephen, Rachel's brother. We know no negotiators. Omar also tells us that the seven pirates who disappeared from *Lynn Rival* in the two skiffs were captured by a warship. We try to hide our glee. It's a small comfort to know that they were stopped in their bid to catch another ship.

Omar comes back in the early afternoon brandishing his mobile phone. Buggas is with him. Other gangsters crowd the doorway to the hut. Omar wants Stephen's number. We don't have it – it was on our mobile phones. Buggas gets Paul's mobile out of his pocket.

They find Stephen's number, and Omar taps it into his phone. Stephen answers. Paul speaks briefly to him, then passes the phone to me. Heart in mouth, I tell Stephen that the pirates want to negotiate money. Stephen responds quickly that we have no money and that the Foreign Office has told him not to discuss money.

I can tell he knew this was coming. I'm not surprised by his response. I'm also conscious of my listening captors. I need to appear desperate. I plead with Stephen to ask the Foreign Office to find someone to talk to these people. If nothing else, someone needs to communicate with them in Somali – Omar's 'English' is flawed and laboured, often incomprehensible. We give him Omar's telephone number. Stephen promises to do what he can.

Afterwards, we mull over the situation. Surely Stephen will be getting advice and help from the authorities? And surely they know how to handle these situations? All we can do it sit tight and hope. We know we can't believe a word Omar says (even if we can understand it). Who knows what's going on in the background?

Two cars come back late in the afternoon with new tarpaulins. A big orange one is pulled over the hut, to try to complete the coverage. The tarp is secured with ties made from torn-up plastic bags and strips of old rags, with branches laid against the roof slopes to hold it down. That will work well when the wind gets up, won't it! We try to improve it, pulling it into better shape, scrounging extra bits of string for the eyelets. It looks as if we'll be here for a while, so we can settle a bit and contemplate. Omar brings us a large mozzie net. He must have noticed Rachel itching from bites before dawn yesterday. It's easily installed and covers both our mattresses, with plenty to tuck in at the edges.

Wednesday, 4 November
Rachel's diary

> Get up for loo 6.30. P lies in until 7.30. Have 'shower' wash with new bowl. Do some clothes washing. Hang outside on line. Only available line is filthy so have to clean that. No lunch. Go for walk at dusk. One guard asks if we have goats at home. Buggas and others return after dark but don't speak to us. Fed at 6.30: rice & potato sauce. Play crib. P wins but only small margin! Go to bed under net approx. 7.30.

We settle down for a few days of waiting, keeping a lid on our emotions. At least the hut is lighter and more spacious than the gloomy village room we had for our one-night stopover. The brushwood sides allow good ventilation. The new tarpaulin works well. Some of the men join us when it rains – an uncomfortable hour or two in their close company. The open doorway is a problem, but Paul holds up a blanket when Rachel wants an all-over wash. Sleeping under the mosquito net provides an illusion of privacy from ever-prying eyes.

As on *Lynn Rival*, Buggas places great emphasis on us

eating. Apart from breakfast, the cook offers us '*briis*' or '*basto*' (spaghetti) for lunch. We make our choice, and it arrives with a potato-based sauce, often with onion or tomato paste, or even chilli. Mid afternoon we're given a flask of hot water, then the same choice for supper. We can add tinned tuna to the sauce for variety. We also have biscuits and sometimes one-off treats of bananas or watermelon.

Most days they allow us out for short walks in the undulating landscape. We can see quite far into the distance, over the small hills and hollows. We watch two women weeding the bean field, and we wonder about life in the nomad settlement we can glimpse in the distance – a dome-shaped house, made of brushwood, cloth and plastic sacks next to a small brushwood compound where they pen their goats for milking. The bush is thick in parts and the soil heavily imprinted by a variety of hoof prints. Occasionally there's a large tree, though nothing to rival the beautiful one with large bell-shaped flowers in our compound. When we pass the cooking area, we catch a glimpse of activity. Is the kettle on for tea? Have they killed a goat this morning or is it just bread for breakfast? Sometimes we stumble across the entrails. While walking we talk and – in moments when our guards linger behind – find things to joke about. Brief bursts of quiet laughter subdue the gnawing anxiety inside.

We can only walk comfortably in the early morning or late afternoon. The heat of the day and the sand in the air take some getting used to. If there's no wind, we lie listless, wishing it to end. When it's windy, the sand blows everywhere, aggravating Paul's sensitive eyes.

Thank goodness we have books, playing cards, crosswords, paper and pens. We talk, agonising over what is happening, searching for hope, and finding mutual reassurance. Using Rachel's yoga book, we follow a sequence of exercises in the mid-morning to help keep us supple and calm.

The bush surroundings are peaceful, but our guards are always noisy, unless they're sleeping off a *chad* session. In the afternoon, they gather in the shade of our hut, sometimes cleaning their guns, always clamouring and arguing. We can't get away from them.

Apart from the constant feeling of helplessness and anxiety, we struggle with more immediate aggravation. Attacks of diarrhoea are part of the normal process of acclimatising to a new environment, but now the gripes are more upsetting than usual. It's miserable lying listless in the heat of the day, not knowing if it's just a 24-hour bug or something worse. If worse, what chance is there of medical help?

Saturday, 7 November

The guards are irritable and obstructive, saying, 'Big problem,' and not letting us out for a walk. Then Buggas comes into the hut, smirking.

'British soldiers in Somalia. Five killed.'

We question him, but he grins and saunters out. Rehearsed? He must have known what he was saying, but is it fact, rumour or plain fabrication?

We can but get on with more mundane matters. We need a new washing line, the original having been used to tie down the tarps. The Somali gangster solution is to throw things onto the bushes to gather thorns and sand as they dry. We can do better. After all, Omar has brought us some clothes pegs, as requested on our one and only shopping list. But no line. What can we do? The goat bleats. Of course. She is tethered to a tree with a length of rope. Her soul mate, today's breakfast, must have been similarly restrained. Yes, there's the line, hanging from a tree by the cook's area. We help ourselves: problem solved.

Buggas stays away from us, only coming to look slyly into the hut twice a day, saying nothing. He sits with the group of gangsters outside the hut in the evening, telling stories by the sound of it, annoying us with his snarl; the sycophantic laughs of the men adding a further jarring note.

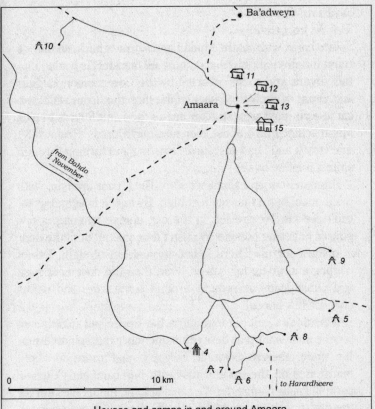

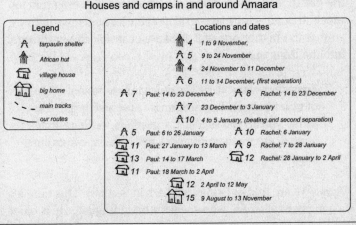

Houses and camps in and around Amaara

Legend

- 🏠 tarpaulin shelter
- 🏚 African hut
- 🏘 village house
- 🏠 big home
- - - - main tracks
- —— our routes

Locations and dates

🏚 4 1 to 9 November,

🏚 5 9 to 24 November

🏚 4 24 November to 11 December

🏚 6 11 to 14 December, (first separation)

🏚 7 Paul: 14 to 23 December   🏚 8 Rachel: 14 to 23 December

🏚 7 23 December to 3 January

🏚 10 4 to 5 January, (beating and second separation)

🏚 5 Paul: 6 to 26 January   🏚 10 Rachel: 6 January

🏘 11 Paul: 27 January to 13 March   🏚 9 Rachel: 7 to 28 January

🏘 13 Paul: 14 to 17 March   🏘 12 Rachel: 28 January to 2 April

🏘 11 Paul: 18 March to 2 April

🏠 12 2 April to 12 May

🏠 15 9 August to 13 November

0   10 km   to Harardheere

from Bahdo
1 November

Monday, 9 November

5.40 a.m. First light

'Up! We go. Quick!'

Into convoy again; the khaki Land Rover is back, so there's room for all the fighters and guns. All our stuff is hurled into the Toyota, and we're escorted by the Commander, Buggas and Omar again. We go back in the direction from which we came eight days ago, stop for one of the Land Rovers to pick up a machine-gun outpost, then turn north, cross a (relatively) main track and head eastwards, twisting and turning through almost pristine bush.

After an hour and a half, we stop. The area is low lying with thick bush, more than six feet high. By now it is light, but we can't see far. We are left in the car, engine running, a few guards lingering outside. We don't dare get out until the door is opened for us. There is activity just out of sight, lots of coming and going for half an hour, then the door is opened and Omar leads us proudly around some trees and points ahead: 'New house!'

New prison cell. Orange tarps have been put together to form a makeshift tent between some taller but spindly trees. It's quite enclosed, which is good: just room for both mattresses on the ground mat with our bags and 'kitchen' paraphernalia alongside. We can stack the mattresses during the day to make more room. OK. We hope it doesn't rain too much, though – they've overlapped the tarps the wrong way, so that the higher one will shed water inside the lower one, into the living space.

> First priority is a toilet. Buggas points us to an area where there is less bush. I squat down for a pee and then realise to my embarrassment that a guard is watching from beneath a tree a short distance away! Next time we go the other way.

Again we are told of British soldiers in Somalia. This time it's a gangster called Ali, who speaks a bit of English. He is older and has the look of an experienced fighter. He wanders off and returns having shot a baby deer – a treat for supper. He is proud of being a good shot. The gangsters reveal a desire to impress, to show off, and we are offered the pick of the cooked meat, which is very tasty. Perhaps we should be charitable – the instinctive hospitality of bush dwellers has come to the fore.

At the end of the day, we are no wiser as to what is going on. Dare we hope these British soldiers are real – and can help us?

Tuesday, 10 November
Paul's diary

> No liver today. Thought I heard a plane to SE about noon; no reaction by the gang.

Wednesday, 11 November

> Remembrance. Much more than 2 minutes of silence! Again thought I heard a plane – so did the gang. Exercise cancelled!

Thursday, 12 November

A quiet, hot day. I finish reading John Gribben's *Science: A History* and start Freddie Forsyth's *Avenger*. Gribben's book is particularly inspiring. Being reminded of the great scientists and how they struggled to give us the knowledge that underpins the civilised world is humbling. Why am I complaining about a bit of hardship? I'm a slow reader and not fast at cryptic crosswords, so have plenty to keep myself occupied.

We struggle in the confined space under our shelter. Compared to our previous 'house', there is less shade from the midday sun and less ventilation. The bush and scrub are so thick that we keep getting lost going to the toilet. The heat and lack of exercise are taking their toll on our morale, but we congratulate ourselves on how well we are managing. It'll take more than this to beat us! Soon our hair will need a trim, so we ask for a comb and scissors. It will be another task to help fill time.

Omar is rarely present, but Buggas comes and goes. This afternoon he sits right in front of our tent, shouting down his mobile phone but saying nothing to us. When he's there, I can't think, can't read, can't do anything. I feel closed in and intimidated. I'm overwhelmed by his presence. I'm sure he does it deliberately.

Tonight the gangsters all bed down around us with two machine guns directly outside our tent door. Are they nervous about an attack?

Friday, 13 November

Omar turns up. He and a sulky Buggas come into the shelter. Omar explains, 'No contact from family. We make video. You have camera? Show me.'

I retrieve my camera from the depths of a bag. I've been careful not to be caught using it; I'm sure they will smash it, and probably me, if I'm seen taking photos. But on occasions, when the close guards are asleep or distracted, I sneakily capture what I can. Every time I take a few photos I remove the memory card and hide it away, inserting an empty card, so if challenged I could show them – no pictures. The camera is new, an Olympus DSLR, which I haven't had time to master. I offer it to Omar. He plays around, obviously with even less idea of how it works than I have.

'Can you make video? Connect to computer?'
'It only takes still pictures; no video; no sound.'

Omar shrugs. He informs us that we've been on the TV news in England. It was reported that we have a son, and a house in London. When we deny this, Buggas barks, 'Liars!' Paul tries to explain to Omar that what money we have is tied up in a pension fund. Omar says, 'These people are tired and angry. All they want is money. They want someone to start negotiations.' Omar also makes a point of saying, 'There are no elders, no government. This man [meaning Buggas] only.'

We worry about the lack of contact. Surely someone should be talking to our captors, even if they won't discuss money? We hear another plane in the afternoon. Someone is looking for us! Can we hope for rescue?

I dream of hunky men in black, parachuting down, shooting the lot of them and whisking us away.

Sunday, 15 November

It's day 24 of our captivity and our existence has become uneventful. The gangsters wear our Musto waterproofs and my diving watch – frustrating reminders of where we might have been. Had our passage not been interrupted, *Lynn Rival* should now have been safely moored in Tanga, our port of entry for Tanzania. We have long had a plan to meet Scott, an American friend of many years, on the summit of Kilimanjaro, and we were hoping that my cousin Lynda would join us for a safari trip, or a visit to Dar es Salaam and Zanzibar. Now we have no control over our lives, except for the mundane matters of existing, making ourselves as comfortable as we can, developing routines to pass the time, keeping healthy and looking after each other. It seems to take several weeks for the mind to accept such a traumatic change in one's existence. After three weeks, my mind knows this is the new reality. It's given up seeing it as a nightmare, hoping for an awakening. I must not give up; the 'thinking thing' that is me must nurture hope, not worry about what I cannot control, concentrate on what I can do so that we both survive. I wish I had studied philosophy.

Monday, 16 November
Paul's diary

R has the runs. Scissors and comb brought pm. Important. Look after appearance.

Wednesday, 18 November

Paul has his first go at cutting my hair freestyle without clippers. It's now very short and we are laughing about it, reassuring ourselves that it will soon grow, when Omar appears with a small point-and-shoot camera.

'Your situation is very bad. These people are very angry. You must search man to negotiate.'

He tells us again that there is a 'fanatic' group searching for us and that there are no 'elders' to help us. We must use 'sensitive' words and ask the British government, the British people and our families to help us. He says he has borrowed money to pay for all the things he's been giving us. 'These people' will stop feeding us and we will 'perish'. We ask him if he means they will kill us – and he replies, 'Yes.'

We choke back the despair and once again try to explain our situation – we have little money, no jobs, and the British government will not negotiate. He tells us he knows of Italian people ransomed for millions and Britain is wealthier than Italy, so we should be worth millions too. They think we are worth more than the *Kota Wajar* with its African-bound cargo! They won't accept 'only one million dollars'. We have no hope of raising anything near a million dollars. We ask to speak to Stephen but Omar says Buggas won't allow it.

Clearly he's trying to wind us up, but we're getting more of an idea of the crude way they think and operate. Apart from the linguistic difficulties, the gulf between their expectations and our reality will not be resolved easily. We try not to worry about the prospect of making a begging video. Anyone watching it will surely realise we're not doing it of our own free will.

We follow Omar and Buggas, picking our way through the thorny low bush away from the camp towards the north – a direction we haven't explored on our occasional exercise walks. We're followed by several guards, two of them laden with machine guns. These are light machine guns, using the same calibre cartridges as the AK-47s, and have a bipod attached near the front of the long barrel. It's quite a load for a skinny Somali gangster if you add a belt of about 200 cartridges. The machine gunners are the taller men, mostly with powerful shoulders. They put on a light jacket, then drape the ammunition belt diagonally over a shoulder, round again, over the other shoulder, then two or three times around the waist. Ready for action! Or just for show? When test-firing they shoot from the waist, although you'd think that any more than a few rounds would knock them over. And how on earth would they feed the ammo belt? Another two have RPG launchers, fully assembled, red lights glowing, each with a juggling club-like grenade loaded. After about 400 yards, we stop. Another five or six men closing around us have not only their AK-47s but also carry spare magazine holders, leather shoulder slings with three or four pockets for the distinctive curved magazines, each holding 20 or 30 rounds.

So, an impressively intimidating backdrop. We are told to stand near a tree. The men are jostling for position; they want to be in shot. Or do they? Buggas, the Commander and another more senior character we've nicknamed Fat Boy stand behind the cameras. Omar gives us instructions: 'Say you are well, you have been well looked after, but water and food will soon run out. Ask your family for money. Ask your friends for money. Ask the British government for money. Ask the British people for money. Say we will kill you if there is no money.'

Take 1: Omar starts filming, as he prompts first me, then Rachel, to speak our lines. He seems to want mostly headshots, holding the camera close, hovering above us. All done. Omar fiddles with the camera – he and Buggas peer at it. Not happy. Omar: 'We must do it again. Use sensitive words.' He reminds us what to say.

Take 2: Halfway through my spiel, Omar turns away, shaking the camera. Technical problem. We are getting fed up. The sun is hot, and we ask Omar if we can go into the shade. 'Just one more time,' he says, putting new batteries into the camera. Again he briefs us: 'Ask for money. Say your situation is dangerous. Say the people here will reduce your food, your water.' He is looking for more emotion, but it's farcical. He moves around, for a new angle. We try again.

Take 3: Omar is wielding the camera intrusively. Rachel glances at the thugs behind me. I look too; I hadn't been aware of the armoury pointed at me until now. Keystone Kops or what? Now I can't keep a straight face. Halfway through, I have to smile. Omar is cross: 'You must use sensitive words. Again.'

Take 4: The strain is getting to me. This time I give a good enough performance for them. I don't have to pretend; I am not concerned about the guns, but anxiety makes my voice waver. Omar shows Buggas. Yes, we can go now, back to the shelter.

I am angry and humiliated. I try not to say any more than I feel necessary to keep them happy, but Omar keeps chastising us for not 'crying'. I think he means begging. I don't know what more I can say. I won't say that these are poor, deserving people. I won't beg for our lives. I want to say they are greedy criminals and I don't want them to have a penny, but that will upset them. When I see the men standing behind us holding machine guns to our heads, it all seems so surreal and ridiculous, I have difficulty not laughing. I try to look glum, all the while thinking they are so stupid. If this is shown on TV people will laugh! It's so obviously a set-up. What do they think the British people are? Fools and suckers?

Omar tells us the video will be sent to Channel 4. He takes off to his home, four hours' drive away, where he has a computer and Internet access.

Up until now I haven't contemplated the possibility that our plight will be getting publicity. I've always been a private person, but I realise I'll now have to come to terms with notoriety. I fight the feelings of shame. We comfort ourselves that everyone in the UK, all our family and friends, will realise that it's a set-up – and that the government will be supporting our close family. I can't help worrying about Paul's father, living on his own.

I wonder what other people will think. They'll probably assume that we're a rich couple on a luxury yacht who were fools to be sailing without an armed escort. But maybe some will look at our blog. Then they'll see that we're quite ordinary people who love to sail and travel.

We are taken back to our tent and Fat Boy gives us a watermelon! Is this our treat for being good? It's time to return to our coping routine – and to dream of rescue.

Friday, 20 November
Rachel's diary

Gang noisy & irritating. Deliberately annoying with loud music? Or just boys? Feel intimidated when right outside. Moonlit night. Contemplate the worst and write letter in my spare notepad.

To Sarah & Stephen, and all I have known and loved,

If the worst does happen I want you to know that I am at peace with the world. Please try not to mourn my death, but celebrate my life and get on with yours. I've had a good life, especially the last 30 years with Paul.

You have done everything you could possibly do in the circumstances. I do not believe we should give in to criminals and I support any action the UK Government may have taken to secure our release without paying a ransom, even if it resulted in my death. I could not have lived in peace if a large ransom had been paid for our release.

All my love,

Rachel

Monday, 23 November

Hear possible aeroplane in afternoon. Sudden rush of activity & shouting from guards. Shots fired! Guns on everyone. Machine guns outside our tent again, plus

grenade launcher! Plenty of shouting. Darkness
descends. Guards have chad – much hawking & spitting
in night. Also fags. Easy come, easy go!

Tuesday, 24 November

Everything seems to be back to normal until mid-afternoon
when Buggas storms in.

'Pack things. Go another where.'

We are driven by Baby Face, one of our attackers who we've
hardly seen since abandoning *Lynn Rival*. Never mind the fact
that he's too young to drive and we've no idea where we're
going, or for how long! We're soon back at our African hut, and
a smirking Buggas asks if we know where we are. We resettle
into a familiar place, happy to have the better shelter and more
spacious accommodation. We congratulate ourselves on
coping and even joke about how much money some people
would pay for this kind of experience: travelling around the
countryside, camping with the locals, seeing isolated places no
ordinary tourist would venture into. We compete in conjuring
names for the travel brochure. 'The hostage trail' is Rachel's
favourite.

Wednesday, 25 November
Paul's diary

I have runs. Stormy. Little rain. Dusty.

At bedtime, we usually visit our toilet area together, for
reassurance and also for star-gazing. A couple of hours
after dark, we make our way to the bushy area, about 200
yards from the camp, and enjoy the night sky, shutting out
the noise of the gangsters. On a clear night, the Milky Way
is astounding. There's no light pollution here. The stars are
as bright as we have ever seen from mid-ocean. But now,
with the extra frequency of trips required, I decide to make
my own way at night.

OK, business done, now which way is the hut? Fire out.
No torches, not even the glow from a mobile phone. I'll

navigate by the stars. I'm supposed to be able to do that. There's the North Star, just above the horizon. I need to go about west. That way. Is that the glimmer of the white Land Rover? No. Let's go right a little.

'Paw' – I hear someone call out of the night. A gangster leads me back to the hut. So they do keep an eye on us, and their night vision is fantastic.

The next day, at 6.30 a.m., then at 10.30 a.m., we hear planes flying low. The gangsters see the second one and with much angry gesticulation they drive the white Land Rover further under a tree and cover it with an orange tarp. The other two cars stay away. Two more flights, at 2.15 and 3.30 p.m. Then the sky clouds over. Despite concealing the Land Rover the camp would be easily visible – they make no effort to hide the cooking area, the washing, the mats, etc.

Sunday, 29 November
Rachel's diary

> Thunderstorms nearby. Heavy rain. Fat Mohamed joins us in tent with SW radio. Ask to listen to World Service. Hear programme debating the future of the Commonwealth. Camp subdued.

I awake in the early hours, listening to the silence of the bush. Suddenly there's a low but distinct whistle. It's about two o'clock and for almost an hour I hear four or five whistlers, as if they were individuals, passing stealthily through the camp. No animal sounds, no disturbance of the bushes or the trees. My imagination runs riot. What, or who, could they be? Surely not the SAS? Birds? Some sort of owl?

Tuesday, 1 December
Paul's diary

> More stormy rain from time to time. Only one LR [Land Rover] on camp. Possibly heard plane late pm.

Every morning when I go out to visit my toilet bush, I peer up into the skies in hope of seeing a plane. I want to believe that someone knows where we are, or is still looking for us.

The first few days of December are wet and cooler. A respite, though the camp is damp and everyone is bedraggled. All manner of plants sprout up and bloom. Our guards look bemused when we pick wild flowers and take an interest in them. We have fruit – bananas, mangoes and limes – to supplement our diet, and the gang is more relaxed. Buggas isn't around much, and there's no sign of Omar. We hear few sounds of planes but always try to put out washing in the dry spells to increase our visibility. Also, our toilet area has become littered with discarded paper, and I deliberately scatter it over the bushes. Surely someone looking down on us will be alerted to this unusual evidence. Little things please belittled minds!

I wake up with an agonisingly throbbing toe. Gout. I have had it three times in ten years, always the big toe on my right foot. Luckily I have pills, kindly passed on by a good friend, but no idea of the dosage! I can't put a sandal on, so it's flip-flops only. And my flip-flops have lost half the soles through wear, so thorns will be another problem. Never mind, I won't notice them over the pain of the gout. My first toilet trip of the day takes some time – I can just about hobble, with care. Of course the gangsters notice.

'Problem?'

'Yes. Problem.' I manage to indicate that I haven't been bitten, stepped on a big thorn or stubbed my toe. 'Three days OK,' I say, optimistically.

They are sympathetic. Soon Buggas hears of it and appears. By then I am lying down again.

'Problem?'

'Yes. Gout.'

'Medicine?'

'Yes, OK after tomorrow,' I say. They think we have pills for everything – another myth that misinforms their idea of the Western world.

Monday, 7 December
Rachel's diary

Cloudy all round, but hear plane twice, fairly close, at about 1000 and 1200.

Wednesday, 9 December

Goat bleatings. Lost mate? Tomorrow's food. Another uneventful day. Mr F says 'translator here tomorrow'.

Mr Fastidious (aka Mr F) is one of the gangsters we've come to recognise and given a nickname. He's a more senior figure, who understands a little English, and is uncharacteristically calm and organised. If we need something, there's a chance he'll try to help. He sleeps under the tree immediately outside our hut and is very particular about laying out his bedding. He has his own foam mattress and even a mosquito net! In the morning, he carefully folds everything up and puts it out of the way. He doesn't share it with the others. Most of the gangsters just have a blanket, which they keep in a black plastic bag with their *ma'awiis* and leave hanging in the tree.

When it rains they have a problem keeping themselves and the guns dry. Some come and crouch in our hut. Others use a tarp, which they spread out and crawl under, but now Mr F has rigged up a proper shelter under the tree. He's obviously more practical.

Thursday, 10 December
Paul's diary

Heard plane at 0815. No exercise. T arrived 0900 with B.

Omar is quiet but impatient. His voice is a whine: 'No contact from UK. Family not speak. Government not speak.' Beside him, Buggas snarls angrily.

We explain again to Omar that the British government have a rigid policy – they will not pay ransom; they will not deal with criminals. Omar appears to accept that now. He says he has a call 'booked' with a businessman in Nairobi; that one of our family is in Nairobi. What on earth can he mean?

By now we are used to Omar's patter and despair at his naivety. The gangsters have no idea how they are going to make money out of us, but, driven by greed, they're clutching at straws. They persist with the tactic of making us uncomfortable and threatening us, in the hope that we will find a way to raise the money they want. Omar is completely flummoxed when we say we can do nothing, that we know no rich people who might be willing to help us. Thankfully they do seem to realise it's in their interests to keep us alive.

'I am your friend,' he says. 'I will arrange for you to speak to Stephen. You must ask for money. I will speak with "these people". I am not one of them. I am not pirate. I will help you.'

Paul decides to test him. We often hear the gangsters listening to a radio. Paul asks, 'May we have a radio, please? Listen to BBC?'

Omar agrees and disappears out to the Toyota, parked outside the compound. He returns with a little shortwave tranny and hands it to us. Buggas looks as if he will explode. He rants and raves at Omar, but Omar shakes his head, leaves us with the radio, then brings us batteries.

Omar is back at three o'clock and hands us the phone. The rest of the gangsters hover outside. I take it first, though I have no idea what to say. With Christmas coming I want to speak to our family, to reassure everyone we're OK.

Rachel: *We finally got them to agree to let us have a word with you. We want to find out you're OK.*
Stephen: *We're OK, we're worried about you of course. How are you?*
Rachel: *Yes, yes, I know. We're OK. We're bearing up. We*

want to say Happy Christmas to everybody.

Stephen: *And I wanted to say the same to you. Paul's father is very well. He's got a nurse calling on him regularly. Helen has got the Land Rover in a good garage.*

Rachel: *I don't understand.*

Stephen: *Helen, Paul's niece, has got the Land Rover in a good garage . . .*

. . . Think about it. Talk to Paul about it. He'll understand.

Rachel: *I'll pass you to Paul.*

Stephen: Hello. How are you?

Paul: OK, thank you.

Stephen: Good, good. Helen has got the old Land Rover into a good garage.

Paul: Yes.

Stephen: Yes, just think about it. How is the weather?

Paul: Cloudy, we've been having rain on and off the last few days.

Stephen: And are you being treated all right?

Paul: OK, we're OK. They've given us a radio today for the first time. They are anxious to know why you have not contacted them.

Stephen: They want us to contact them?

Paul: Yes.

Stephen: On this number?

Paul: On the number we told you before.

Stephen: Fine, fine. We have had problems getting through.

Paul: Right, fine. Do you have that one on your phone now?

Stephen: Yes, I will have it on there now. That's the number which ends in 613 not 322.

Paul: That's correct, yes. And they want you to contact them on that number.

Stephen: Right, tell them I will contact them in a week. Any particular time?

Paul: Any time on this number, any day . . . because the *reception on that phone is very poor, the area is bad. You know, it's a bad signal. They only have mobiles here.*

Stephen: *Yes, I know that. We try to emphasise that you are only poor people and you've only got a small boat and you have no other money.*

Paul: *I'm afraid we've been told to stop now, Stephen. Give our love to everybody.*

Stephen: *Everyone sends their best wishes. We hope that they will understand you are only innocent tourists. We are working as hard as we can for you. Is there anything you need?*

Paul: *Not at the moment. We are OK on medication and so on for some weeks more. We need to get out of here really.*

Stephen: *Yes, I'm sure you would like to, yes. How is the food?*

Paul: *The food is OK. He wants us to finish now. I think we have to get off.*

Stephen: *We're all thinking of you.*

Omar is furious that we didn't quiz Stephen about what's happening. We explain once more that there's nothing we can do. We have only little money and no jobs. We can't hope to raise the millions they demand. Omar tells us that he knows of hostages being held for months and that governments eventually find a way to pay up 'under the counter'. We don't know what to say. Clearly Omar and Buggas haven't a clue. They are such amateurs!

I realise from Stephen's promise to call back in a week that he is playing a waiting game. I've heard about aid workers being kidnapped in Somalia and held for months but can't believe that millions have been paid for their release. If that's what Omar and Buggas believe, then we'll certainly be here for months. Surely they don't want to keep us here for long? They run the risk of us dying on them, with stress-induced stroke or heart attack – though there are two of us, so it's less of a risk.

If one dies, they've still got the other. If Paul were to die, I don't know how I could carry on. My mind starts pondering that scenario and I have to block off that avenue of thought. I return to the still bleak realisation that we could be here for a long time, maybe six months.

Afterwards, we discuss what Stephen meant by the coded message: 'the Land Rover is in a good garage'. Paul cracks it. He thinks it must mean they know where we are. The photos taken by the surveillance plane have shown up the white Land Rover under its tarpaulin tent and tree – a garage of sorts. Yes! That's it. They know where we are! Wonderful! If they know where we are, we can hope for a rescue! But wasn't it a bit rash of Stephen to risk disclosing that? Never mind. We have hope!

About an hour later, Omar comes back with the phone and hands it to Paul. Yet another call. What a busy day!

'Speak to journalist. Answer questions. Don't talk about your position.'

With the usual difficulty establishing to whom I am talking, I think the caller may be a freelance journalist doing an article for the *Sunday Times*. He asks whether I know of a reported incident of pirates shooting each other, whether I know if our family has been prevented from paying a ransom by the Foreign Office, and if I have any request for the government. My response is no, no and please use every possible method to get us out by Christmas.

We are then cut off. He has obviously been given strict instructions by whoever set up the call. I have a hunch someone other than Omar was listening in, on the pirates' side. Tiresome, not very reassuring, but I feel that all publicity could be helpful.

We are so thrilled to have the radio, so desperate to hear news of the outside world. In trying to find the World Service, we find an interesting Radio France International feature on the Somali piracy problem. There are 285 hostages at present. We are not alone.

Friday, 11 December

As I go for my early-morning trip to the toilet bush, the guards are starting to pack up. Buggas wakes Paul, and I return to find him struggling to put in his contact lenses, take down the mosquito net, washing line and all the paraphernalia we've accumulated.

Precious books, torches and the radio are hurriedly squashed into bags. The gangsters are excited – grabbing bags, tossing them into the back of a Toyota, hustling us into the back seat – a guard either side, machine gunner in front. The usual convoy packed with men, arms, kitchen equipment and food stocks rolls off. How far this time? Just 20 minutes or so – along an established track, then a short drive picking our way through dense bush. It's the same pattern as before. We wait. Men go off into the bush. Soon Buggas comes to retrieve us, and we walk a short distance to be shown our new 'home' – another tarpaulin shelter constructed under some bushes. It's cramped and awkward, but we grumpily do our best to make ourselves comfortable. We are allowed to go for a ramble. We walk up to a high point near a large field where we can see for miles around. Despite feeling very alone in the world, it's another fascinating excursion in the Somali countryside to wonder at. If only we had some reference books!

Time passes. Not only do we have a radio to listen to but two plastic chairs arrive – as if to compensate for our reduced accommodation. We can hardly stand up, let alone swing a cat. Now we can sit outside in the afternoon shade – a small comfort but nothing to assuage the utter dismay. 'They' knew where we were. How will rescuers find us here? Again we try to make ourselves as visible as possible, putting up a washing line and distributing our used toilet paper with gay abandon. We hear only one plane in the distance.

Monday, 14 December

Everyone is doing washing. Our line is full. The guards drape theirs over the bushes. They're cleaning their guns, oiling the RPG launcher. Buggas arrives and reads them the riot act. They all seize their guns and gather around our shelter, squatting as if to hide, looking nervous. A plane comes over, low and loud. They sit tight and it passes. Then they jump up, shouting, gathering up the weapons, dressing up and strutting about. Acute fear pervades the air. Buggas shouts on his mobile phone, barks at the men, then growls on the mobile phone again. We sit tight and listen to the radio. What is going on? Lunch is served: more spaghetti.

Buggas, snarling, makes the on-duty guards – about 12 of them – form up in ranks and . . . well, sort of present arms and do a bit of 'marching'. It's pretty shambolic – Dad's Army – but quite frightening: a completely different atmosphere from any we have experienced before. Buggas is frightened too, and he communicates his fear to the gang. He has them cleaning their guns again, and when they're not doing that, they parade back and fore past our shelter, looking daggers at us, staring, saying nothing.

Buggas himself storms up: 'British soldiers fighting. Fighting these men! You want us killed! You big problem.'

He moves away, but we can't relax. Ali comes over and makes gestures indicating a helicopter and men dropping out: 'Soldiers from plane. Five soldiers. Fighting.'

It's unusually quiet for an hour. Everyone's nervous. Buggas comes back.

'Pack bags – one, one. You go – one, one. Quick.'

He grabs the radio and takes it away. We can think of nothing but to comply. We have our separate bags for clothing but need to split the medicines, the books (six novels, one non-fiction) and our hard-won household goods. Thermos? Paul. Crossword book? Rachel. We sit glumly on the chairs, waiting for the inevitable, holding hands, trying not to cry, thinking: this can't be happening – we were coping so well!

Buggas returns. The khaki Land Rover stops 20 yards away.

'You go. RUN!' he shouts at Rachel. Three of the men grab Rachel's bags, her bedding and box of bits. We hug, hating it, hating this damned country, these horrible men, but wanting it to be over.

> 'Go!' shouts Buggas, and I watch Rachel walk up to the Land Rover and climb into the cab. Despite the strain, Rachel maintains her composure; there is defiance in her poise as she walks with great dignity up the gentle incline. I hold back the tears and shout after her, 'Don't worry! I love you!'
>
> I watch Buggas get in beside her and the Land Rover drives off. I am left, stunned, numb, unable to do anything. I sit in my chair and wait for the world to end . . .

Threats and lies

Monday, 14 December continued

Ten minutes later two of the men start picking up my stuff and walk off towards the west with it. Two more take down the tarps, grab everything else and follow. One man points with his gun: 'Go!'

Meekly I follow, carrying my chair, at gunpoint. We walk, in the heat of the day, up a gentle incline and then down the other side, across a cultivated field where only weeds show, then zigzag through a bushy area until we reach a dry wadi bed. I am 'encouraged' to go down into the wadi until I reach a dead end, blocked off by thorny brushwood, with a single orange tarp rigged up as shade. The wadi is about three feet deep and eight feet wide, with trees growing from each side, soil eroded from around their roots. There is just enough room under the tarp to spread out my mattress, with the bags alongside, but it's on quite a slope, so no need to think about where my head will go – uphill. Misery. The men stay away. I sit on the mattress.

There's no sight or sound of a car, but Buggas turns up before dusk accompanied by the Commander, who looks dejected.

Buggas is in a fury: 'British soldiers fight this man. From plane – attack these men.' He mimes the dropping of soldiers from a helicopter. 'The last where.' Does he mean the African hut? I ask if Rachel is OK.

'NO! Rachel NO OK! Rachel go Somaliland. Other militia!'

I can't bear to think of Rachel. I ask for *Omo* (the word they use for detergent, although the packets are labelled TOP) to wash my food bowls and clothes.

'No! No! You liar! You speak again, kill you! Fuck you! You speak family. Get money!'

I lie on my mattress and cry.

Tuesday, 15 December

God, it was cold in the night. I must have cried myself to sleep. The chill from the ground was intense in the wadi bed, lying only on a thin mattress. Arthritis pain in my hips woke me. I have to try to get myself sorted. Tea is brought by a different cook – another Ali – but no breakfast. It's quiet. I can see only eight or nine men. I busy myself, trying to smooth out the ground under my mattress, organising the bags. Rice and sauce come for lunch, so I know they are going to feed me. But there's no sign of intelligent life; I'm being guarded by the juniors. Ali comes again with more rice, no meat.

'Where Buggas?' I ask. 'Must speak to Buggas.'

He shrugs. One of the other men comes: 'Problem?'

'Problem,' I confirm. 'Speak to Buggas.'

'Tomorrow.'

Somehow I survive the day.

Wednesday, 16 December

My hips are in agony again. As yesterday, no breakfast, but a new variant – 'high-octane tea'. They are using a petrol jerrycan for the well water! I drink it anyway. In a bid to establish a routine – I know I must to keep my sanity, my self-respect – I tentatively walk down the wadi. One guard comes over, looks questioningly, gun pointed in my direction. 'Exercise,' I say, miming a walking action. I manage about 30 paces down the wadi, round a bend, to a point where it is blocked by another tree. Down and back, down and back, 40 times. It's slow going, as the ground is soft. I take my anger out on that loose sandy bed. Stamp, stamp, stamp! Better exercise too. That occupies half an hour before it gets too hot in the sun. What now?

I sit in my chair and try not to cry . . . but fail. One gangster comes over, not unfriendly: 'What?' Another one comes. I sob. What can I say?

'Problem?'

'No wife,' I say. 'No life.'

'No problem,' they respond. How can I communicate? These guys must have feelings. How can I explain to them that Rachel and I are an item? That we have never been apart in our lives together? That we cannot survive alone? I must learn to speak their language.

'Must speak to Buggas.'

'Tomorrow,' comes the inevitable answer but with no nastiness, no hatred. I get a small sense that these men are human, beneath it all.

Almost dark – what's that? – a small bird flies out from behind the tree roots, circles the nearest thorn tree and returns via the shelter. A bird? No. It must be a bat, no three, maybe four. They've become used to my presence. They flit so fast, circling for almost an hour, then all is peace again.

Thursday, 17 December

After morning tea, I exercise and enjoy breakfast – a bowl of liver. A small portion, so maybe Rachel is not far away and is eating the other half? I hope. I don't believe Buggas's threats about Somaliland. He wouldn't want to lose half his valuable prize, or let it go far from his sight. But I am very depressed. I want to speak to the family, to get things moving. I'll do anything if it will make Buggas happy and let me see Rachel. Again I ask a gangster if I can speak to Buggas or Omar. 'After,' comes the unsympathetic response.

I'm still very down. I can't eat. I refuse goat meat at midday.

Buggas turns up early in the afternoon. He has my mobile phone and shows me the numbers in the contacts list. 'Who this? Who this?' he demands as he scrolls through. I ask about Rachel. He says, 'NO Rachel. You speak family.' And points at the phone again. He picks through the list. I manage to gloss over most of the entries, but he homes in on the women's names: 'Sarah, who Sarah?'

'Rachel's sister.'

'Lynda, who Lynda?'

'My cousin.'

'You sister where?'

I crave news of Rachel – I'll do anything this thug wants. I plead: 'Can I speak to Stephen?'

'Stephen waste time. Stephen follow government. Stephen no negotiate. Stephen no speak, Paul no speak Rachel!'

With that he stalks off. I follow, but he turns round angrily, 'Go your position!', making clear with a gesture of his AK-47 that I must stay under the tarpaulin shelter.

In the early evening, he approaches again, more relaxed. I ask to speak to Stephen. 'No,' he says. 'No translator. Translator run! Too much fighting.'

I plead to speak to Stephen, to get negotiations going. 'OK. We find another translator. You speak sister, all family, ask money. Tomorrow, after tomorrow. No money these men kill you! You too much money. Big house London! Sleep.'

I wonder if there really is any fighting? I'm not surprised if Omar has run away – he's not a fighter. But how does that affect us? My spirits sink lower and lower. The skies are clear all day, but there are no overflights. Have our rescuers landed and been fought off?

Friday, 18 December

One week to Christmas. I don't think it will be a happy one. How can I find out about Rachel? There's no sign of

Buggas; just the eight guards, half of whom are asleep. They're relaxed now; no planes heard for several days. Ali comes when I am only halfway through stomping up and down the wadi. *Sagara* and *brr* (bread) for breakfast. He lingers – he wants me to learn Somali words. OK, it's a small beginning, but if I have to live alone with these scum, I will try to communicate. The other Ali, who arrived with a new group of gangsters this morning, comes over and asks if I like the meat. Politely I reply, 'Yes, very tasty, thank you.' He indicates that he shot it, then repeats '*Halkan*' several times, with a gesture encompassing the immediate area. I take it to be the name of the local region. I point at them both, saying, 'Too much Ali!' They laugh; the taller one points at the cook – 'Ali Yeri' – then at himself – 'Ali Deri!' ' Big man,' he continues, indicating his height, '*af Somali – deri*'.

More meat at midday and in the late afternoon – goat this time. They're feeding me up again.

At 4.30 p.m., Buggas and Omar turn up. 'Come. Speak family.'

Buggas throws a sheet over me, wraps it around my shoulders so that only my face is exposed. We walk back across the field, up to the ridge, with Buggas uncharacteristically solicitous – pointing out thorny outcrops, holding aside branches when we reach the edge of the field. There is the khaki Land Rover, a door held open for me. Buggas and Omar jump on the back. I am in the cab with the driver, Land Rover Man. He is older, quieter than most of the gangsters, polite and almost friendly. As we set off up the hill, he passes me a bottle of water to drink.

Across the scrub, down the 'main' track towards the south-east, then off into the bush, towards a small clump of trees. We stop; I'm told to wait. The others deploy. We have only the one car but plenty of firepower – four guards with AK-47s, one machine gunner, as well as Land Rover Man, Buggas and Omar. Only Omar is unarmed.

I'm led out of the car, to a spot under a spindly tree. Omar has his phone ready. Buggas gets my old Nokia out and peruses the numbers. He wants me to speak to the women. More pressure. Omar dials Sarah's number. Her partner, Adrian, answers. Sarah is out. Buggas shouts, 'Speak! Speak! Tell want money!' I don't think about the effect on Adrian; I want to speak to someone, anyone, to get the message through. But I manage not to be too hysterical. I say we have been separated . . . I am desperate . . . I have no news of Rachel . . . the kidnappers say Stephen is not helpful . . . the family must speak to Omar on 0025255898322.

Omar tells me to ask for Jill's number. I do. Adrian says he doesn't have it – he is not in the loop. Omar cuts the call.

Then Omar dials Lynda's number. I don't want to do this. Lynda is my closest cousin. I remember playing together at the stream near my parents' house in South Wales when I must have been nine or ten. Vivid pictures play through my mind, of us building dams, creating armadas of tiny ships, fire ships! She has had a tough time over the last few years. She doesn't need more stress, but she will cope. Luckily the answerphone takes the call and I get away with leaving a message.

Buggas's plan is not going well. He exchanges words with Omar. The men have formed a perimeter, 40 or 50 metres away from us, looking out for wandering goatherds or women returning from a day's weeding.

'OK. Speak Stephen.' Omar dials and hands me the phone.

'No money you dead!' says Buggas, in case I hadn't got it. Stephen is driving and unable to say much. I tell him Rachel has been taken away . . . I can't stand it much more . . . I am lonely and very, very depressed. I have no one to talk to. Why won't they speak to the kidnappers?

The signal is poor. I have great difficulty in understanding, and I'm not sure Stephen can hear me. I tell him it's horrid here, the food is awful and the weather is terribly hot. 'Why is nobody negotiating with the gang? Rachel has been taken away – I've no idea where she is, or even if she's alive. There's no government here, just the gang and Omar. They won't talk about anything but money.'

Stephen tells me they have tried twice to contact Omar but can't get through. He says the kidnappers have not made any demands. I stress that it's just the gang and Omar; that there's no Mister Big. 'You must speak to them. Please at least start negotiation. They have said $7 million dollars. I know it's silly but that's an opening bid. Can't you at least make a silly offer to them? Please? Otherwise we will die here.'

I tell Stephen that it's no good doing it through the bloody Foreign Office and that he must get the police involved. I repeat my concerns for Rachel – that she may be dead for all I know. Stephen tries to reassure me that they're good people essentially and won't harm their captives.

'Yeah, they're nice people all right.' I can't help the sarcasm.

The Foreign Office vis-à-vis police point has been worrying me ever since we were brought ashore. In going over various kidnap scenarios in my mind, I remember the rash of criminal kidnappings in Western Europe in the 1970s and 1980s, when it seemed that the European police forces had cooperated and got on top of the situation. Surely that expertise is available via Special Branch? I am afraid that if the Foreign Office gets involved they won't make use of it. They'll treat our case as a political one, about as effectively as a one-armed paper hanger.

Buggas and Omar have words again. Omar dials and passes me the phone. Who has he called? Sarah.

Paul: *You must start negotiating . . . I don't know what has happened to Rachel . . . she may be dead.*

121

Sarah: *I don't think so. Rachel will be OK.*

Paul: *No one is speaking to Omar. No one makes telephone calls.*

Sarah: *Stephen has made telephone calls. He is good at making calls. Often he can't get through. It's a shame there's no landline.*

Paul: *Omar's English is not good. You must give him more time to understand. It's difficult on a mobile for him to understand. It is not political. They just want money. They are used to getting millions from shipping companies.*

Sarah: *But you aren't in that position, you don't have big companies behind you. You are just tourists. We are just a family.*

Paul: *They don't understand. They know we have a little money. You can sell everything. We don't need anything. They are feeding me slops. I might as well walk out into the desert. I am going out of my mind.*

Sarah: *No, you're not. You can be strong. Be strong. Be strong.*

Paul: *It's easy for you to say that.*

Sarah: *We are strong together as a family.*

Paul: *They don't care. They are just a gang of men, no more than 25 years old.*

Call over. It is now almost dark. We make our way back to camp, exhausted and dejected. Omar promises to bring me *Omo*. He gives me a radio – a welcome gesture, but a measure of my despondency is that I can't feel excited about it.

Buggas interrupts, 'Sister you – speak.'

I respond wearily, 'My sister Jill; no number.'

Buggas insists, 'You have number? Get number. Rachel have number?'

Omar asks if I can remember Jill's address – he can get her number then. Directory enquiries? He says I must call Jill tomorrow.

'Don't worry – once negotiations start you will be with Rachel.'

I hope so.

Sarah and Stephen both told me it would be OK. They didn't seem to understand the situation. But I remember Sarah's *'Be strong . . . Be strong.'* That is a powerful message and I take it to heart.

Saturday, 19 December

The day starts quietly with some cloud cover and a little wind, so not uncomfortable, and only six or seven men about. At 11 a.m., the khaki Land Rover and Omar's Toyota roll into camp. Omar hands me a scrap of paper. Fantastic news – 'prickly-heat powder' written in Rachel's distinctive hand! How good is it to see that?! I could shout for joy. Buggas frowns and says, 'What? You have?'

I root out the powder and give it to him. Now both Rachel and I know we are not far apart; that all the threats and lies are just that. Omar brings me back to earth with a jolt. He points at the paper – there is Jill's number. We head off in the Land Rover again, travelling 45 minutes in a different direction on a quest for a good signal. I'm led up a small hill, to a little shade beneath a thorn tree. The gangsters spread out, Omar plays with the phone. It's very windy, blustery, and it will be even more difficult to communicate. Buggas refreshes my memory – 'Speak money. No money these men kill you!' – as Omar dials and passes me the phone.

I don't want to beg from my sister, or to plead, but I am sure she will be supported and briefed by police specialists in kidnapping, so I go ahead with a pleading call, similar to yesterday's calls to Sarah and Stephen. I ring the changes a bit: I tell her that when I sleep there is a machine gun within a few feet each side of me . . . that I am desperate . . . that I can't stop worrying about Rachel. I ask why no one has spoken to the kidnappers for eight weeks and explain that they only want to talk about money. I say, 'I know seven million is ridiculous, but there must be some response, otherwise we will be killed.'

Jill tells me that Father is OK . . . that they have had two feet of snow . . . that she will be going to Dartmouth for Christmas with Pa. In her matter-of-fact way, but with an edge to her voice showing how hard she is trying to control her emotions, she tells me, 'Father says, "Stay calm."'

It's another of those life-saving moments. I can imagine Dad saying that, standing in his living room in Dartmouth, worried to death about the whole business, struggling to stay up-to-date with the news, relying on emails from the family, unable to talk it through with anyone because he is totally deaf. So, for Pa, I will . . . *Stay calm*.

I tackle Omar about the difficulty in communicating using mobile phones. How well does he understand Stephen? How can they negotiate like that? Why not use email? Omar agrees and dials Stephen again. Buggas seems unconcerned; for him the day's dirty work is done. In a short exchange with Stephen I give him Omar's email: eid-2010@live.com. Stephen promises he will contact Omar on Monday or Tuesday. They want to have a family conference, but they can't travel because of the snow, so it won't be before then. Buggas loses patience, grabs the phone and ends the call. I try to explain snow to Omar and Buggas, without success.

Down the hill, I follow Omar, who opens the car door for me. I am about to get in when Land Rover Man shouts, 'Paul!' and covers his ears, then points behind the Land Rover. Just in time I cover mine. Ten paces away a gangster fires the machine gun, from the hip, at about forty-five degrees into the air – a burst of about fifteen rounds. I am grateful for the warning – the AK-47s are noisy, but this is something else.

I'm back in my 'cell' by about 1.30. Buggas and Omar talk together calmly, so I ask if I can see Rachel. 'Can we be together? No planes for many days.'

Buggas and Omar discuss, then concur, 'OK. Tuesday, after negotiation start.'

They seem good humoured, so I ask for *Omo* and water and they say, 'Tomorrow.'

Sunday, 20 December

I've endured a bad night. It's bitterly cold in the early hours. I manage to keep the radio but have frequent arguments with the gang. One of them will 'borrow' it – 'Five [minutes]; Bee Bee See Somalia.' And it's gone. I have to wait until one of the more sympathetic gangsters is close, then I ask for it back.

Buggas appears briefly, and a man brings a box of bottled water from the car, and a washing bowl! But no *Omo*.

Monday, 21 December

Another bad night. I don't sleep at all, suffering hot and cold spells. I'm going down with something. I get up at dawn, sit in my chair and cry. I'm very depressed, not at all strong. Three of the gangsters come over. I am beginning to give them separate identities, differentiate the characters, recognise the mean ones. These three are sympathetic.

'Problem?' they ask.

How to start? 'No Rachel. No wife.'

'Tomorrow. Rachel OK. No problem.'

They mean well. Liver for breakfast cheers me up a bit, and I vent some frustration on the wadi march. Buggas comes briefly after lunch, with a different subset of the gang. He assures me, 'Rachel OK, sleep well. Rachel, you, after tomorrow. Wednesday.' He sounds genuine, but who knows?

Tuesday, 22 December
Paul's diary

New gang very noisy and using torches at night, shining into my 'tent'. Exercise 3,100 (paces) in half

125

hour. No meat today. Right toe getting sorer all day, take two ibuprofen at bedtime. May have to cut down exercise?

Wednesday, 23 December

0900. Early b'fast – liver and chapati arrive before I am up. R arrived! Great relief and joy!

Rachel arrives! Before we hug, I only register her big smile and that she appears to be unhurt. In one day, a roller coaster – the mundane and the emotional. Sometimes one *can* believe Buggas! We are so very happy. There's no privacy, so we're a bit circumspect with hugs, but we share such incredible relief. I make room for the extra bags, then move everything out, to start again with the floor. The gangsters are happy too; they bring a shovel and help make a flatter, larger floor area. We move things back in, rearrange the bags, put the chairs side by side, hold hands and talk.

Alone but defiant

Monday, 14 December

I walk a few steps to the waiting Land Rover and look back at Paul. He says something, but I can't make it out. They take their time loading up. I walk back to Paul and give him a final hug, reassuring him, 'I'll be OK. Remember not to believe a word they say.'

I'm not afraid, just numb. We were stunned to be told we were to separate, but I'm strangely excited at the prospect of some action. I find it hard to think straight, but I hope that somehow this dramatic turn means we are getting near the end.

I sit in the front of the Land Rover, with Buggas and nine other gangsters in the back. We drive along tracks for about 45 minutes, then veer off into the bush and stop. They unload everything, and we walk a short distance into the bush, me carrying my chair, the others carrying the rest. We pause – they stand under a bush and I sit – while Buggas makes phone calls, then we continue walking along goat tracks further into the bush. We pass some nomad homes and eventually stop. Buggas rigs a tarpaulin under a tree, making a lean-to shelter, open to the north and west. There'll be no privacy for me here. He tells me to put down my mat, and I sit with my bags around me. Paul is not far away, but we might as well be a million miles apart. Buggas soon goes. The men are apprehensive, not friendly. They chatter and argue while I sit and weep. I long to lie down, but I'm on a slope. I set about excavating to make it flatter, using a piece of wood to scrape away the hard sand, pulling up roots, doing something to take my mind off worrying about Paul.

We are used to being together, working as a team, supporting one another, relying on one another. It's not that we don't disagree on things, or even bicker occasionally, but in times of need we're there for each other. I'm afraid they'll put pressure on him to give up everything we have. I'm afraid that without my support he will give in to their demands. We should refuse to get involved. We must leave it to Stephen and his advisers.

I'm less worried about Paul keeping his spirits up. He is good at occupying himself and perfectly capable of fending for himself.

The tarp is already flapping in the wind. There are no suitable stones around, so I weigh it down with full water bottles. Paul would have done better. I refuse food. How can I eat without Paul? One gangster offers me some *chad*, and I respond by crying.

Don't sleep well worrying about P. Lots of taunting – psychological warfare.

Tuesday, 15 December

I refuse breakfast. Buggas comes and sits in my chair with his gun in his lap, pointing at me. He demands, 'How you feel?'

'Alone, miserable. No Paul.'

He snarls back, 'Paul another where.'

Then he declares, 'British troops in area . . . You have me dead!'

You bet I do. I didn't say it, but I'm not a good liar. It must have shown on my face. I say, 'YOU want to kill ME!', pointing at him then at me. Does he understand my meaning? He's the one with the gun after all! He scoffs, sneers and almost laughs, in a high-pitched, nervous way, then falls into a sulk. I'm not only intimidated but frightened. His command of English is so bad that it's dangerous having these exchanges with him. Who knows what he's trying to say and what he makes of my response?

'No food,' he barks. 'Why?'

'I can't eat without Paul.'

'You want to die?'

I'm frightened to say anything.

'No eat, troops kill you!'

I don't know whether to laugh or cry.

'Family? Phone?'

'What can I do?'

He wants me to beg, and I don't want to. I know our family will be doing their best. They don't need more pressure from me.

Buggas suddenly bursts out, 'You no old. Baby!'

Again, I almost laugh. Where did he get that from? We've been telling Omar that we're old people with little money and no jobs to go back to. Maybe it's sinking into Buggas's thick skull that we are not in a position to raise money on expected future earnings? He goes away, and I'm left none the wiser, just exhausted. I try not to think about the fact that now we're apart, our dreamed-of rescue will be much more difficult, if not impossible.

I struggle to come to terms with life without Paul. I know I must get my act together, but it's hard not to think about him whenever I try to do something, making me cry. I know I must eat. When we split, Paul made me take the last mango, so I have it for lunch.

Have siesta then try & wash under sheet! No privacy at all. Guards are their usual taunting selves. Find it hard not to cry when thinking about Paul, but start talking aloud to him. I write him a letter in my notepad:

My Darling Paul,

I miss you very much. It is the season of goodwill but I

am finding it very hard to be cheerful. I love you very much and hope you are OK.

If I don't make it out of here I want you to know that I don't want you to grieve for me or be bitter about what has happened. Please get on with re-building your life and planning for future happiness. Don't regret anything. We've had a wonderful time together and I don't regret a thing.

I love you lots and always will.

R

Wednesday, 16 December

Woke up with mozzie bite on left eyelid. Also rash under left knee. Clear & windy so not too hot. Sit outside as much as possible. Lie down at 12.30. Mr Fastidious brings mosquito net. Ali says, 'War is better because it brings cars, guns & money.' Sleep until 2.30. Find I've got spots appearing on my legs and trunk. Prickly heat? Ask to have private wash & allowed to go into bush for strip wash. Mr F erects new post to tie back tarp. Guards more cheerful. Chad again? Not for long! Late supper again. And enough for 2. Go to bed by 7.30 but have trouble sleeping because of itching.

As the days pass, I start eating regularly. Even if I don't want much, I accept what they give me. So long as I don't refuse food, the guards don't worry, and they don't check what I throw away. They are all around me, noisy as ever, but I take my time when I'm allowed to walk into the bush to go to the toilet. I go far enough to get away from their noise and enjoy the freedom to think. That little bit of 'space' helps me keep my sanity, to rally the mental strength to carry on, to cope with the worry and, above all, to believe in myself. Whatever they do to me, I must take it on the chin and keep going, for Paul, and for our family and friends.

Thursday, 17 December

Summoning up mental strength, I force myself back into a routine. Tea, breakfast, wash and laundry, read book, yoga, lunch, siesta, crossword, read book, play patience, supper, bed. I daydream as much as possible, especially after dark, conjuring up happy thoughts. I train myself to think about Paul and the fun times we've had together, without thinking about what I'm missing. I wonder about friends and family and visualise what they might be doing. It's somehow comforting to contemplate that while I'm here, under a stretch of orange tarpaulin in the Somali bush, they are going about their everyday lives in their homes or offices. The very idea of Christmas shopping and chilly weather makes me appreciate being in the warm! For days on end, I try to remember as many Christmas carols as possible, writing them down in my notebook. I sing them to myself in my head, with perfect pitch!

The guards are mostly stand-offish, but I begin to pick up some of the names and personalities. Mr F, a calming influence, is in charge. Ali, tall, fit and wiry, who knows some English, is a bit of a stirrer. Sharif, also older, but aloof, sleeps in a brown blanket with UNHCR (the UN High Commission for Refugees) emblazoned on it and always wears trousers. Sireet, the cook, again older, has an unusual stooping gait and sneezes a lot. Sayid, a quiet youngster, is another fastidious one. Senick, also young, has a cleft palate which the others tease him about and, perhaps because of that, is exceedingly noisy.

On Thursday morning, they have a row. Senick points a gun at Ali and yells at him aggressively. Others grab the muscular Senick and the gun goes off in the air, just beside Mr F. They scream at each other a bit more before Senick stalks off in a sulk. Mr F remains remarkably calm, me less so! It's the first fight I've experienced and a demonstration of how volatile these men are.

The next afternoon most of the gangsters disappear,

leaving a new man to guard me. He's chubby, about 30, with a strangely stiff gait. In broken English he tells me his name is Oman and asks how I am. He settles himself in my chair right next to my tent, with his gun pointing at me. I'm feeling stroppy and don't want to humour him. I shoo him further away. After much gesticulation, he takes my chair away a few feet and sits down again. I stand up and say, 'Give me my chair.' He doesn't move. I walk towards him and he panics, pointing his gun at me and cocking it. I retreat! He shouts to the other men in Somali, mentioning 'chair'. One says *'kursi'* and eventually Oman gives me my chair back. I win, just.

I struggle with the heat and humidity. My tarp shelter makes a poor sunshade and a fickle wind provides inadequate ventilation. The itching of the prickly-heat rash drives me mad. When I lie down at midday, I keep a bowl of water to hand, sponging myself to cool down.

The sound of the Land Rover approaching always unnerves me. Whenever the Land Rover comes, there's a row – most frequently over the *chad* delivery, or who knows what else?

Saturday, 19 December

Buggas arrives with Omar, who is quick to show me a piece of paper with Paul's writing on it showing his sister Jill's address. He wants her phone number. I dig out my address book and write it down. Omar asks for a mobile number. I say Jill has no mobile. He looks incredulous. I say, 'Jill's an old lady. No mobile phone.' I am angry that they want Paul to phone Jill, who will be occupied with looking after Paul's father. No doubt they are putting pressure on Paul. I find it hard to believe how sick these people are. I ask Omar to pass a note to Paul. He has our stock of prickly-heat powder, and I want him to try to get it to me. Buggas notices and snarls, 'No money. No medicine!' A loitering gangster, a devious character called Samata, repeats, 'No money. No medicine,' as if he's learning a new phrase. Omar walks off, but Buggas sits menacingly in my chair, staring at me. I look down and wait for him to go away, breathing deeply to keep myself calm.

Sunday, 20 December

5 days to Christmas! Must do last-minute shopping!

Buggas turns up with bottled water and the prickly-heat powder from Paul. He sits in my chair again, looking angry, saying nothing. He cuts a ridiculous figure. Will he ever give up hope that he can threaten and intimidate us into finding the money he wants? As a bully and a coward that's all he understands. Eventually, he moves off.

They are determined to keep their 'asset' healthy. I'm fed well, and as the days wear on the portions become larger. I'm often given extra snacks of meat and plenty of vegetable (potato and onion) sauce, which I eat in preference to the copious amounts of spaghetti or rice. The men are sometimes chatty, and Oman asks about the book I'm reading.

'Bible?'

'No. Wilbur Smith.'

Monday, 21 December

Winter solstice. Wake at 6. Feel nervy, on edge. Everyone relaxed in camp. Ali chewing chad. Guns left lying around. Singing. Old man visits but not welcome. Band of nomads turned away too. Given large bone of meat to eat at 10, just when doing yoga. Buggas comes about 3 and asks what I want. Answer: my husband. He says, 'Where husband?' Idiot that he is, trying to provoke.

Tuesday, 22 December

Suspect something afoot as larder stocks getting low. Itchy and restless night. Guards noisy at midnight.

Wednesday, 23 December

Breakfast is unusual: meat-and-potato stew. Ali announces we're leaving. The Land Rover arrives with Buggas, who greets me with the news, 'Go Paul's position!'

At last! Land Rover Man, who always looks serious, gives me a scarf to cover my head – he must be worried about someone seeing me through the windscreen.

We return to a slightly different location, on a distinct rise, looking down into a valley. Buggas opens the door, points his gun at me and then down the hill, grunting, 'Go.' I pass the cooking fire on one side and barrels of water on the other. Down we go, past a tree where some of the gangsters are squatting around a machine gun, and then make a final steep descent into a wadi bed. And there is Paul, the love of my life, coming out of his shelter, partially hidden under the bush. Buggas follows with my bags. His mood is light.

'Happy?'

'Yes!'

Not a merry Christmas

Wednesday, 23 December continued

Reunion is sweet. We hug and share an enormous sense of relief that we have both survived. There's so much to talk about. Where have I been? What's it like here? We discuss how we've coped in our respective captivities.

When apart, I imagined Paul would manage better than me. He's good at occupying himself. I'm the restless one. If he decides to do something, he gets on with it and doesn't get distracted. But we're a team – with *Lynn Rival*. Pursuing our passion for sailing and travelling is a joint endeavour. Until now, I hadn't realised how much we've come to rely on each other.

Paul has been desperately lonely. I feel guilty when he tells me about the great pressure he's been under from Omar and Buggas to make begging phone calls to members of the family. Buggas has been goading and threatening him until he's at the end of his tether. He can't bear the thought of going through that solitary experience again. I had it easy.

We soon get down to the practicalities and re-organise our accommodation. Making ourselves as comfortable as possible is important to our survival, and the process is time-consuming. I do a recce to check out my new surroundings, though the guards are not keen on me exploring. The wadi is yet another fascinating environment. I find many new plants and insects to ponder over, including some captivating stick insects. We walk up and down the flat and scrubless wadi bed for

135

exercise. It's just as hot here in the middle of the day, but one of the gang brings an old blanket and hangs it under a thorn tree to create a shady spot to sit in. To show our appreciation, we use one of Paul's recently learnt Somali words: *mahatsenit* (thank you).

We settle down into our joint routine again. No problem – we've adapted to being hostages, and two is infinitely better than one. At suppertime, we grumble that the food is very plain and meagre. We've become used to having as much tea and food on our own as we get between us when together. It's good to listen to the World Service and play crib again. I'm enchanted by the bats, who come at dusk, but not so sure about the cold at night when we shiver under our blankets.

Christmas Eve

We're left alone and hardly notice the full gang merging together again while they argue over favourite spots. There are few signs of any order; sometimes they sit close to us and other times not. Buggas is away. In the evening, we pick up the 'Festival of Nine Lessons and Carols' from King's College, Cambridge, on the BBC World Service. The reception is terrible, but we listen on defiantly. Rachel has tears running down her cheeks: grief for a life lost. She joins in the carols, and I joke that the reception is so poor I'm not sure if she's singing the same ones! We try not to dwell on where we should be now: at Lamu, in Kenya, with *Lynn Rival*.

Christmas Day

Rachel has saved silver foil from the gangsters' discarded cigarette packets. We put it on the thorn tree to decorate the entrance of our little home. Our Christmas Day starts with petrol-flavoured tea for breakfast, followed by spaghetti for lunch. For a festive treat we eat some of the walnuts and chickpeas that Captain Zaidi gave us. We hope he is now free. Buggas appears briefly at midday to say, 'Family no speak.'

He has a new toy, a pistol, which he swaggers about with, but no pockets, no holster, so he can't put it down or do anything useful with his right hand. He is preposterous.

He asks, 'Why no food? No meat?' He wants to goad us about not having any meat on Christmas Day. Later we cut into a watermelon, another treat kept for some time, which is deliciously sweet. All afternoon we check the radio for the Queen's speech but can't find it on any frequency.

Boxing Day

Another quiet day. We start our yoga routine again. We mustn't let it slip. One of the young gangsters mimics us. When he comes with our food Ali Yeri stands and stares, fascinated by everything we do. Or bored? Another – a keen machine gunner who was behind us in the video – joins in, saying, 'These men crazy.' He shows us his finger, which is badly bruised with a rag wrapped around it. We offer him a better bandage but he's not interested. Afieri, our on-board cook, wanders over later to steal some of the communal cigarettes kept – along with the bullets – under our shelter. He is a painful reminder of our final days on *Lynn Rival*.

Sunday, 27 December

Another day of 'high-octane' tea and washing in dilute petrol. We hear a plane – coming quite near at 1.30 p.m., then again at 2.15 and 3 p.m. They must be flying a search pattern. Our guards shout 'House' when they hear it and make sure we go under the shelter. Buggas appears in the evening and stares at us from a few paces away. 'Family close communication. Say no speak robbers.' He must have memorised the phrases, but he isn't very worked up.

Now Christmas is over, what next? We await their move, convincing ourselves they don't want to split us up again. Surely it's more hassle? On Tuesday we hear – and Rachel sees – another plane at noon, then 12.45 and 1.30 p.m. The gangsters are annoyed. Buggas visits afterwards and takes all the empty water bottles but says nothing. We're always excited by the planes but worry about the effect they have on the gangsters.

On Wednesday we monitor yet more flights: at 11.45 a.m., 12.30 p.m., 1.15 p.m., 2 p.m. and 2.45 p.m. Afterwards Buggas turns up with several men in tow. They stand in the wadi and argue for a while, then Buggas comes over and announces we are to be separated again. He says, 'Plane big problem . . . Stephen liar . . . Family 60 people. Big money!'

We deny that our family is large. He must have misunderstood. We beg him not to split us up, desperately trying to think of ways to persuade him otherwise. Paul pleads with him, aware of the audience of gangsters, some of whom have said kind things to us recently, like, 'Be happy.'

> I warm to my theme, saying they are cruel and asking how they can call themselves kind Somali people when they torture us? Pointless, or is it?

Buggas turns away for another heated discussion with the gathering, then leaves. Most of the gangsters disperse, but one comes over and says, 'No problem.' It's a small comfort. It must have been a spur-of-the-moment decision and we have won some time, but for how long?

Our fears – hidden below the surface – are confirmed. We worry about another separation and the new tension in the air. If they decide to separate us again, what can we do? We feel miserable and powerless.

New Year's Eve
They stay up talking loudly, playing the radio and chewing *chad* until after midnight. Do they celebrate the New Year?

> Planes fly over again, six times on Friday, four times on Saturday, but further away. Every time the roar is heard, up goes the shout, 'Paul! Rachel! House!' and we must hurry in under the tarp. Never mind that the chairs, the washing, the water barrels and the cooking site remain

138

visible. Buggas comes and asks how we are. I peer at him from a foot away, point at my eyes and try to explain about windblown sand, contact lenses and sore eyes.

We have difficulty calming ourselves. I can't concentrate. I notice Paul is the same. When we play cards, he just stops and loses track. Every time we hear a car arriving, we fear the worst. The sound of an engine reduces us to quivering wrecks.

I have to do something about it. I can't live in a state of fear. The problem is I'm afraid of dying. I don't like to think about death, about its finality. I don't believe in an afterlife. How do people who risk their lives for others cope – like our soldiers fighting in Afghanistan? They must train themselves not to fear death. If they can do it, so can I.

We all have to die sometime. I've had a good life, longer and happier than many. I have never sought to do any harm. I have no reason to fear death. It would be a release from this. And I want to die with dignity.

When Buggas is around, and I feel my anxiety levels rising, I say to myself, 'He can but kill you,' and feel relieved. When I can control my fear I feel stronger, more empowered. His hold over me is diminished.

Buggas ignores us. He has reduced the gangsters in number and is taking more care at concealment.

Sunday, 3 January

No planes, no hassle, until 6 p.m., when Buggas saunters over and shouts, 'Go another position. After two,' gesturing a circle on his watch.

Mr F drives with his gun across his lap. Buggas sits with his rifle and an RPG launcher in the front. One man comes in the back with us. We head north and north-east, back towards the village we recognise from before, where we pick up a 'guide'. We then travel west, fast, on a fairly good track. The convoy pauses to assemble the rocket launchers, ready the guns, then we dash through a hamlet, guns bristling out through all the windows, foot to the floor for a few moments. Heaven help anyone who puts a head out! We turn off the road and are told it's not far to a 'new area'. A mat is thrown under a tree. 'Sleep,' they order. No argument. We all bed down in the open.

Just another place in the bush. I've been wondering why they don't take us back to a hijacked ship. If they're worried about a rescue attempt, surely it would be easier to guard us there? As we set off, I imagined we might be heading back to the shore but soon realised we were not.

At least we are together.

Monday, 4 January

A new week, a new location. We are disorientated, worried, nervous and frightened – a horrible cocktail of emotions made more potent by lack of sleep. We wake to find gangsters moving around, close by our feet. Buggas comes over: 'Up.' We follow him to a spot a few yards away, under the low branches of another large tree. The orange tarp is being strung up, the mat thrown down. Our mattresses and bags are handed in.

'Dangerous! This tree. Dangerous,' Buggas explains.

There is a low bough over the 'entrance', covered with long, brittle and very sharp thorns. Is he stating the obvious, the low headroom? Or does he mean the thorns are poisonous? We are well used to the scratching and pricking variety. And our sailing life has taught us to be aware of low obstacles. We wonder if it amuses them to tell us to be careful not to scratch ourselves while they point lethal weapons at us. I hang my oldest shorts over the low branch to act as a warning. We move in and dig out the worst of the prickly growth from the ground under our mat, feeling increasingly unsettled. The men loiter, uneasy. We watch . . . and wait.

We are determined to resist another separation. I'm conscious that Paul suffered so much last time, and I can't imagine how we will cope with another. I'm fearful of the pressure he might be put under again by Buggas, who has always been more demanding of Paul than me. From the beginning, Buggas has assumed that Paul is in control. And no doubt he thinks I'm less likely to have access to millions, being a mere woman. Inevitably they will separate us by force, but at least we can make a stand, to show them all how painful it is. If any of them have the least bit of compassion, of shame for what they are doing to us, we will remind them.

Two Toyotas arrive. Buggas, the weasel-faced Commander and the other cheerful, chubby villain we call Fat Boy have a conference with Omar, out of earshot. Something must be afoot, as we only see them together at 'events'.

Omar comes to us, alone, and doesn't bother with pleasantries: 'These men are angry. They are angry because your family refuse to start negotiations. Your situation is very bad. They will kill you.'

I remind Omar of the British attitude and repeat there is nothing we can do: 'These men were robbers. Maybe that is not so bad; people can sympathise and understand. But they have moved on to kidnapping and extortion. That is a huge step up – taking a person's freedom rather than his property. There is no excuse for that. In every culture it is a big crime. Now you say they will be murderers. How do you feel about that? Is that OK in Somalia? To take ordinary people from their families, then kill them? Is that accepted by the elders in this evil, evil country?'

Omar insists he is not one of them, not a pirate; he is our friend.

'They are *not* pirates,' I scream. 'They are armed thugs, kidnappers, extortionists. You understand kidnap? You understand extortion?'

Omar says he will try to help: 'I will talk with them, maybe I can persuade them not to kill you, but I am not one of them: I have no gun, I cannot tell them what to do.'

Omar argues he was the one to persuade the gang to bring us together after our separation, but now they are losing patience. He won't be able to hold off another separation unless we find someone to 'name a figure'. He asks for Jill's phone number and says he will call her again as a last resort. I'm angry and fed up with his nonsense. He keeps trying to make us feel responsible for finding the money they want. How many times do we have to keep telling him there is NOTHING we can do?

In no uncertain terms we also tell Omar that we won't survive another separation. They will be murderers if they separate us again. Omar looks frightened and angry. He goes on about the British people helping us. I tell him the British people will be very angry about their threats to kill us, especially the video showing guns at our heads. He says that was Buggas's idea, not his. He asks if the government will send troops to rescue us and I say, 'Possibly.' We are still hearing planes and still entertain hopes of a rescue. Omar cries, 'That makes no sense. You'll be killed and I'll be three hours' drive away.' He is worried for his own skin! Good!

Omar rejoins the other three; they have a long, argumentative conference. We can hear the raised voices, the anger. The rest of the gang stay out of the way, minding their own business. They, and we, know this is a crisis point. Eventually the leaders and Omar leave, without coming near us.

What will they do next? Paul wonders why Stephen does not at least offer an amount that we can afford. Are our family still hoping for a rescue? Don't they realise by now that the reconnaissance flights aren't getting anywhere? All they do is make our captors jittery. We realise the risks of putting men on the ground here must be huge. Perhaps our family are struggling, as I am, with the prospect of paying these evil people money. For all my fear about what will come next, I still can't come to terms with the idea that they will make money out of us. We'll end up penniless and spend the rest of our lives in debt. If our family donate their savings, how can we live with that? And why should the British public pay criminals to release two ordinary people from Tunbridge Wells when the same money could save thousands from hunger?

I muster my thoughts to control my rising fears. In our cruising life we enjoy simple pleasures: meeting people from all walks of life, sharing experiences, learning about different cultures, spending a bit of money in poor coastal communities. We are not bad people and don't deserve this treatment. Who does?

We hear two more planes, not very close, in the afternoon. Our guards are more vigilant, with RPG launchers to hand as well as machine guns. A Land Rover brings supplies and the cooks set up their area. We are brought spaghetti, but we have little appetite.

Tuesday, 5 January

There is an undercurrent of tension. The men are avoiding us and a kerfuffle breaks out among the group on close guard. Fisticuffs! And a knife. Men pile in and separate the combatants, who are bloodied but both standing. One is the older cook, shy Sireet, who doesn't seek our help. Other gangsters would be asking us for a bandage and sympathy. He and his sparring partner are led off, separately, to calm down. This is the first serious fight we've witnessed.

At about 4.30 p.m., Buggas turns up with the Commander. Most of the gangsters gather around; they make their way just out of sight, but we still hear them. Fifteen or more have a big, noisy pow-wow. Not their normal high-volume discussions but real anger and impatience is evident in the exchanges. The mood is unnerving.

We are brought rice – early supper – but only have time for a few mouthfuls before Buggas strides up. He looks straight at us: 'You go. One. One. Quick. Bags.'

We stand up and say, 'No.'

Buggas snarls. He is visibly taken aback, but soon recovers: 'One out! One in! Now.'

Only the low branch of the thorn tree is between us. We walk out to the branch, holding on to one another.

He screams, 'One in!'

We say, 'No' in unison. We have made the challenge. What will *he* do?

He turns away, picks up his AK-47, swivels back and aims it at us, low, about waist level. I turn, trying to keep myself between him and Rachel. We are still clasped together. Out of the corner of my eye, I see that the gangsters are gathering around. Some race towards Buggas.

'One out. NOW.'

'No. You might as well kill us.'

He splutters, his voice now shrill in anger, 'You want dead? OK. KILL YOU!'

I tighten my arms around Rachel, feel her gripping me. I'm vaguely aware of the sound of the AK-47 being cocked. The men are shouting, incomprehensibly, and two grab Buggas from behind.

Crack. Crack. Crack.

Three shots. He has fired into the air. From only a few feet away. We are stunned, but cling to each other even more tightly, resigned to dying. There is nothing more he can take from us. We are tearful but not afraid. He flings his gun to the ground and storms off. Mr F and Baby Face come up to us and say, 'You crazy?' They pull on our arms, and we stagger further from the shelter.

Buggas yanks up an exposed tree root, finds a knife

and peels the outer layer. It's about three feet long, the thickness of my little finger.

Ktsh – the first stroke hits my shoulder, protected only by my thin T-shirt. I move my arms up, trying to protect Rachel's neck.

Ktsh. Ktsh. Ktsh. I lose count of the strokes. Some are high. Is he aiming for our heads? I sense six or seven red weals developing on my right forearm and wrist, more on my shoulders and upper back. Awareness of time ceases. Consciousness of surroundings vanishes. I just try to protect Rachel from this vicious thug who has our lives in his hands.

I hear nothing.

Two strong arms grab mine and wrench me away. Rachel and I make a last desperate attempt to cling together. But Rachel is grabbed as well. We are being pulled asunder with overwhelming strength – we can't hold on – and are thrown to the dusty ground. Two men continue pulling at my arms. They drag me away. I can see Rachel pinned to the ground. Buggas picks up his AK and deliberately smashes the butt down into Rachel's face. This is the end.

Whipped and separated

Tuesday, 5 January continued

Three men drag me away, 20 paces or so, behind the trees. I can't see or hear Rachel. I am pulled roughly to my feet and held. Facing me is Mr Fastidious. He looks stunned, so stunned he finds some words of English: 'Are you mad?'

'No! *You* are mad! All of you are crazy.' I spit at him; he ignores me. The men pull me further, another 20 paces. I crane my neck, but there's no sign of Rachel. They bundle me into the back seat of a Toyota.

'Sit!' One man stands close each side, guns at the ready.

It's dark by now. Two men turn up with my bags – we had hardly unpacked and had maintained the split of the medicines and books from before. Mr F asks what's missing. I don't care but force myself to look at the bags, the mattress, pillow, sheet, etc. I mime eating and drinking, and realise my contact lens solution is missing – I'll be lost (literally) without it. I gesture at my eyes. They are now familiar with the ritual of lens wearers, but they don't realise that I have keratoconus – my eyesight cannot be corrected by glasses. 'Small white bag,' I say. Size: OK, I can mime that. Colour: I don't know the word; there is nothing white around. Buggas comes over, and I explain again. He disappears but comes back shrugging. They want me back in the car, but I can't go without my lens solution. Mr F rushes up, bearing the Jiffy bag. I'm shoved back in the car with only two guards and Mr F driving. I won't cry, not in front of these thugs. What have they done to Rachel?

A fast drive, back the way we'd come, through the dark village with the distant glow from the light at the mobile-phone mast, out towards the south, sticking to the 'main' track, turn off, cross the bush, lurch to a halt. Mattress on the ground, bags thrown onto it – 'Sleep.' The car drives off. I sit, disconsolate, on the ground. There is no moon, no stars. Has the world ended? Mine has.

Time passes. Mr F walks up. He offers a mosquito net, ties it to a tree branch, levels the ground and spreads the mat and mattress out. 'You have water?' I nod. 'Rachel OK,' he says. 'No problem.'

Does he realise the irony? But I'm grateful for the small sign of humanity. I summon the effort to take my lenses out, lie down and long for oblivion.

Wednesday, 6 January

The worst day of my life dawns. My mind is in turmoil. My brain wants to analyse yesterday's action – what could I have done? What should I have done? Perhaps accept that there is only so much a nine-stone weakling can do against thirty armed thugs. But my heart wants me to sit quietly and think morbid thoughts. Is Rachel alive? Will I ever see her again? How could I have let this happen? I have failed to protect my woman. Now the Somalis have reason to despise me. But what of them? How could they let Buggas be so violent? They have families, most of them don't seem to be gratuitously violent or hateful. How could they stand around and watch?

The hatred builds in me: we can beat these bastards. I somehow know that Rachel is not dead. Together in mind and spirit, 30 years together, we must live for each other. Be strong. A part of my being wants to divert me towards practicalities. Survive, take stock, make plans. Do the laundry.

Food? No. Why does state of mind affect one's ability to eat? I don't feel that I can eat; I don't want to eat, and I will not eat until I am with Rachel again. So there. Take it away.

Behr, brr, briis, basto, whatever.

I put up the washing line; hang out the sheet to air. Will they tell me about Rachel?

Soon after nine, Buggas and the Commander arrive. The Commander joins the men; Buggas walks towards me.

'How are you?' he says. I can't believe it. What does he expect me to say? I shrug.

'How is Rachel?'

'Don't know.' He stares at me, mouth half open, chewing. 'You speak family! Speak sister.'

'How?' I ask. 'Where is Omar?'

'No Omar. You have phone?'

This is crazy. I try again: 'Call Omar. Tell me how is Rachel. Where is Rachel?'

He spits and turns away. I run after him. He turns, barks at me, 'Go your position! Sleep!'

I don't know how the time passes. Buggas and the Commander have left without me noticing. Mr F brings me a spoon and fork. He won't tell me about Rachel. I plead with him, 'Where Omar?'

He pulls out his phone, dials and hands it to me. It is Omar's distinctive voice: 'I cannot come. They will not let me come. I will make conference call for you to family.'

I ask about Rachel. 'I don't know. These people are angry. I cannot tell them what to do.'

I get through an unsettled night – hot sweats, but cold in the early hours. My mind manages to close down and I get a few hours of disturbed sleep.

Thursday dawns. I make tea and refuse liver. I empathise with the goat tethered close to my shelter. 'I am not going to eat you. You are my only friend here. And you have lost your mate.' She lets me stroke her head but soon tires of this new entertainment when she sees I have no food for her.

Buggas and the Commander return. Same mantra as yesterday: 'Call sister. Call Sarah. No speak Stephen.

Stephen fucking. Omar come tomorrow.'

They walk away but return angrily: 'No food. Eat! Eat!'

'No. Not hungry. Sick.'

'No eat, I beat you!' Buggas shouts, picking up a stick. I am scared, tired and weary beyond belief. How can people do this hunger-strike thing? They must be so strong. I can't. I can't overpower the organism's need to survive. I take a little *hilip* (goat meat) and chapati. Buggas calms down. 'Rachel come – after tomorrow.' He isn't convincing. 'Stephen delaying. So that, so that soldiers search you. NO speak Stephen. Speak sister.'

I'm left alone again. It's quiet except for the cicadas – the pulse of nature in the bush. I hear the distant drone of a light plane. Three flights at forty-five-minute intervals but quite far away. They are still looking for us! There is hope of rescue. The six or seven remaining gangsters don't seem bothered. After dark a man comes to the shelter, thrusts a phone into my hand and squats on his haunches. Omar is again trying to set up a call. It may be Jill, but we lose the connection. Omar says he will try again. I return the phone and hear nothing more.

Friday, 8 January

I try to cheer up. I eat a little breakfast and set off to walk around a big group of trees – 'Exercise' – managing a circuitous route of about 250 paces on trodden paths. I can walk fast, for half an hour or so. It's getting windier, so I have to take care of my eyes. Windblown sand is a problem in this camp.

At midday I'm offered a phone again. It's Omar. He says he will make the call to Jill: 'You must tell your sister to negotiate. These men will kill Rachel. Rachel has broken head. She not eating. Maybe she die. Stephen is wasting time. Family must find another negotiator. These men will not let you speak to Stephen.'

I take the phone, reluctantly, but what can I do? It is, unusually, a good line. I tell Jill about the beating, the separation, I explain that the gangsters won't deal with Stephen, that they are angry and impatient. I say she must appoint a negotiator, plead with her to at least make a starting offer: 'Jill, I know you have little money, but Rachel and I have about $250,000, please put it on the table. There is no other way out. These thugs only want money.'

I explain that I will not be found by the planes as there are no cars at camp and that anyway I would be moved within hours of an aeroplane coming within sight. Jill – calmly and with immense restraint – promises the family will discuss and call Omar tomorrow.

Omar cuts off Jill and speaks to me. I am distressed by his news of Rachel. But I don't know whether to believe him. He says he will call Stephen, but I mustn't let the gangsters know! 'These men say no speak Stephen, but I will help you.' What is going on? Is he genuinely trying to help?

I tell him there's a problem. 'In my family, the only man is my father who is 98 and completely deaf. Stephen is the only one who can negotiate.'

Paul: Hello, Stephen, this is Paul, can you hear me?
Stephen: Yes, I can hear you, Paul.
Paul: Yes, just, things have changed out here, Stephen. We've been beaten. We were put together again for a short time and then beaten – I've got weals on my arms from trying to protect Rachel's head.
Omar prompts me: 'What, what he can do?'
Paul: Stephen, because it's gone on so long, the gang are not prepared to speak with you officially. Can you appoint a professional to negotiate, please?
Stephen: I'll see what we can do but, um, it makes great complications. This is a normal bargaining ploy, Paul.
Paul: I know. But these are not normal people, Stephen. They have a one-track mind – they don't understand.
Stephen: We can't touch your funds, as solicitors say you're under duress.

Paul: *I'm a captive, I'm not under duress; everything I've said to you has been true – you can't put off . . . you can't delay any more – it's not on. Find another fucking solicitor.*

Omar: *Paul, Paul. I mean, they see another some, er, people of another, some Somali people I mean, er, contacting us and Stephen. I mean saying, er, we are another people . . . I mean, Stephen, this is untrue. There is no anybody who understands – we are these people and who able to solve this problem. Another people, Somali people, I mean, they, er, they are telling something, they are telling I mean we are to well, um, leave them these people out . . .*

Stephen: *I must go now, I've got to catch a train. I will speak to you later today. Thank you.*

Omar cuts Stephen off and speaks to me.

Omar: *OK, OK, and, er, Rachel, she well, fine. I speak her this morning. She's eating a little rice. She very well now.*

Paul: *I do hope so, Omar. Thank you.*

Am I to believe what Omar says about Rachel being well today and eating a little rice? Is he saying it to put me in the 'right' frame of mind to make these distressing calls? I take it positively – Rachel is not too badly hurt. I hope they will reunite us now I've done the dirty business.

Before dusk, the Commander comes; no sign of Buggas. He brings a big bunch of *chad*, which the gangsters squabble over. He comes to me: 'Rachel OK. She sleeping, eating, OK.' I ask if I can see her. 'You have money? No money, no Rachel.'

The *chad* party goes on into the night, a few feet away from me. The night is difficult on every level: the noise of the gang, the wind dropping sand on me every few minutes, my own fretting about these agonising phone calls. I get up and try to make more of a screen with my bags, the cardboard water-bottle box and an empty jerrycan, but it doesn't help. The phone conversations torment me. I was speaking from the heart, so worried about Rachel, but then afterwards it seems that I had just been wound up. I cry myself to some sort of sleep.

The next morning is quiet – I recognise the aftermath of a *chad* session. Seven or eight sleepy men who show all the symptoms of a night on the town. They creep around gingerly. There's no shouting, just the sound of retching from behind a tree. Late service – water for tea after eight o'clock!

I am depressed, my low spirits exacerbated by trouble with my lenses.

At 11 a.m. a gangster hands me the phone. Here we go again. But he is grinning. Why? It's Rachel! We're only allowed a few moments, but she says she is OK physically, she is eating, but she is being tormented. I tell her to keep positive. We will be reunited. We *will* survive, together.

The white Land Rover arrives with three big oil drums of water and two goats. Buggas saunters over, nonchalantly chewing a *chad* stem. He doesn't look angry but not pleasant either.

'Family. How much money?'

I say maybe 300,000, with a little from my father and family absolute max $500,000.

He spits. 'No money, you dead.'

I try to explain. Again. 'Family little money. Old people. Finish work. Small family. Government no money.'

He falls silent – is he inventing the next lie, or rehearsing the next memorised statement? 'British soldiers fighting in Somalia – BBC radio speak soldiers search two hostages.' Another pause, then: 'Rachel come this place after sister speak well.'

I tell Buggas we will die if we are not together. 'We will give up hope and die. You will have NO MONEY.'

Sunday, 10 January

The meaning of solitary confinement sinks in. No one to talk to. No one to engage with. No interaction. Of the gangsters guarding me only Ali Deri speaks a little

English, and he keeps away. He has a machine gun, usually set up under a tree about 50 yards away. I sink into depression again.

One night there is a crack, not a violent gunshot but the snapping of a tree branch. Mozzie net, tarp and branch crash down on me. I make a DIY repair, groping about in the thorny branches, tying together scraps of string, reaching over the tarp that I am trying to tie up. No concern is shown by the gangsters. It's the spur I need to while away an hour in the morning, adjusting the shelter, making it more robust and improving the windshield. That takes me to midday when . . . my chair arrives! The blue plastic chair I had given up hope of seeing again. My euphoria lasts only minutes. What use is a chair when I have no Rachel, no life, no hope? It's just somewhere to sit and cry in a little less discomfort.

I put it under the tree opposite my shelter, where the shade is better in the late afternoon. I have a book, but turn the pages only occasionally. On the radio it's *Newshour* on the World Service, but I can't concentrate. I try so hard not to cry. The gangsters notice my distress. One of them comes over.

'Problem?'

Well, yes, actually, since you mention it. How can I get it across to these stupid, stupid people that what they are doing is inhuman, cruel, *torture*? But they *aren't* stupid. They're ignorant, mostly illiterate, but they must have feelings, a conscience. They must have been brought up to know right from wrong, to respect elders. I have a rant. The words mean nothing to him, but he gets the drift. I mention Rachel a lot.

'Rachel OK,' he says, softly. He goes away, returns with a dark blanket and hangs it carefully under the tree, using the thorns as hooks. He gestures to me to move the chair into the shade.

'Hassan,' he says, pointing to himself

153

'*Athiga* Paul,' pointing at me; '*Aniga* Hassan,' pointing at himself again.

Two others join him. They squat in front of me. They are quiet and appear sympathetic – Ali Yeri, the young cook, and Senick, with broad shoulders, easily capable of lugging one of the machine guns around. My first words of Somali: *athiga, aniga*. You, me.

Ali Yeri, pointing at the others in turn – 'This man name Hassan, this man name Senick.'

I become a willing pupil – '*Inglisi* "name", Somali?', with what I hope looks like an interrogatory shrug. Ali understands and teaches me my third word – '*Maga'a* . . . *athiga maga'a* Paul.' Ali grins, looks at me, points at one man, then the other, 'Name this man? Name this man?' I pass that test, and they head off to get the fire going. I am calmer. Have they been told to be nice? Or is it genuine now the bosses are away? I must be careful not to get too friendly. But I can't stand the loneliness. I must take advantage, make the task of existing less intolerable.

I'm getting used to solitude. Buggas stays away. I dread his arrivals, but my need for information, to know what is going on, to know that *something* is going on, becomes overwhelming. With no other 'leaders' about, and the gangsters being 'friendly', I have time to settle, to contemplate the cruelness of fate and plan how to survive. It is important to stay fit. So, every day, I embark on my after-breakfast march around the trees, six circuits each way, before the sun becomes too much. In the evening, an hour or so before dusk, I do a yoga session. Retaining suppleness is as vital as aerobic fitness. And while the half hour of marching allows me to vent anger, the yoga poses require me to shut out the world. I move outside the shelter for the standing stretches. There is a smooth, thorn-free patch of sandy ground. The sun is low, and I do the side stretches, watching my shadow in place of a mirror. Ali Yeri laughs. What's up? I turn and see Hassan in a perfect pose behind me. It's easy for him, with the suppleness and strength of youth. I finish with a long forward stretch – and he can't do it! He can't touch his toes. Neither can Ali. I am smug: proud that this wrinkly is as supple as they are.

The stormy weather continues. When the wind does drop, the lack of clouds makes it stifling under the shelter. At night I alternate between shivering in the wind with copious showers of sand, and sweating, willing the wind to come back.

Tuesday, 12 January

I am feeling sorry for myself. If I think about Rachel it reduces me to tears, so I blot out all musings on our former life. The days seem endless. And I can't sleep; the heat and humidity is too much when the wind drops. So I sit in the chair, re-reading *The Fiery Cross* by Diana Gabaldon. We brought three of her *Outlander* series, and I have two with me. I get a lot out of them, even on the third reading. The eighteenth-century gung-ho adventuring is an absorbing distraction. But there is a downside: the romantic interludes reduce me to tears. This is a love story between time travellers that goes way beyond their wedding day. The way the hero Jamie rescues and protects his wife Claire makes me contemplate my inadequacy again.

The following morning is overcast. I think I hear a plane, far away, but then a gangster hands me a phone. Is this it? Will there be news of Rachel? Has someone started negotiation? Omar briefs me, 'Speak Stephen. Tell him not to waste time. These men beat you because Stephen make silly offer. Only 20. Family must give money. They must make proper offer.'

Stephen: *Hello, Paul. How are you?*
Paul: *I'm OK, except I'm alone and in solitary confinement. Jill spoke to you, I expect, about our beating.*
Stephen: *Yes.*

155

Paul: *I spoke to Rachel on the telephone on Saturday. She said she was being tormented all the time, and she said she was giving up . . . They will beat us again if we don't come up with something that end, so I need . . . it's nonsense to say you can't use our money. If a solicitor says that, tell him to bring the gravestone out here personally. It's no good to us there. We have to put all our money on the table. I have said that our money would be maybe 300,000 and with a bit of help from my father and Jill, I know that the rest of you, you don't have much money.*

Stephen: *Ssshhh.*

Paul: *They might possibly expect half a million, but if they have another . . . what they think of as a silly offer, they will beat us again, and I don't think we can stand it much longer [voice very strained]. You understand, Stephen?*

Stephen: *Yes . . . yes . . . Where is this money?*

Paul: *. . . My money? Our money?*

Stephen: *Yes.*

Paul: *. . . You would have to borrow against it. There is a file on our computer, which is in my father's computer room in Dartmouth . . . called 'Investment' . . . It's an Excel spreadsheet . . . and it's saved with various dates. That summarises all our resources.*

Stephen: *Yes, yes . . . That's fine as long as we know that, um, but we're obviously negotiating . . .*

Paul: *Yes.*

Stephen: *Keep your spirits up, Paul.*

Paul: *I'm so worried about Rachel.*

Stephen: *I appreciate that.*

Paul: *We've been beaten now with rifle butts . . . It's not funny. We're coming up to the end of 12 weeks, you know.*

Stephen: *I know it's awful for you.*

Paul: *It sounds so silly.*

Stephen: *We are doing our best . . . keep something to* *occupy your mind . . . try practising your Greek or something like that, you know, because anything which exercises your mind would help.*

Paul: *[very miserably]* I know . . . but 24 hours a day, everything I think makes me think of Rachel, and that makes me cry.

Stephen: Of course it does. But it will end soon.

Paul: Please . . .

Stephen: I can promise you they want to be rid of you as much as we want you back . . .

Paul: Yes *[muffled]*.

Stephen: Yes, we think of you all the time, Paul. I'll try to speak to Rachel as well if I possibly can.

Paul: I don't think they'll let you.

Stephen: We're working for you.

Paul: Please, we're desperate.

Stephen: We're working for you 24/7, I promise.

Paul: Please just make them an offer of half a million, you know . . .

Stephen: Yeah, it's not that easy to put our hands on that sort of money, that's the trouble.

Paul: Yes, I know.

Stephen: I will do my best. Don't worry.

Paul: If you can get a big sum, a decent offer, they say they will put us together again. I'm so worried about Rachel.

Stephen: Yes.

Sebulay *[accomplice of Omar's]*: While Paul is online, can you tell us what you can come up with?

Stephen: Is this Sebulay?

Sebulay: Yes. Can you come up with the number?

Stephen: I can't come up with any number till I've spoken to the family.

Sebulay: Ah ha.

Paul: Stephen, please do it quickly, please.

Sebulay: OK, OK, do it quick Paul is now saying . . .

Stephen: But we can't, we, er . . . You know there's no

benefit to you to keep these two separate. It doesn't make any difference to the negotiations.

Omar: Hello, Stephen, this Omar. Can you hear me?

Stephen: Yes, I can hear you, Omar.

Omar: Paul's on the line, please I mean, Stephen, you are saying 'other time', um, or 'I'm contacting the family' . . . Please, we are two months in that idea, so we are contacting somebody else and doing something, so I mean, the pirates with Paul now, they are now waiting a number. Paul gives them the telephone, they are asking us the number . . . Which number do you have, they say?

Stephen: I told you earlier.

Omar: OK, Paul, please he is on the line and you are on the line, so please come up a number to tell the pirates now . . .

Stephen: We, it's no . . .

Paul: Please, Stephen. We can't, I can't, we can't get anywhere otherwise.

Stephen: I know, Paul, but these negotiations have to take a certain form.

Paul: Honestly, they don't understand that here. Can you not just say half a million? We'll work it out . . . It can be borrowed against our portfolio?

Stephen: We can't do that, Paul. The banks won't allow you. I can't borrow money against your portfolio because they won't allow us because you're under duress. The banks just won't do it.

Paul: Well, there must be some way. I mean, this is stupid. This is stupid.

Stephen: Well, this is how our government protects people like yourself, because they say the banks must not give money against this. They won't even release your own money because they say that if you want to borrow this money you've got to be able to put your signature on it . . .

Omar: Stephen, please, Stephen, with Paul, Stephen, listen, please. These people, they don't need any money from the government. The government are not ready to pay money. We have Paul and his wife; they have their money.

Stephen: What I am trying to say, Omar, is that the banks won't give money to people who are not in control like Rachel and Paul. They won't give the money because they say they are not in control of their lives. They say the pirates are forcing them to ask for this . . . so they won't do it.

Omar: No! Paul can now and he's saying, telling us, no, there's no anybody forcing him to tell a lying. Paul even told me that he has this money.

Stephen: I know what I'm saying to you.

Omar: You are playing about, Stephen. You are playing. Stephen, please, if you are not the solution, please, if you are waste of time, and on our telephone we are consuming our time and our money, so please ask now anyway. Please, you are to tell them Paul and the pirates . . . my fear is they will die . . .

Stephen: Omar, you told me yourself earlier that you wouldn't threaten them. You said you would look after them well, and you'd feed them, and you said they wouldn't come to any harm.

Sebulay: Yes, now time is very tough. Better to end negotiations now and taking longer . . .

Stephen: Right . . . Yes, yes. I agree.

Sebulay: So you . . . I know they have savings in their accounts, so you have to start on their savings, then you go to other relations.

Stephen: Yes, but I am trying to explain to you all that we can't get at the savings. The banks won't let us touch them because Paul and Rachel are being held against their will.

Paul: Stephen, this is Paul. Can't you work something out, because you know it's reached the point where we will die here? If something isn't sorted . . . somebody must have some assets they can borrow against, I mean . . .

Stephen: *We're working on that, Paul, don't worry. If we speak to the banks, they say you can't borrow under these situations. They will not lend us any money.*

Paul: *No, but there must be some way. Have you spoken to Special Branch, because they know about kidnapping?*

Stephen: *We have spoken to everybody we can. The trouble is that any government agency won't speak to us because it's talking money. They won't help us at all. You know, they simply say, sorry, we are not allowed to talk money, it's government policy.*

Paul: *So they'll cry at the graveside, will they? This is what it comes to, Stephen. I'm not joking any more. They are going to beat us again, and they will kill us eventually, and it won't be very long. They are very impatient and angry.*

Stephen: *The pirates have no history of badly treating their captives. They know it's not good . . .*

Paul: *I know, but this is a new game to them because, remember, they take ships and on ships the people are just a human shield. They have no real value. With us, they stepped into a different league, and they are angry, and they're worried by the aeroplanes and so on, and they're running out of patience and I . . .*

Stephen: *Well, we are trying to explain to them . . .*

Paul: *They don't understand, Stephen, because they are only interested in money.*

Stephen: *Yes, but there is no benefit to the pirates holding on to you if they are not going to get any money . . .*

Paul: *I know, I know.*

Stephen: *. . . And we offered them all reasonable expenses.*

Paul: *Think about it in terms of face for the leader, the gang leader.*

Stephen: *Yes, yes.*

Paul: *It's very much the prep-school gang with the leader. His reputation is on the line.*

Stephen: Yes, yes, well, we are telling him that he can get a lot of kudos by releasing you. Everyone's going to look well on him. They're trying to say that they are only doing this because they have no fishing left. If they let you go, they would see the benefits from the international community, our government and others . . . you know it won't do them any good if they hurt you.

Paul: I know. The level of understanding is not that high, Stephen, not with the people I've met.

Stephen: No, I . . .

Paul: The man who demands the money . . . if he doesn't get it . . . then there's anger and . . . I don't see any way out, I really don't.

Stephen: We just don't know . . . how to take it further . . . but we are investigating, I promise you.

The phone battery runs out. I am despondent. It's so depressing that they don't seem to understand the position. 'All reasonable expenses' – I can imagine Buggas's reaction if that were to be translated to him. I don't know – maybe if there is an offer, not an insulting one, but a starting 'bid' of around 100,000 then a negotiation may get to about half a million. We would be wiped out, but we would be free. And that is priceless. But we have been held for 12 weeks, and there is no serious negotiation. How can that be? I wonder whether to expect another call. Nothing happens. After an hour, Buggas comes, but not near me. I peer out from the shelter, I don't know what to do. Am I brave enough to go out and speak to him? Too late. He's gone. He left *chad* with the men, so it will be a noisy night but a quiet day tomorrow.

Thursday, 14 January

The gangsters are hungover but wake up in time to entertain three locals to a late breakfast. They find me amusing. It's not mutual. I skip exercise and mope in my shelter. After lunch Buggas comes in a Toyota driven by Mr

F with the usual water jerries and a goat in the back. The tailgate won't open – cue much struggling to extract the goat, over the back seat and out. Poor thing. They don't give her much more respect than they give me. Buggas ignores me again. As they prepare to leave, I rush out and ask him if I could be with Rachel. He snarls, 'Rachel have money? No money, no Rachel. *Go your position*!' His tone brooks no argument.

The next day, Buggas comes again in the supply Land Rover. He radiates less anger; he's just sullen. I've had another tearful morning feeling sorry for myself. The loneliness is getting to me. I rant at him. I say I am alone, no one to speak to, no Rachel, no friends. 'These men your friends,' he says with a dramatic sweep of his arm and walks off, smugly satisfied.

More quiet days. Yoga lessons continue – when Buggas is away – with four or five eager participants. I get to know the names of all the gangsters who are guarding me, and something of their characters. There are the youngsters: Afieri, the 20-year-old cook who was in the attack on *Lynn Rival*; Senick, 20; Hassan, 22; and Ali Yeri, 22, another cook; the older Ivarr, 34; and Deli, 30, both have some quasi-military training; Ali Deri, at 40, the most experienced fighter; and Sharif, 38, the serious Muslim, the only one who prays the required five times per day.

I now realise why this camp seems familiar. I extend my exercise route a little and come across a small pile of used Lipton tea bags and a Boots dental-floss stick. There is only one way that could have got here! Further along, a pile of shiny fragments, the broken internals of a thermos flask. I remember that breaking. I check my diary – yes, Rachel and I were here from the 9th to the 24th of November. But why hadn't I recognised it? Surely my mind isn't that far gone? Over the next days I ponder during my exercise and toilet trips, looking at the features from different angles. Maybe that was where our shelter had been? And, over there, was that the route to our toilet area? It's amazing how the place has changed in a few weeks.

One afternoon I see three little squirrel-like animals. They have thin bodies, long legs, a non-bushy tail and they sit up to see further, like meerkats, peering around for any tasty morsel. I ask Ali Deri, who is close, what they are. '*Dabagaale* – no good eating.' Ali runs towards them and they scurry away, dropping their trophies, small pieces of old chapati.

A new item appears on the evening menu – *digir*, Somali beans. They are boiled for a couple of hours, then rice is added for bulk and sugar to taste. Most days I manage to get Ali to serve my bowlful before adding the sugar, then I add a few spoonfuls, rather than the multiple handfuls that the gangsters like. I still have no appetite, but Ali reports to Buggas, and I will eat rather than incur further wrath.

Most afternoons a few of the men sit by me. We have a 'name check'. I learn more Somali; they learn a little English. Ali Deri doesn't join in these basic lessons. He learnt English 20 years ago, in Mogadishu. When the country fell apart, he chose the life of a fighter and has had no use for English. He is keen to practise, though, and has a language course on his mobile phone. He doesn't let the others use it but sits by his machine gun, practising, and then comes over to try a new phrase on me. It's not easy, but we learn – *kiss, kiss* (step by step). Hassan is also keen to learn, but he's very shy. He's been taught to write – he carefully forms the letters in the sand – and can pronounce English words. His smile of simple delight when he masters something new is infectious. Occasionally, it shocks me back to reality, and tears. I am *not* a tourist exchanging strange words with friendly locals, but just for a moment we empathise as fellow men. Who knows? It may make my life more bearable. It may even give me a chance to make these guys realise what they are doing, to see me as a human being rather than an asset.

The days pass. I'm still not feeling well but am buoyed

when a plane comes over – one every other day perhaps. At least someone is still looking. Surely negotiations will start soon, and I'll be together with Rachel again.

I can't get used to the noise. Somali gangsters don't have volume control, just an on–off switch. And it's rarely off. Every evening, after I have gone to bed, four or five of them settle down on the mats, a few feet from my shelter, and talk. And talk. And talk. And watch videos on their mobile phones. Most nights they run out of steam by 11 p.m. One night, I can't stand it any more. I creep out from under the net, stand up and shout, 'FOR FUCK'S SAKE, SHUT UP!' There's stunned silence.

'Problem?' asks Senick, quietly.

'Yes,' I say. 'Problem. *Jabber jabber jabber*. All day, all night. Too much.'

'OK. No problem,' several of them say. Amazingly they quieten down and, apart from the occasional eruption, keep it to a bearable level thereafter.

Sunday, 17 January

Buggas appears again, only for long enough to order me to sleep. 'Omar come tomorrow, after tomorrow search Rachel.' I am pleased to see him go. I've heard two flights today – I can dream of rescue tonight.

In the afternoon I make a start on learning Somali numbers with Ali. Senick and Hassan join in and Sharif becomes interested. He has been aloof until now, ashamed, I think, that he has no English. He doesn't take any interest in learning it, but he's a thinker, and one of the storytellers in the gang. He knows Arabic, at least from the religious texts. I remember my Arabic numbers, learned in Saudi Arabia in the '70s; my desert cred improves a little. But the gangsters are from different backgrounds, so the varying pronunciation makes it difficult for me. The answer is provided by Hassan – he writes the words in the sand, so I can copy them into my notebook, for old-fashioned rote learning.

Wednesday, 20 January

Another rough night. Although the temperature is better, I can't sleep. I suffer something like a panic attack. I feel I am suffocating. I get up and go to the toilet area, then sit quietly for an hour. Eventually an overcast, threatening morning dawns and, sure enough, there are rain showers by lunchtime. There shouldn't be rain at this time of year; the rains come in two distinct seasons here, and surely we are between them?

Soon after the midday delivery of well water and a goat in the white Land Rover, I'm handed a phone by Ali Deri. It's a nice new phone with a big colour screen. Most of the gangsters have similar ones with freshly charged batteries delivered every few days. A man I haven't heard before, speaking good English, introduces himself as Ali, the new translator. He asks for family phone numbers. I give him Sarah's and Jill's and say I don't have Stephen's. It will be good to have a new translator after Omar, one who can speak intelligible English. I have a long chat with Ali. I tell him about our small families, that we sold our house to sail, that our boat has been our only home for the past four years. I tell him I am terribly worried about Rachel and long to see her. He says he will try to make that happen. I feel comforted to know there is someone who will move things along, who genuinely understands English and maybe has experience of the world beyond Somalia.

Buggas and Mr F turn up, like bad pennies. I tell Buggas what I had said to Ali, and ask if I can be with Rachel. 'We wait,' he says. 'Family must speak well to Ali.' They go.

More rain in the evening. Ali Deri shoots a *sagara*, so we have nice meat. I have the biggest portion; they are treating me well. All in all, a good day. My definition of 'good' is of course relative.

That night, soon after midnight, I'm woken by a rustling, close to the edge of the tarp. Deli's arm reaches through, thrusting a phone towards me. I disentangle myself from the net and rub my eyes. Translator Ali tells me to speak to this man – a correspondent, he says, for the *Sunday Times*: 'Tell him the pirates have set a deadline – three or four days – for the family to start negotiation.'

When the connection goes through, it sounds like Stephen. The man tries to make it clear he is not Stephen but Angus Walker. I am tired and confused but talk to him anyway. I must use any contact with an English speaker to try to get the message across that we are being left to die.

Angus: *Paul, this is Angus Walker here, not Stephen.*
Paul: *So, yes, Angus, we were split up just over two weeks ago. Now the food is irregular, the shelter is bad, it's been raining, everything is wet. I'm just hanging on in hope. If there is nothing sensible from that end, I am afraid they will kill us or abandon us in the desert here.*
Angus: *Why do you think that there's only a matter of days before you are killed?*
Paul: *Because they are angry. They were angry when they separated us, and they are having to look after us, keep us captive, and they've run out of patience. I wouldn't say they are simple, but they're not sophisticated. They're not interested in knowing difficulties – they don't have any rational understanding – it's like a gang of nine to ten year olds.*
Angus: *Did they give any reason why you were split up?*
Paul: *Yes, it was because of hiding better from the aeroplanes. I don't know whose clever idea it was to send low-flying planes to look for us. Daft idea. We move within a few hours when one comes looking.*
Angus: *What do they say about negotiations?*
Paul: *The last thing they said to me was that there had been an offer of 20k. They are looking for a substantial amount of money. But they need a proper offer, you know, a quarter of a million dollars, to start things moving at least. But they don't understand we have no company,*

no insurance, that nobody cares for us except our family, and our family have very little money. It's been 91 days, so they've run out of patience with us.

Angus: *Do you have a message for the Foreign Office?*

Paul: *Not the Foreign Office. It's Special Branch that should be involved, because it's straightforward criminal kidnapping. It was accidental; they didn't mean to kidnap – just loot – like they do with the ships. We are going to die because the government will stand back and wait for things to happen and hope that they won't kill us. But the gangsters have lost patience.*

Angus: *How worried are you about Rachel?*

Paul: *I'm terribly worried – about every three days I see a guy who speaks some English, and I ask him every time about Rachel and he says, 'Don't worry.' I guess Rachel is in the same state as me, but she is a woman alone, with a gang of Somali men guarding her and tormenting her. I was allowed to telephone her about 12 days ago. She said she was being taunted, and she said she was giving up. I have no hope of getting out of here, but I would love to see Rachel again . . . why we should be apart, I just don't understand.*

Angus: *What was last thing you said to her?*

Paul: *[Pause] I can't remember.*

I spend the rest of the night thinking, my mind racing. It was OK to open up to Angus; more pressure from the press will be no bad thing, and I have no reason to hide anything. Will the pressure of these calls influence anybody at home? I hope so. I don't take the deadline seriously; they won't kill us. But they may do something awful to Rachel, to put more pressure on me. What if they do send her to Somaliland, or hand her to al-Qaeda? But how would I know? How would they convince me? It doesn't make sense, so I am sure they won't. But what if they injure her and show me photos on their mobile phones?

Sleep won't come. I think back to Angus's question,

about my last words to Rachel. I honestly couldn't remember; events were such a blur. But I know what I would have wanted them to be: words that Diana Gabaldon put in the mouth of her hero, Jamie: 'If my last words to you aren't "I love you", ye'll ken that it's because there wasn't time.' I can't do the Scots accent, but the sentiment is spot on. I spend most of the morning in tears.

By the afternoon, I have regained my composure. A Toyota drives in, filled with the bosses: Buggas, the Commander, Omar and Fat Boy. Oh, for a grenade! They form a huddle a few paces away, then Omar approaches. Omar, whose whining voice I had hoped never to hear again: 'Stephen [always with a very soft f sound rather than a v – the little things starting to annoy me] . . . Stephen is not acting to solve the situation. His latest offer is only 90. I have not told Buggas – it is not worth it. These people will not allow you to speak again to Stephen. What can I do?'

'What can *I* do?' I reply. 'Our family cannot access my money. The law in Britain stops them. I can't do anything.'

He doesn't understand.

'Can I speak to my sister?' No response. They turn away and go to sit in the car, where they talk for a long while. The gangsters are quiet. Eventually, they get out; they don't come near me but sit behind the oil drums with the gang, eating watermelon. Hassan quietly brings me a piece. Has something changed? Their quietness is almost worse than their previous boisterousness. The bosses prepare to go. Omar comes my way again: 'Last night – Ali – who you speak to?'

'Angus – some journalist,' I reply. He turns towards the others, laughing, saying something in Somali. I catch the word 'journalist'. Is there something going on between him and Ali, competition perhaps?

Saturday, 23 January

A few days of peace and reflection. Shy Sharif speaks to

me. 'Ali good,' he says, referring to translator Ali.

'Where Ali?' I ask but 'where' is beyond our common language.

In the evening the gangsters want me to sit with them. They test my knowledge of numbers. I master counting up to 1,000, *cun* in Somali, not a word they use often, such is their distorted view of values. Their first multiplier word is *million*, which is the same in Somali. They never say *cun*. *Shun bocol*, 500, means half a million (dollars). Using Arabic, I have a very limited means of communicating with Sharif. He is a bit of a religious philosopher. We argue, comparing Islam with Christianity. I try to bring out the common ground: we have one god, common values of good and evil. He understands that Jesus was a prophet, that he is mentioned in the *Q'ran*. 'Christians are people of the book, according to the *Q'ran*,' I say. I am sure this is right, but we flounder, especially when discussing prayer. 'Muslim five [times],' he says, 'Christian?'

'It is between you and God,' I explain. 'One time, two times, no problem.' I choose to keep secret my atheism – I don't think they would understand or respect that.

One afternoon, Senick struggles across to the white Land Rover, his foot swollen to the size of a watermelon. He doesn't come to me for medical treatment; they know Rachel is the specialist in that department. As the car drives off, Ali Deri hisses theatrically and draws a wiggly line in the sand. Snake bite.

In the evening, a new face appears. A little more of a leader perhaps, and in the middle of the age range of the gangsters. Another Ali. My blossoming language skills are helpful. Ali Ad – Ad, short for *adan*, meaning white. Well, actually he's a pretty dark coffee colour, but, relative to the skins of most of the others, it's apt. Ali Ad has a few words of English. He dresses smartly, still in the vernacular dress of a wraparound skirt, *ma'awiis*, over long, brightly coloured football shorts, and vest. But whereas the others top it off with a T-shirt, Ali Ad always wears a freshly ironed collared shirt. He is friendly but doesn't join in with the banter. He notices my appearance and is not impressed! He mimes hair cutting. I shrug. '*Baree,*' he says. I look blank. 'Tomorrow.' I scrabble for my notebook and write it down. I've started a page for useful words.

Sure enough, the next morning, I am directed to sit in the plastic chair in a shady spot. A small vanity mirror is thrust into my hand, and the hairdresser approaches. It is Afieri, a man of many talents. '*Magas?*' he enquires. More miming. This must mean scissors. I am expected to provide them. A two-hour delay, while Ali Ad is found and a pair is spirited up from some semi-communal hiding place. Afieri cuts my hair short but not quite the number-one cut that most of the youngsters sport. They leave me with the scissors and mirror, to trim my facial growth to match.

Another recent arrival is Abbas. Like Ali Ad, he is a little older (26), better dressed, and slightly aloof from the youngsters. He is clearly well fed, reserved, but never nasty to me. In fact, he often tries to cheer me up. 'Be happy' is his common greeting – when the boss is away, of course. He has had military training, and he's at ease with, but not excited by, the weapons. One afternoon, the language class drifts into talking about armies and marching. I feel the need to be silly, so I impersonate John Cleese. Of course, I don't have his stature, so the Ministry of Silly Walks loses some of its impact. But Deli gets the idea, and when Abbas demonstrates a perfect goose-step, the bush comes alive with hysterical laughter. It's another moment when reality is set aside and I realise that these men do have feelings – what can I do to make them see that their thug of a leader is a Bad Man?

I'm left alone for almost a week. Buggas visits occasionally, never staying long, and not coming near me. I'm suffering from a sore throat and gargle with aspirin twice a day to ease the pain; just one more irritation.

Tuesday, 26 January

An hour before dawn the tarp strings are pulled free and I have to crawl out from underneath, find my lenses and get dressed. Hurriedly, I collect the valuable bits and pieces of string, washing lines, tarp tie-downs, etc. and make sure I have all the utensils and clothes pegs. My bags are always packed and ready to go.

We pile into the white Land Rover – Land Rover Man driving, no sign of Buggas, six gangsters in the back. After only a 20-minute drive, south-westwards, we jump out and the Land Rover leaves, returning within an hour with the supplies and men. Ali Ad is in charge of erecting the tarp. It's not well orientated, so I pitch in to help, and we end up with the best of a poor job, a compromise between shelter from the midday sun and from the wind.

Why the move? I wonder whether we might be on the way to join Rachel. Who knows? I lie down for an hour to nurse my cold.

I hear a plane, unusually just after sunset, then the white Land Rover comes back, bringing Buggas, who holds a small pow-wow under a tree ten feet from my shelter. I have spent most of the day arranging my area, putting up the washing line, clearing the ground, finding a spot for the chair where a blanket can be fixed to the thorns above for shade. Now I feel unwell and go to bed early, snuffling and with a headache as well as the sore throat. Buggas's pow-wow makes me uneasy. I get up, walk around my shelter for half an hour. Suddenly there is silence.

'What?' says Buggas. 'What you do? Sleep!'

Not for long. Two a.m.: 'Up! Up!' All the packing up palaver again. Into the white Land Rover and off we go. Another 20-minute drive; this time we pass through the village and stop on the outskirts, the car door three feet from an open gate in a fence. I am ushered into a compound, across a small yard and into a single-roomed 'house'. My mat, mattress and bags are handed in.

'Sleep.'

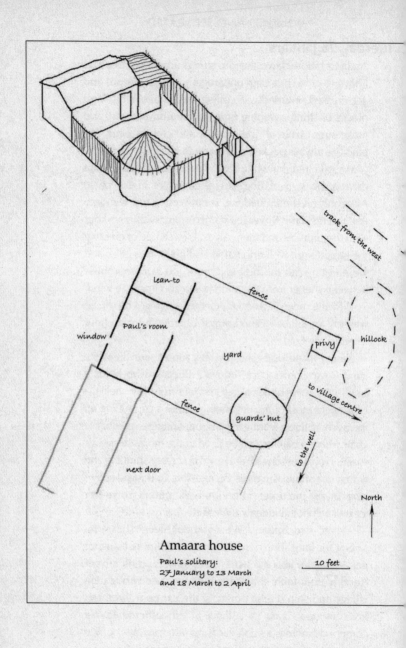

track from the west

lean-to

fence

window

Paul's room

yard

privy

hillock

fence

to village centre

guards' hut

to the well

next door

North

Amaara house

Paul's solitary:
27 January to 13 March
and 18 March to 2 April

10 feet

Wednesday, 27 January

I take stock in the daylight. My new prison is a room, 16 foot by 12, with a single door to the yard and a small square window, sealed shut with wire, in the opposite wall. The floor is smooth compacted sand; the walls are wattle and daub, with a smooth-ish internal finish; the door and window have sawn timber frames with steel sheet from flattened oil drums carelessly nailed on. The pitched roof is of crinkly tin, with no ventilation at the ridge or eaves. The yard is bounded by a seven-foot-high fence, stoutly made of substantial branches buried into the ground, with horizontals and smaller infill dense enough to completely block vision. In one corner, opposite my doorway, is a privy, a five-foot-square enclosure with no roof. It has walls of oil-drum sheets nailed to sawn timber framing and a similar door. There's a 'hole in the floor' formed in cement render. Next to the privy, I spy the only exit from the yard: another 'oil-drum door', serving as a gate. Built into the compound fence is an African hut, which the guards use as their daytime base. The front wall of my house extends almost to the fence, forming a small area covered with a lean-to roof of branches. This is taken over for the cook's stores.

Several gangsters are lying on the ground, in the yard, cocooned in their blankets. I ask for washing water – for the toilet. One of the men takes a five-litre can outside the compound and returns with it full. There is evidently a well nearby. There's still some shade, under the front yard fence and the African hut, so I start walking. 'No! Go house,' calls Sharif, gesticulating with his AK. 'Exercise,' I say. This usually allays their fears that I might be making a run for it. 'NO! House.' That's clear then. It will be too hot in the direct sun to be outside after 9 a.m.

I turn to settling in the house. The men seem happy not to come in – it's quite private compared with what I have been used to. The sun streams in, and it's getting hot already. I'll need ventilation, but last night, when we arrived, Sharif had checked the window to make sure it was securely wired shut and said, 'No,' pointing at it. It looks as if opening it won't be allowed.

Before I can worry any more, Buggas comes in clutching a sheet that he throws over my head. 'We go,' he says as he leads me out. The yard gate is held open and I am ushered into the front seat of a Toyota. We rush off – only about 200 yards, out of the village and up a gently inclining sand dune. Buggas and two gangsters are in the back. I haven't seen the driver before. He is sophisticated – dark glasses, gold watch, courteous air, and wears a flat cap. He offers his hand. 'I am Ali.' We brief each other – it's almost civilised! He says we need to resolve the situation: 'Speak to your family. Find out why there is no progress. What do they have in mind for you? Tell them that I am the only approved contact with the pirates. They must stop the aeroplane flights.'

He picks up his phone, dials Jill, then Stephen, but reaches an answerphone both times. I suggest it's too early – not yet six – in England.

'We try later,' he says, as he drives me back to prison. Two hours later, off we go in Ali's Toyota, just up the slope again. Two calls to Stephen, Ali prompting me to get things moving:

Paul: *Good morning to you.*
Stephen: *I've got a very poor line, Paul. I can hardly hear you.*
Paul: *OK, I'll shout. Is that better?*
Stephen: *Yes . . . it is.*
Paul: *I'm with Ali, the new translator. His English is much better than Omar's. You'll be able to understand him. I must tell you there is no one else to contact. I'm sitting here with Ali and the gang leader himself.*

Stephen: *Right.*

Paul: *There is no other contact, so if anybody else speaks to you saying they can help – they can't – there is no other connection. OK?*

Stephen: *Right, fine. Can you pass me to Ali?*

Paul: *I will in a moment. He wants me to tell you two other things first.*

Stephen: *Yes.*

Paul: *They would like you to tell the government that these aeroplanes flights are very dangerous for us.*

Stephen: *I have spoken to the Foreign Office about this, Paul, and the Foreign Office deny it's anything to do with them. They say they're American drones.*

Ali: *All right.*

Paul: *You know – something nasty might happen.*

Stephen: *Paul, can I just tell you that Rachel is fine?*

Paul: *Good. Have you spoken to her?*

Stephen: *I haven't spoken directly, but I heard her tape, but don't pass it on, please . . .*

Paul: *I'm worried about Rachel.*

Stephen: *Yes, of course you are.*

Paul: *I last spoke to her about 18 days ago on the telephone, and she said she was alone and being tormented, so she was giving up, and I haven't heard from her since.*

Stephen: *She's eating, she's fine, and she's being well looked after.*

Paul: *OK. And the other thing is, what can you do to help us? I know it's difficult. You can't get our money.*

Stephen: *We've been negotiating, I promise, Paul.*

Paul: *Yes, with Ali?*

Stephen: *We're negotiating with the man who we've always been negotiating with – Omar.*

Paul: *Yes, well, Omar is not involved any more. It's Ali now. Ali asks if Omar has contacted you in the last few days?*

Stephen: *Yes, he . . .*

Paul: *What time? Ali wants to know.*

Stephen: *He spoke to me last at 1.40 our time yesterday afternoon, which is twenty to five your time.*

Paul: *. . . And before yesterday?*

Stephen: *We've been speaking to him, um, we spoke to him about four days ago.*

Paul: *I mean, the thing is, if the government won't help, I don't know whether the press can help us at all.*

Stephen: *If you're thinking financially, Paul, there is nothing there. We've spoken – no sensible money anywhere.*

Paul: *So what is the future for us?*

Stephen: *Paul, I can't negotiate with you. We can only negotiate with one person. I'm sorry. I know that sounds awfully hard.*

Paul: *That's true enough. Can I pass you to Ali?*

Stephen: *Yes, please.*

Ali: *Hello, you are speaking.*

I only hear Ali's side of the rest of the conversation:

Ali: *Yes, I have another number.*

Ali: *Omar was dismissed because they could never understand, and that's why you should not contact him. If he contacts you, he has nothing in hand. He is dismissed.*

Ali: *I am with Paul and other pirates.*

Ali: *Which way the negotiation is going on at home and help us overcome the problem. What can we tell these young people around him? So I need only to ask you what is the situation? Have you any progress so that we can solve the problem? Have you any money that we can tell these young people?*

Ali: *90,000?*

Ali: *No more money?*

Ali: *Yeah, they are talking about millions. What do you mean 90,000?*

Ali: *What about the government?*

Ali: *Paul has told me that he has himself 300 and the*

family will have another 200, so 500. What about that?
Ali: *You mean nobody can take his money?*
Ali: *OK, OK. We understand each other, you and I. It's just your offer, 90,000 dollar. It's very, very small for these people. If you're talking about two million, three million and above . . . 90,000 are very different offer, so what else can we do? OK, we're going to discuss.*

We sit in the car for 20 minutes. Ali and Buggas talk. Mostly Ali. They don't mention money. Ali calls Stephen again.

Paul: *Right, OK, we must try to sort this out, Stephen. There's a war going on out here. It's not a nice situation to be in for very long, and I've said to you I'm quite happy for all my wealth to be used. I know that there is a difficulty, but can we resolve that in some way because is there a power of attorney that can be used?*
Stephen: *No, there isn't, Paul. We've tried it.*
Paul: *Yes, we can communicate here, you know. I can do fax, email, whatever. I don't understand why not?*
Stephen: *It's because, Paul, you are under duress.*
Paul: *Yes, I appreciate that, Stephen, but what's the money going to do? Buy me a super memorial?*
Stephen: *Paul, they don't kill people. They don't hurt their hostages.*
Paul: *There must be some way forward.*
Stephen: *Well, yes, we have to negotiate it and there are ways of doing it which they are fully aware of . . .*
Paul: *I am not so sure about that. They're not sophisticated . . . and they don't understand.*
Stephen: *Well, Paul, it's quite simple. There are running costs. They're going to get to a point when they realise it's not worth carrying on and they know that they could be doing this same work on a big ship and making lots of money . . .*
Paul: *I know . . . but there's a matter of face. There has*

to be a reasonable amount of money. This is what's so stupid; they know I have this money because they have my computers.

Stephen: *Paul, you are not helping. Sorry, but you're not helping. I don't want to sound hard, but it's not helping you joining in the negotiations.*

Paul: *But I'm put in this position. It's down to me to make something happen. That's why they give me the phone. I don't know what I can do, Stephen. What can I do?*

Stephen: *Tell them they have got to bring their demand down. We can't talk millions. Paul, you know we can't raise millions.*

Paul: *I know, I know. I just heard them. You've tried all ways to get at my money and it can't be done?*

Stephen: *It can't be done. I promise you. Sarah has been working on it, and it can't be done. The solicitors have said no. I mean, Paul, Paul, please understand they know you're a valuable commodity. It's no good them killing you or hurting you, because we won't pay out if you're dead.*

Paul: *I know that, but, Stephen, they have a completely different concept of money. They are not poor – they talk in millions of dollars.*

Stephen: *Yes, Paul, but they're used to talking to ship owners who are covered by insurance. We're not wealthy like that.*

Paul: *I know that, Stephen, and you can rationalise with me, but that's not understood here. It's not accepted. I'm at my wits' end. I don't know what to do. I can't do anything.*

Stephen: *I promise you, we're working on everywhere we can, but until they bring their demand down we can't work with them.*

Paul: *Let me just put that to Ali.*

Ali tells me they may take an offer of 500.

Paul: *Stephen? Ali has said they are now talking about* two million, but he says if there were an offer of half a million they may take it.

Stephen: *Are they talking half a million?*

Paul: *Well, this is what Ali just said, yes.*

Stephen: *So they're talking half a million dollars?*

Again I stress to Ali the difference between a commercial ship and a retired cruising couple.

Paul: *We were just exchanging the information. Yes, they get millions from the ship because of course a ship is worth millions, but I honestly think that a hundred thousand dollars is small change to them. This is the problem – they are so wealthy here you wouldn't believe it.*

Stephen: *In that case why are they worrying about two elderly people like you?*

Paul: *By accident, that's it. They didn't know they were going to find two elderly paupers, and then they realised we were British and they had a long – well, you've seen my satellite phone bill – I expect they had a massive, lengthy discussion. Oh, we've got two rich old people, they'll be worth a lot of money, and of course it's not like that at all. But Ali says if we get to half a million then perhaps they would accept it and we can hit this on the head.*

Stephen: *Well, look. I will talk to the rest of the family.*

Paul: *You don't want me to be involved in the negotiations, but I'm just put in the firing line, as it were.*

Stephen: *Yes, I appreciate that, Paul, and I will call Ali tomorrow at one o'clock Somali time, is that OK?*

Paul: *I will tell Ali you will talk to everybody and you will call him on that number tomorrow at one o'clock.*

Stephen: *Thank you very much. Keep your chin up, Paul. We're all thinking of you, I promise you.*

Paul: *I'll try. The pressure's on here. I've gone through the tearful stage. It's just quiet desperation.*

Stephen: *We understand. Well, I know we can't fully understand what you're going through, but we're*

hoping . . . we're sure we'll see you soon.
Paul: *OK, thank you, Stephen.*
Stephen: *Thank you, Paul. Stay strong.*

They drop me off, and go away. Ali Ad and Sharif escort me to my room.

'News?' asks Ali. 'Money?'

'No news. No money. Leave me alone.' I feel drained and anxious that there is still little understanding of these thugs' mentality. But at least there seems to be a start to negotiation. And surely with Ali involved there will be less misunderstanding? Ali seemed to understand what I told him, and to believe me. I hope he can convince the big brute, Buggas.

I settle in and enjoy the relative quiet. Only when they sit right outside the door is their *jabber, jabber, jabber* intrusive. They do that in the late afternoon, when the house casts a patch of shade, but they are usually quiet by nine o'clock.

It seems to be the same sub-gang guarding me. The four on watch spend most of the time outside the compound, on a small hill where there is shade from a tree. The others are either asleep or they dress up and walk into the village, to meet wives and girlfriends, boast to their mates, or even go home to Mum for laundry. Apart from breakfast and late-afternoon supper, when there is some gathering, I am left mostly in peace. Sometimes after dark, I can't believe it – there is no one else in the compound for an hour or so.

But it's awfully hot and humid. The tin roof and lack of ventilation set up a micro-climate in the house. The humidity rises steadily through the day and evening. I have to stay inside from about nine o'clock onwards; there is no other respite from the sun. I partly close the door, to reduce the heat build-up, but the claustrophobic effect negates that. It's far too sticky to lie down. So I spend time sitting, reading, listening to the radio, with the chair just inside the doorway, where there is an occasional zephyr of breeze. I tear off a side of the water-bottle box for a fan; it doubles as a swat – see how many bastard Somali *doxi* I can kill each day (unfortunately only flies!). I have a restless night. Just can't calm down.

I get up at about 10 p.m., pull pants on, go out into the yard and wander around, trying to clear my head. There are bodies everywhere, cocooned in their blankets. I don't have a lens in, so I stumble. A hand gently takes my arm. It's Hassan. He guides me to the privy. I don't want to go there, but he means well. After a suitable time, I emerge. He is waiting and guides me gently back to the house.

Thursday, 28 January

Off we go again. Is it to be a repeat of yesterday? No. We drive off the other way, through the village, for the first time in daylight. I see rows of houses, a few shops, men sitting outside in the shade of big trees, carefree women and children about, but we rush through and stop on the far side, near a large building, perhaps a school? This time I am in the back, a gangster each side, with AK-47s pointing out of the windows. Buggas is in the front with Ali. A white Toyota roars up, passes us and heads out to a big sandy area to the east of the village. We follow, past the mobile-phone mast, on for a few miles, stopping in a cloud of sand.

'Sit.'

The men get out and look around suspiciously. The door is opened, and I'm guided to the front of the car. Three men are waiting, one with a case – a doctor who says he needs to examine me. The others have cameras. They ask if I mind them taking pictures. I shrug. I ask the doctor who has sent him. He whispers, 'I can't talk now, I have come from Mogadishu.' I sit on the ground, and he conducts an examination: stethoscope, blood pressure, etc. I tell him I have a persistent cough. He says he will exaggerate my condition to put pressure on for release. 'I am working for your release. I will try to get you reunited.'

One of the photographers asks if I have a message for the government. The words tumble out. I don't even think about what I am saying. I am confused. Is this an opportunity, a genuine medical check, or a show? I don't know. On the way back in the car, we stop at the mobile-phone mast. Ali goes into the building at the base – to renew his credit. Then it's back to prison.

I'm left alone for the next few days. I have a quiet celebration – 100 days in captivity; 25 days in solitary. How will it ever end? Our wedding anniversary is two weeks away. Can I persuade Buggas to reunite us for that? Or at least have a phone call? I must start asking him whenever I see him. Maybe I can explain to the gangsters. It will be our 29th.

The humidity is hard to bear. After dusk, while the yard is empty, I sneak over to the window, carefully remove the wires and ease it open a little so it won't be noticed in a casual peer through the doorway. I am shaking with fear of being caught. I jam it with a twig, so the wind won't blow it open. Gosh, that makes a difference. Now I try lying down at about 9 p.m., and although the humidity is still high, it is much better than before. I wake two or three times in the night to pull on more clothes as it gets cold, and I must remember to close the window otherwise Ali will see it when he brings hot water at dawn.

My gout flares up again. It's too painful to do yoga, and I can only just hobble to the privy. I have only one of these orange pills left, so when Buggas comes in the afternoon I ask for some. I offer him the empty blister packaging. He peers at it – 'Diclofen, OK' – and throws it on the ground.

Within an hour, he comes back with two packs of

ten. I'm amazed, and grateful, despite my hatred of him. Now I know they are available I will try two at bedtime, one at breakfast and one with lunch. The next afternoon he comes again, on foot this time, and asks how I am. 'Better,' I say. 'After tomorrow OK, *insha'allah*.'

He nods. 'Stephen speak Ali after. Pictures you TV – AFP [Agence France Press].'

He is in good humour, so I dare to ask about Rachel, and he says she's OK. I ask when we can be together. 'Ask Ali' is his enigmatic response. As I am getting ready for bed, Ali Ad brings a phone to me. Ali the translator speaks: 'Man on telephone is Steven, not Rachel's brother, another, but don't worry, you will speak with Rachel.'

I don't care who it is. It's such a relief to hear Rachel again. We manage to exchange 'love you's' and 'miss you's' for ten minutes! Rachel is also in a house now. She sounds distraught, but it's wonderful to be in contact. After she's cut off, the other Steven speaks to me. He tells me that Ali is a good man, that they have dealt with him before and they will press him to get us reunited. He says things are moving, not to worry. I ask if he can get me any contact lens solution, and he says he will try. Afterwards, when the euphoria of hearing from Rachel has subsided, I wonder who this Steven is? Who is the 'they' he refers to? Are 'they' helping Stephen, our Stephen? Who knows?

Another week passes and tedium tries once more to set in. One day, an old man turns up. He is welcomed by the gangsters, but he's not part of the gang. He has no gun. His hair is dyed orange; I take that to mean he is a *Haji* – he has made the pilgrimage to Mecca. I learn his name is Boor. He is seventy-two, has four wives and fifty-three children! He extracts a shirt from the wooden box in my room – perhaps this is his house. He comes and goes, always leaving with something stuffed under his *ma'awiis* in a plastic bag, some rice, sugar, or even meat and bread. Ali Yeri warns me to keep an eye on everything – 'Boor *tuk wain* [big thief],' he says, with no irony at all.

One evening, we play 'this man Muslim'. Ali and Deli come up with a variation on the 'this man – name?' game. I'm not sure if they want entertainment at my expense or to cheer me up. Ali and I have 'discussed' the seriousness of religious observance in Somalia and in Britain. He surprised me, saying the attitudes in the gang are typical: most Somalis are relaxed about it. Only a few are regular prayers, like Sharif. 'Somalis half Muslim,' he said. Now he points at Deli, 'This man Muslim?' I haven't seen Deli praying, so I shake my head doubtfully: 'Quarter Muslim'. Ivarr and Senick come and join in. Duly prompted, and to much hilarity, I respond, 'Ivarr full Christian, Ali half Muslim, Sharif full Muslim.' It's harmless enough, I hope! Buggas isn't around, but inevitably Ali asks, 'Buggas Muslim?'

'*Maia, maia, maia* [No, no, no],' I reply. 'Buggas *maia* Muslim.' I mime having a hand cut off, 'Buggas *tuk wain*, but no hand cut off, so no Muslim.' They all laugh.

Now the gangsters are calm, and mostly uninterested, I wonder if I dare take a photo. After lunch all is quiet, so when Ali Yeri goes out I carefully unwire the window. I get out the camera and put in the memory card, which I keep in my trouser pocket. Check again that all is quiet. Ease open the window, fully now. Poke the camera out. One, two, three shots. Close the window. Camera under pillow. Calm down. Breathing back to normal. There's still no life in the yard. I hide away the memory card, put the camera in my bag and tie up the window. Guiltily, I resume normal life. It would not be good to get caught!

The humidity is getting worse. It's too hot and sticky even for yoga, which, now my gout is receding, I try to do last thing before bed. But I cannot concentrate. In the bush, I would enjoy finishing with the 'corpse' pose

– ten minutes, or even half an hour, when I could reduce everything to simple breathing. Now I can't even work through all the parts of my body without being distracted by racing thoughts or having to swat a fly.

Buggas is still in a good mood. He visits most days, often not speaking to me, but one afternoon he asks if I have eaten lunch and was it OK. 'They give you vegetable?'

'*Maia, hilip y briis* [No, meat and rice],' I say.

He harangues Ali Yeri, shouting at him, then turns back to me, 'You ask what you want.'

The area is getting busier. There is always activity just after dawn and at dusk: a passing donkey and cart, with a squeaky wheel; goats being herded to and from a milking pen, and children coming and going from the house next door. Every few days, an ancient lorry passes. This morning, one got stuck in the sand outside our compound. You'd think there were enough bodies on board (the lorries double up as buses, even when fully loaded) to lift and push it out of the sand. But no, instead they make a palaver. I stand on my chair, peering over the fence. No one objects. There is digging, much revving, grinding of gears, clouds of thick black exhaust and a very polluted atmosphere for two hours while the driver and his wife extricate it and move it back to the firmer surface, watched by the 30 or so passengers who have retired to a shady spot under a tree.

But there are other, more worrying noises. The occasional gunshot doesn't disturb me now, but increasingly I've heard sounds of fighting, coming closer in the late afternoons. I stand on my chair again, but see nothing – it can't be that close. This evening several convoys pass by at speed, each comprising two 'technicals' and a Toyota Land Cruiser. Nobody worries, so neither will I. But the next day, in the evening, a machine gun is set up just outside my doorway, pointed at the yard gate, so they can pick off the enemy as they come through in single file! This becomes the 'normal' night-time set-up. Until now they haven't worried about being attacked in the village.

I told Buggas that I was having difficulty sleeping, and he triumphantly produced a bottle of Promethazine Elixir. On the label it says, 'Antihistamine with sedative and hypnotic effects'. Wow. Do I have enough to sedate the whole gang? I could pour it into their tea kettle. The dosage is given only for children. I try the minimum dose and sleep like a log but wake up feeling awful. My nasal passages are clear OK, but my mouth and throat are so dry it hurts. My head is spinning, and I think I'm going to be sick. I won't try the elixir again.

There's a campaign to feed me up. Ali Yeri gives me larger and larger portions – not only liver and chapati for breakfast but meat with rice at mid-morning, spaghetti and sauce at lunch, and *digir* in the evening. Finally, my stomach rebels. I'm stuffed, constipated and can't eat another morsel. I ask Ali Yeri politely for no more food today. Panic! Calls to Buggas. Both translator Ali and Buggas phone me to ask what is wrong. 'No problem,' I explain. I will be OK 'after tomorrow'. That's a good phrase – turned back on them – and it seems to satisfy them. Ali says he has my contact lens solution – he will bring it tomorrow. I tell him our anniversary is next Sunday. He says he will visit Rachel and will arrange a call.

We all relax again; the machine gun stays hidden. They even let me traipse up and down across the yard just before sunset, when it's cool outside but light enough for me to see where to step to avoid the obstacles.

There's a new young lad in the gang. Sugal is 22 but looks younger. He's mates with Ali Yeri, and the two of them have made room for my chair in the cook's lean-to, so I can sit there during the day. The shade is adequate and the ventilation good, so it's more tolerable than my room. Around extended mealtimes this area is full of gangsters and food, often two of them asleep there. They will always make room for me, but it's uncomfortably crowded. Sugal clears it out, mostly by chain smoking! Then we sit and do more language lessons. He asks how long I am here. First I must supplement my knowledge of numbers with the words for days and months. I already know *sano*, years. The Arabic *kam* seems to work for 'how many' – I can't get the Somali phrase. And the universal crossed-arms gesture indicates prison. They say prism – I think this is a corruption.

We start again – '*Kam malmod prism*?' (How many days in prison?)

'*Bocol yr toban yr lobo malmod*,' I say faultlessly, and try: '*Sadden yr shun malmod maia nagti*.' (One hundred and twelve days, thirty-five days no woman.)'

'No problem,' says Sugal, '*Aniga lobo bocol yr contun malmod*.'

He was in prison in Djibouti for 250 days. I don't understand what for.

Back to routine: Ali goes shopping; Sugal puts the last charcoal embers into an ancient iron and starts pressing his shirt on the sand. I tune in to *Newshour* on the World Service and continue compiling my critique of the BBC. The radio is a godsend for me, but I don't hold the BBC in the same high esteem as the Somalis do. I rate Radio France International and even the Voice of America a lot higher quality.

Tuesday, 9 February

Buggas appears at dawn. After an hour, he hands me his phone. Ali says I must speak to this man, from the Somalis in England:

Man: Paul, this is Ahmad from Universal Somali TV. The majority of the Somali people in Europe and the UK especially are really concerned about your situation and we are doing our best to get you released. Are you OK at the moment?

Paul: Thank you. Well, I'm physically not too bad. I've lost a lot of weight, and I'm having difficulty with the heat in the house I've been living in the last few days – mentally I'm very low – and I'm very worried about my wife.

Ahmad: I spoke to Rachel five minutes ago. She's OK. She said you've been separated more than five weeks now. Is that right?

Paul: Yes. It's awful. We've never been apart this long. We will have been married 29 years [voice breaks] next Sunday.

Ahmad: The Somalis in the UK are very concerned, and we're doing our very best to get you released. We've been talking to everyone. Don't worry. Things are OK.

Paul: Thank you. I mean, is anything happening?

We are cut off. I know not to expect any attempt at re-connection. A lost connection seems to be accepted as a natural end to a conversation. Good to hear that Rachel is OK. I believe that. I don't know how Ahmad fits in, but I don't see why he would lie about Rachel. We'll chalk today up as a good day – it's overcast and so it's been tolerable to stay in the house, the first such day for ages. And there's a special treat, five small green tomatoes, handed over the fence to Ali by the woman in the house next door. I put them carefully in the sun to ripen.

I am alternating periods of fairly good health with bouts of sickness, unsure if it's genuine or psychosomatic. When I'm down, I suffer a general malaise, sometimes the runs, feverish spells, loss of appetite, and hyper brain activity. Yoga 'corpsing' is impossible. It lasts a day or so. The mental trauma continues, but I've come to terms with it. I know I can survive, and Rachel will too. I trust Ali to move things on with Stephen. We'll be together soon. I must keep asking for an anniversary call. Ali Ad delivers a packet of multivitamin pills. Good, I've been getting worried about the lack of greens and fruit. Is it six months before one gets scurvy?

Something seems to happen every few days to kindle the flame of hope. Today it's *Newshour* on the World Service – a five-minute slot about us, including an interview with a lady from the UK Somali Solidarity Group for Paul and Rachel Chandler. Owen Bennett-Jones, the presenter, was a little patronising, but it's good to know that someone cares, other than our family and friends of course. Perhaps Somali 'peer pressure' will help.

Sunday, 14 February

It's Valentine's Day, our 29th wedding anniversary – day 115 in captivity.

I have a bad stomach and the runs again. Lie in until 10.30 – it must be overcast, the heat less intense – and put myself on a water-only diet for 24 hours. Buggas comes in the afternoon. 'Stop going on about me not eating!' I rant. 'I must speak to Rachel. Today special day.' I might even have sworn at him. He was certainly taken aback. 'We'll see,' he says, and after a few moments passes his phone to me. Only a two-minute call, but it cheers me up no end. Rachel sounds as well as could be expected. No food and early to bed.

Monday, 15 February

I shrug off the sickness, and Ali starts to build me up with plenty of meat. I'm worried about a chipped tooth. I don't want to risk any dental problems here! So I borrow the cook's knife to cut up the meat chunks into manageable sizes. It would make a good weapon, but they all realise that I'm not going to attack with it. I wonder if they have thought that I might take my own life. I've never considered that. Perhaps I'm afraid that I'd make a mess of it, but really I just couldn't inflict the pain on Rachel or my family. Does that make me a coward or the opposite?

Another quiet spell. Ali Yeri says he is going away for ten days. He hasn't had a break for a long time. Afieri is back and he will cook. That's fine – Afieri is a good cook. Buggas and the Commander visit and ask how I am. They say I must eat. Afieri cooks the *digir*, but it's very late, not ready until 8.30. The next day there's no breakfast. The fire is lit, the charcoal burning bright in the *pochuko* (asbestos barbecue), but where is Afieri? Gone. The gangsters are angry – they want breakfast too. Sugal takes over. Misshapen chapatis are served after an hour, overcooked rice later. No liver or meat arrives. Buggas turns up.

'Where Afieri?' Many shrugs. He storms out. Half an hour later, Ali Yeri appears. Normal service is resumed.

'Afieri problem,' says Ali, pointing at his head.

Ali Deri comes back from a trip. There's a lot of phoning. He and Ali Yeri say I go to London in 30 days. Sharif comes over: '*Ali tadobo malmod* [Ali (will come in) seven days]. You London *lobaten malmod* [20 days].' Is something happening? Will Ali really come in seven days? Or are they winding me up?

Buggas now comes only two or three times a week, usually on foot. He ignores me, sits with the gangsters in front of the house, chewing *chad* and telling stories in the evening, then leaves. I am happy not to speak to him. I will wait until two weeks after I last spoke with Rachel, then challenge him to let us speak again.

Sugal solves a mystery. I have occasionally heard gangsters shouting 'Alero' as if calling someone, but I can't work out who. 'Ali,' says Sugal, pointing at Ali Yeri. I am puzzled, then it dawns on me – the vocative in Somali adds an 'o' to men's names: Buggaso, Sharifo and so on. Sugal repeats slowly, 'Al-er-o . . . Ali-Yeri-o.' I think of happier days: sailing in company with Jean-Louis and Denise, who became great friends. Will we ever see their Canadian yacht, *Alero*, again?

The next day I have a haircut. This time, Sugal is the master hairdresser. He makes a better job of it than Afieri. I ask how he learned. We converse by gesture, mime and our few words. He says he trained as a barber before he went to fight. I hear more shooting in the afternoon; the machine gun is set up again for the night outside my door.

Ouch – is that a mozzie bite on my arm? I haven't seen any, but with this high humidity and rain, perhaps there are mosquitoes. I start taking Malarone tablets, hoping it's not too late. Also I will avoid using the privy other than in the middle of the day. If there's no cloud it's terribly hot then, but better sunburn than getting malaria.

Excitement in the afternoon, much shouting from outside, women and children screaming. Ali Yeri and a couple of the others rush out, leaving the gate banging open and shut. When they come back, Ali is covered in sand and scratches. A baby had fallen down the well. Ali climbed down and brought him out. The wells are only two feet in diameter and more than twenty feet deep. He'll be the village hero. The gangsters celebrate noisily through the night.

Monday, 1 March

I am sitting in the lean-to. Sugal is smoking, Ali peeling the potatoes for lunch. Ali's phone rings and they both go out. When they come back into the lean-to, it is with a woman. She is introduced. I can't remember her name, but I stand and offer my hand, which she shakes. Ali gestures and she sits on the mat, giggling. She lowers her headscarf. She is young, perhaps 20, very attractive with long black hair. We are both dumbstruck by the situation. Sugal and Ali banter with her. Ali gestures to me – to take her into my house.

'Make babies,' he says, with a big grin.

I don't know how much she understands, or what they have been saying to her. They try again, to coax me into action, but I stay resolutely stuck to my chair. She puts on her scarf, gets up and moves gracefully out. Rejected? Sugal and Ali escort her away. Later, Ali comes back and teases me. Was it a wind-up? Or, heaven forbid, a genuine offering? Some of my recent language sessions with Ali have covered parts of the body, so he knows how to say what he was expecting me to do. I wonder how far I could have gone? It was tempting to play the game. But I haven't completely lost my marbles.

The days go slowly by. Often there is some event, something to distinguish today from yesterday. It may be like yesterday's temptation, or a gunfight nearby, or the occasional contact with the outside world, or best of all with Rachel. But underneath I rely on routine to pass the time. I discover the benefits of reading aloud. I'm now on my third reading of *The Fiery Cross*. I sense that it's important to hear an English voice, even if it is my own. Every little task must have its allotted time, a suitable pace of execution, one thing at a time. And the hard-won 'luxuries' must be carefully protected. So, a typical day in the 'house' prison, on the western outskirts of the large village I have come to know as Amaara, in the semi-arid bush that forms this central part of Somalia, might go like this:

- 0700: Get up when it gets too hot and sticky to lie in bed.
- Hair wash in bowl (alternate days). Save water for washing up.
- Put in one contact lens (rationing solution).

Rachel's first sailing
experience, aged 26, with
Paul's father.

Paul's first recorded sailing
experience, almost two
years old, with family.

Paul, Adrian (back), Gavin (front), Sarah and Rachel on *Lynn Rival* in
Menidhion, Greece.

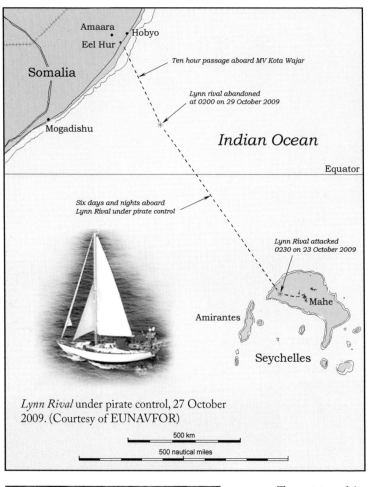

Lynn Rival under pirate control, 27 October 2009. (Courtesy of EUNAVFOR)

The position of the attack, and the following six days' events.

The two skiffs used to attack *Lynn Rival*, later detained after attacking a French trawler. (Courtesy of EUNAVFOR)

Inside the African hut, early November 2009.

Our close guard sleeping off a *chad* session.

Our patio in the wadi, Christmas 2009.

Tomorrow's breakfast and machine-gun station.

Paul's house in Amaara.

Yard and guards' hut.

'Four-day house' yard and privy.

CRYPTIC CROSSWORD Nº 1 (Nautical theme)

M	A	S	T	E	R	M	A	R	I	N	E	R	
C	B	R	A	B	C	L	A
O	R	A	T	I	O	N	O	V	E	R	E	A	T
M	L	S	G	O	A	F	M	A
P	R	O	P	A	N	E	R	O	L	L	E	R	S
A	N	I	O	D	O	N	T
N	E	E	B	L	E	P	B	E	R	T	H	A
I	I	A	S	T	E	R	R	R	A	N
O	C	T	A	N	T	I	B	R	O	A	D
N	H	O	A	C	T	A	V	S
W	A	R	S	H	I	P	R	A	I	M	E	N	T
A	O	O	O	U	U	T	R	I
Y	A	W	N	I	N	G	B	R	I	S	T	O	L
S	U	S	E	E	N	L	L
S	P	O	T	T	E	R	S	G	O	Y	A

ACROSS

1. Expert at sea, confused Marr in steamer. (6,7)
8. Nelson, headless with a point, gives speech. (7)
11. Scoff too much, six balls each time. (7)
12. Sounds like a good plan in port (3)
13. Rather rude, soft replacing strong fuel. (7)
14. Walker loses time, start to finish, for waves. (7)
15. The god of pilots? (3)
17. Sewer off the I.o.W. (6)
20. First sleeping place for girl (6)
22. Reverse, pointless bloomer. (5)

DOWN

2. Single sailor, swimmer. (7)
3. Storm canvas, strongly disturb...
4. Patrolman in state of bitter anger makes arrest. (6)
5. One tack on the ship. (6)
6. Danger in high latitudes – strange eco-life! (3,4)
7. Part the French compiler in hospital department. (7)
8. Familiar's methods : steps? (7)
9. Info. losing 500 is upright steering lever without hesitation, possibly aground (2,1,10)
16. Lens initially cooked in the preheated oven upside-down (5)

Rachel's birthday crossword No. 1.

Mohamed Aden, Rachel, Paul, Dahir and Dr Hangul.

Adaado International Airport terminal.

Rachel, Dom and
Paul in the air on
the way to Nairobi.

Our welcome at
the British High
Commission,
Nairobi.

Three of our
attackers detained
in Kenya.
(© Associated Press)

Lynn Rival is
hoisted aboard
RFA *Wave Knight*,
29 October 2009.

Reunion with
Lynn Rival,
27 November 2010.

- Hang up sheet and towel to air on internal line. Put blanket in plastic bag for protection from sand and flies.
- Make tea in flask, which Ali has left by door before I get up. Use *alen*, the Somali substitute for tea. It's fibrous and turns the water brown, but I'm sure it's not related to the tea plant. Add a little *sooker*.
- Find chair outside (the guards will have used it overnight), sit in shade of African hut.
- Ali brings chapati – put half aside for teatime snack.
- '*Baholi. Ken baholi,*' Ali demands the bowl for liver. '*Ho,*' I give it to him.
- Enjoy *courrah* (breakfast), sitting outside in the shade, while the gangsters have their meat.
- Laundry (alternate days).
- Move 'day box' and bowl to lean-to. Day box contains soap and shampoo, which I dare not leave unattended, cups, *alen*, *sooker*, reserve bottle of well water, milk powder, toothpaste, brush, fork and spoon. Also a bag of books, pads and radio, bottled drinking water and a can of well water, which would soon be empty if left unattended. (Although the well is only a few minutes' walk away, the gangsters are lazy and would rather use mine than refill their own cans. The cook is told to keep mine filled, but he also has to fetch water for cooking, so it's not surprising he is sometimes reluctant to make a special trip for me in the heat of the day. We reach an accord – he will get the refills, and I will guard his cans as well as mine!)
- Set up washing line in lean-to, for flannel, rags, sweat bands, all made from torn-up shirts. (Sweat bands, changed every hour, to try to keep sweat out of my eyes, particularly the one I have treated to a contact lens today.)
- Visit privy to empty night bottle (now I don't go there after dusk because of the mosquitoes) and to wash

up breakfast bowl and fork. Loo number twos if possible, as it's still not too hot in there!

- Write diary notes.
- 0900–1200: Alternate spells of reading aloud and listening to radio, in chair, in the lean-to. Have tea and/or water and a walk about in the house every half-hour.
- 1100: Ali prepares vegetables in the lean-to. Language lessons continue. Sugal may come in for a smoke and chat.
- 1145: Morning 'exercise' in the lean-to. Actual time varies to suit weather and food. This is yoga stretches, running on the spot, and forearm clenches, demonstrated to me by Sharif.
- 1200: Sometime between 1030 and 1430, Ali serves *cadu* (lunch). Usually *basto yr ghodarr* (spaghetti with vegetable sauce), occasionally *briis* instead of spaghetti. But they are kids – they love spaghetti! Often a few lumps of *hilip* (meat).
- Wash up. (This warrants a separate entry; it can be made to take half an hour to wash a bowl and fork!)
- 1200–1700: As for 0900–1200, but . . .
- 1430: All-over wash in the privy. The oven is still on full, but there is a little shade if one crouches down. Any later and it will be occupied by the gangsters.
- 1500: If it is quiet, move chair to the yard, in the shade now cast by the house. Ali brings a new flask of boiled water for tea. Listen to *Newshour* on the World Service.
- 1530: The gangsters in residence, two or three or four, sit outside in the same area. Sometimes chat.
- 1600: Ali Ad 'borrows' radio – BBC Somali service.
- 1700: Afternoon 'exercise' in the lean-to: more stretches and running on the spot.
- 1730: Any time between 1630 and 1930, Ali serves *ashok*, the evening meal.
- Wash up bowl and throw rinse water into fence

when no one is looking. (Don't visit privy this late; higher risk of mozzies.)

- 1800–2000: Prepare for night between radio news programmes.
- Move 'stuff' back into house.
- Make bed and erect mozzie net.
- If possible to be unobserved, open window (always nerve-wracking).
- Final cup of tea.
- Wash cup and rinse out flask.
- Clean teeth.
- 1800: Listen to *Focus on Africa* on the World Service. If the gang are noisy, retreat into house.
- 1900: Listen to *RFI* – news magazine and sport in English.
- 2000: Try for European news on the World Service, usually poor reception.
- 2000–2100: If too sticky, walk about in the yard in nightshirt! (Accepted if no high alert; often there are no men about at this time.)
- Midnight: Close the window sometime well before dawn.

Tuesday, 2 March

Buggas and Mr F visit by car bringing bottled water. Buggas grins and spouts another memorised sentence: 'You go London seven days. Stephen and another give money.'

The next day, Ali Ad hands me his phone. It's Ali again, connecting me to Stephen. Ali doesn't prompt me at all. He has come to terms with our position, and that of our families. The call is easier, and in some way reassuring; maybe things are moving, if slowly:

Stephen: *Hello, Paul, how are you?*
Paul: *Oh, I'm not brilliant, but I'm alive. Still alone.*
Stephen: *How're your eyes?*

Paul: Well, I'm only using one lens to try to make the eye drops last. I've got enough for a few more days.

Stephen: So you still haven't got enough contact lens solution, that's the problem?

Paul: Yes. Ali said they were trying to get some. Buggas seems to have lost all interest. Every time I speak to him, he says speak to Ali and Ali will come, but Ali doesn't come, so I don't know what's happening.

Stephen: I will speak to Ali. Are you being fed properly? And how are the people around you, the pirates? Are they keeping calm or are they aggressive?

Paul: They are calm, normal. I'm losing weight, but there's nothing wrong with the food. I get no real exercise so . . .

Stephen: . . . that's not helping, no. We are making progress with Ali, but it's slow, Paul. The trouble is we know that lots of other people are calling him who say they will give him money, and it's causing problems because Ali thinks he can get more money from them. But we're trying to convince him that I am the only person he can negotiate with.

Paul: Thing is . . . I mean, it's terrible being in solitary confinement. It's terrible. I don't know what's happening, and the weather is getting worse.

Stephen: Yes, I don't understand why they are treating you like this. I don't understand it at all, but I've spoken to Rachel. She was fine, she said she's keeping well and she is being fed properly . . .

Paul: That's good.

Stephen: Yeah, be as strong as you can. Don't give up hope. We are working for you. I'm sure it won't be that much longer, but we're working hard to make a deal with the pirates but they will keep changing their demands and it's very hard to trust them. We have to be careful.

Paul: I know what you mean.

Stephen: We want to make a deal with them that will

stick. Are you still moving around?

Paul: *No, I'm in a house in a village. I've been here for six weeks. It's very sticky when it's hot because they won't let me open the window. But if you speak to Ali, can you ask him to ring me, because I can't get any sense out of Buggas. Every time I ask Buggas to see Rachel because it's her birthday on Saturday, he says, 'Ask Ali' and 'Ali coming after tomorrow,' but Ali won't come and won't speak to me.*

Ali: *Yes, Paul. I'm away now, and I'm busy. I will come soon, and also to Rachel, and you will talk together on the phone. And after a week, maybe the issue will come together, so I'm trying that the negotiation will be better. It's a family who's never negotiated, but the pirates are used to negotiating and still we do not understand each other but maybe somehow we shall understand the family. Also the pirates are requested to bring Rachel a radio to listen, and maybe they will do that and everything will be OK.*

Paul: *Thank you, Ali. It's Rachel's birthday on Saturday. It's a very special day. She shouldn't be alone on her birthday*

Stephen: *We'll keep working hard on it, Paul. I promise you. But we need to make a deal with Ali which will hold, so when it comes to fruition, you know the two of you will be released and no problems . . .*

The line is cut.

In the afternoon – catastrophe! The radio won't work. It has suffered from humidity before but is usually OK after a period in the sun. I use the cook's knife to open it, put it carefully in the sun for an hour. No joy. Ali Ad helps me dismantle it further. Still nothing. I am devastated. I say I will ask Buggas for a new one. Ali shakes his head, 'Buggas, no. Buggas no more radio.' I'm sure he's right. Buggas didn't like me having the radio at all. Ali Ad says, 'OK, no problem,' and walks out, taking the bits of the radio. Within half an hour he is back, smiling as he hands me a new radio and a bag containing the old one, still in pieces.

'You, me,' he says, indicating we will share it. I am so relieved I hug him.

I would have been devastated without the radio – my only regular contact with the world. The next morning Ali Yeri claims the bag of bits, perhaps he can get it repaired. I learn from him that the radios cost about 14 dollars. Ali Ad evidently has money, despite having four wives to keep, but I am overwhelmed by his willingness to spend it on me, and more, by his defiance of Buggas. It is genuine compassion – I am sure of it.

Thursday, 4 March

Late morning. The compound is quiet. Some gangsters are sleeping in the hut, some are in town. The on-watch guards are outside, on the hillock, in the shade. Ali Yeri is peeling potatoes. Two vehicles turn up, prompting shouting and excitement outside on the track alongside the fence. Ali jumps up to see over the fence. He beckons to me, indicating that I should climb up on the fence and peer over. I watch two large Technicals turn and park under the big trees opposite. Serious weaponry here. Ali points to one and says, 'Howitzer.' Then at the other and says, 'Aeroplane,' miming anti-aircraft fire. Men and boys gather round. One of the guns is multi-barrelled, the other looks more like an artillery piece. Both are on the flat beds of large pick-up trucks. Several rounds are fired, very noisily. I hear the explosive bang of firing, then the 'crump' as each shell lands, nine or ten seconds later, perhaps several miles away. They don't care what might be underneath! The men outside cheer as the guns are moved on.

Twice during the morning I hear the big guns being 'demonstrated' to the villagers. In the afternoon a convoy rushes past, six or seven cars making the grinding gearbox noise I associate with the Technicals. There's no firing, but the gangsters are excited and I am told to go into the house. Ali Deri says, 'Family. Trouble.'

At 3 p.m. there is gunfire, AKs and machine guns, some distance to the north. It builds up, with heavier weapons, mortars or RPGs. It sounds as if it's coming closer, maybe within half a mile. Now all the gangsters, eight or nine of them, are arguing, rushing in and out, taking both the machine guns out onto the hillock, firing their AKs. I can glimpse their heads over the fence. Mr F turns up, calms the men and orders them to bring one machine gun back to its usual position outside my door. I am relieved to see Abbas manning it – he will stay calm. Ali Deri rushes back and says, 'Four *mort* [killed], eight shot!'

The fighting dies down soon after dark. Noisy chatter continues. Ali ventures out again, returning about 8 p.m. with more news. Now he says, '70 *mort*, 120 shot.' Afterwards all are calmer. Mr F leaves; the others sit and talk. Ali Deri says, 'Family problem. This family one and half million; other family 700. Mad!' I ask about the family, which I take to mean clan. 'Big family – one and half million, a quarter of Mogadishu, all of Amaara, Hobyo,' and he reels off a list of nine or ten towns that he expects me to know of! 'Family *maga'a*?' I ask the name. I wonder if he will tell me? '*Hawiye* – small family *Suleiman*,' he says. It means nothing to me, but maybe it will be useful to know at some time.

Friday, 5 March

It's calm and quiet, but I have a bad stomach again, so decline breakfast and lunch. I stay in the house, putting the final touches to two crosswords I have compiled for Rachel as a birthday present. We love to do the *Telegraph* cryptic crosswords, working together. When we are travelling, we download them from the Internet and keep a stock on board. Over the last two weeks I have spent time working them up. It takes a lot of my dwindling stock of paper, and it's difficult without a dictionary. I don't want them to be too easy, but they must be correct. We've been critical of the increasing sloppiness of the published ones over the past few years, since sadly the old school of compilers have retired. I decide upon a maritime theme so that the more obscure clues should be solvable. If we are allowed a call soon, I will tell Rachel; she'll be able to look forward to them.

I spend some time in the privy and decide that the biting things are gnats, not mozzies. I stop taking the Malarone, to conserve it in case I am moved to a riskier environment. I have 48 pills left. I move my mattress into the lean-to. The stores have dwindled, and the gangsters now leave it to me, except when Ali and Sugal fancy a lesson or a smoke respectively. I hope it won't get too cold at night, but the humidity won't be so awful.

Saturday, 6 March

Happy birthday, Rachel! Never mind my tone deafness – I can't sing to save my life – today I shout it out. I explain again to Ali, Sharif, Sugal, Abbas and Deli, who are in for breakfast, that Rachel shouldn't be alone today. Do I imagine it or do they look abashed? Buggas comes at 9 a.m. I've been pestering him at every opportunity, and it has worked! He passes me the phone and allows us ten whole minutes. It is so wonderful to hear Rachel. We are both cheered up no end. Rachel says she is coping with the heat, still in the house. We exchange tales of the shooting. It's much closer to me. I tell her not to worry, I'm well defended here! Rachel tells me she has a radio and has heard reports of fighting in central Somalia. I have missed them – you only get one chance on the BBC!

Afterwards, I feel so much better, and I set about

making myself more comfortable in the lean-to. Buggas strolls in after lunch to tell me that lens solution will come in three days. He's in a good mood, but I forget to ask him to take the crosswords to Rachel. I rush out, but he's gone. Ali Ad asks what the problem is. '*Kitab* [book] – Rachel,' I say, clutching a bag with *The Fiery Cross* and my two crosswords. 'Wait,' he says, and after ten minutes he comes into the lean-to and asks for the bag. I give it to him. And hope. Will he throw it away? Or will some of the gangsters pore over it and laugh? Or is it one more small sign of humanity? Only 15 minutes later he's back and hands me the bag. I am crestfallen but look inside – John Gribben's book! Yes! So Rachel has the crosswords, the only birthday present I could concoct. And, best of all, she is close, SO close!

Tuesday, 9 March

Buggas and Mr F turn up with two large cardboard boxes. Various Alis and the others peer in as I rummage through: books, medicines, toilet rolls, more medicines. Buggas says, 'One – one, you – Rachel.' I find a list and start checking what's there. Of course I am looking for contact lens solution. I see all too quickly that there isn't any. As fast as I pick up anything, look at it, set it aside, a stealthy hand reaches for it, a gangster looks uncomprehendingly and puts it down at random. Anything that looks like eye drops is seized by any one of a dozen hands, 'For eyes, yes?'

'No,' I say. 'Well, yes, that's antibiotic eye drops, but, no, not what I need.'

Buggas is saying, 'Quick. Quick,' so I give up any attempt at order, take out half the basic medicaments, the soap and the toilet paper, thinking I'll leave the rest to Rachel. If I keep a list, I'll be able to ask if I need anything more potent.

Books! Five new books. How to divide five by two? No time to think. *Bridget Jones's Diary* – Rachel, unfairly, but my immediate reaction is that it would have to be the last book on earth for me! *A Man in Full* by Tom Wolfe – I remember enjoying one of his novels, so selfishly I'll keep that one. *The Fourth Estate* by Jeffrey Archer – a bit lowbrow for Rachel, so I'll keep that too. *Maxwell: The Outsider* by Tom Bower – a biography, and *Wild Grow the Lilies* by Christy Brown – this looks more like literature, so both to Rachel. I scribble what I have taken on the list (there are three copies) and push the box towards Buggas. Mr F takes it, then Buggas tips the things I have kept onto the floor and takes that box as well. They go away.

Wow. A gift! I calm down and inspect the list more closely. It has come from Ecoterra in Nairobi. I wonder who they are, what they do? Are they safari organisers? There is an element of 'basic survival kit', plus the books. Whatever, it's most welcome. But no contact lens solution! Did Buggas take the box because he thought it might contain a hidden transmitter?

Wednesday, 10 March

In the excitement yesterday I must have lowered my guard; I used the privy late in the afternoon and now I find two suspicious bites. Start the Malarone again.

Once more, gunfire is getting closer, with heavy guns – the Howitzer? – firing regularly. Convoys fly past, and the gangsters are restless. Buggas brings a grotty plastic machine-gun ammo belt and sets Hassan to cleaning it. The mood is tense and fuelled by subdued discussions, not, I think, about me. Ali Deri arrives with the latest death toll: 10 dead and 20 shot today.

Ali Yeri tries to go on leave again – for five days, he tells me. Afieri is to cook tomorrow, but Afieri has 'head problem' again, so Ali stays.

Saturday, 13 March

Fighting has ebbed and flowed for several days. At 8.45

p.m., after a restless and tense day, the call comes: 'Up. Up. Quick.'

It's Buggas. I haven't gone to bed, so it's easy enough to pack and jump into the Toyota. We only travel about a mile. Buggas rushes off on foot, leaving Mr F in charge. I am shown into a pleasant round hut, with two open windows. It's within a compound, rather like a development of sheltered housing! I struggle to tie the mozzie net up and only just get to sleep when at midnight: 'Up. Up. Quick.'

Buggas again. 'No pack,' he says. 'Come. No dress. Not far.' He bundles me into the front of the Land Cruiser again in flip-flops and pants! I can't see much, but we only go a few hundred yards. This time a gate into a walled compound is held open for me, and I'm shown to a lean-to annex of a house. There is a rough slatted bed frame, on which my mattress is placed.

'OK?' asks Buggas. 'OK,' I reply, resigned, and make my bed for the third time that day. As far as I can see, everything has been packed up and brought. I'll sort it out in the morning.

Daylight reveals a similar arrangement to the house I had become used to as home, but this one is more substantially built, with blockwork walls above a high concrete plinth. The main house stays locked; the guards use the round hut, and my new home is the lean-to annex. Although it has a tin roof, there is open ventilation at the back eaves as well as a big opening in the front wall. With the raised bed, it is actually quite comfortable, though there is no privacy. The yard is barren. I realise my old house had quite a bit of greenery. The African hut had green growth over its roof, and all the fences had traceries of life – melon and bean, Ali had told me one day. None of that here. The privy is formed of surplus roofing sheets, nailed to a rough timber frame.

I settle in and explore – not in the usual sense, but I

look around and when the guards are not interested stand on my chair and even on the concrete plinth to see what I can of the surroundings. I must be closer to the village centre. There are two mosques close by. I can hear them calling to prayer and although we've not moved far I haven't heard them before. The road outside the compound is busier; I hear more trucks passing, animals and people walking by morning and evening. It sounds like a group of children going to school. I peer through the gap at the back eaves – there is an open area with two red lorries parked. Beyond them are some large trees, but there are no people to be seen.

Just before dusk, Buggas comes and sits with the gangsters on the plinth. 'You speak Rachel tomorrow,' he says. 'You free soon. Sheikh Sharif give three million. Gordon Brown give Sheikh Sharif 19 million.' Sheikh Sharif is the embattled president of Somalia, although it has become clear to me, listening to the BBC African Service, that he governs only a tiny area, and that only with foreign military support. I have heard on the radio that he has been visiting the UK, but I don't know how any aid he may have been promised by Brown would help us.

A few days pass in this house. It's far too hot to exercise outside, and there's no room in the lean-to, but the nights are not uncomfortable. The privy is horrible – cockroach heaven! Buggas checks in, late afternoon, every day. He is chatty and encourages me to speak to the men every day to learn more Somali. His messages are in the same vein: 'Ali come tomorrow' or 'Sheikh Sharif Ethiopia – tomorrow. He bring money. Ali come after' or 'You speak Rachel tomorrow'. I take him to task on the latter, but, 'Phone finish battery' is his response. Buggas thinks that a deal is in the offing. It sounds like wishful thinking to me.

Wednesday, 17 March

'Move. Pack.' It's back into the Toyota, again no effort to make a convoy, nor even to conceal me although it's broad daylight. I guess we're not going far. I say goodbye to the comfortable lean-to as we head back through town, skirting the centre on less-worn sandy tracks.

In a few minutes, yes, we're back to where we had left last Saturday. Buggas is in good humour, so I ask if I can sleep in the lean-to and use the house if it rains. I am worried that I may lose the house to the gang if I don't establish 'dweller's rights' to both.

'OK,' he says. '*Halkan, halkas* [outside, inside], no problem.'

Thursday, 18 March

No breakfast. Ali Yeri is rushing around like a headless chicken. '*Midi. Midi?*' He seems to have lost the knife. It's no surprise; the last time I saw it, it was half buried in the sand outside the privy at the house we've just left. He comes to me again, clutching the liver in one hand, gesticulating with the other, '*Magas. Magas!*' He wants the scissors now. He is intent, so I hand them over and watch him attempt to cut up the liver. Amusing, but the result is not pretty. He tries to tear it up by hand. He gives up and rushes across to the hut, leaving me to clean the blood off the scissors. I see him dashing out of the gate, having grabbed his *ma'awiis* and a shirt. Half an hour later, panic over, a new kitchen knife has been bought and the liver is cooking.

Ali comes in before lunch to learn, and teach, a little. He is a good learner. While I have to scrabble for my notebook and carefully transliterate every new word, then work hard to learn it, Ali just repeats a word three or four times and it's fixed in his brain: perhaps the only benefit of illiteracy. He is also a thinker. We spend some time discussing Somalia, the fighting and the TFG (Transitional Federal Government). I ask why he doesn't support his government. 'Somalia too much Ah Kay,' he says, using the vernacular for rifle. 'Somali *nin* [men] problem, two minutes speak, then Bim! Bim!' He mimes shooting. 'You know *mahwille*?' he asks. 'Gordon Brown, Bush – *mahwille*.'

'Yes,' I reply. 'Leader.'

'Sheikh Sharif half *mahwille*, Sheikh Sharif *wahir* [little] Somalia, *wahir* Mogadishu.'

Buggas comes as usual just before dusk and offers me the phone. I have a short chat with Rachel. We exchange news about the crossword and book exchange and I tell her about my four days away; we both think it must be because the fighting came so close. Buoyed up again, I pester Buggas for my lens solution. 'We search Ali,' he replies.

The threat of rain lessens. The days are steamy. Ali sweats buckets out in the open, preparing and cooking the midday meal. I suggest he works in the lean-to. He is reluctant – the heat from the *pochuko* will be too much for me. I am sure it will be OK, and from then on we share the space. He appreciates it and makes sure my water is kept topped up, even if only by shouting at Sugal, who is always willing to go to the well.

I'm getting into the Tom Wolfe novel. From it, I add a third item on my list of 'Things to hold on to' after Sarah's 'Be strong' and my father's 'Stay calm'. Now I have my own, an Inner Strength. I have always considered that it's pointless worrying about things I can't influence. One of the characters in *A Man in Full* becomes an 'accidental' Stoic. He derives great strength of mind from reading the philosophy of Stoicism, as related by disciples of the Greek philosopher Epictetus. The parallel is uncanny. Epictetus speaks about being imprisoned; Wolfe's character is in prison, and here am I. It reinforces and boosts my belief in my inner strength: *'I have the ability to reason. I can accept the truth and reject falsehood. I can decide to act or not to act. No one can take that away from me. I will not worry about what I cannot control.'*

Days pass. Buggas is less aggressive. He visits every day, asks if I am OK, and gives me the honour of a proper name. He now addresses me as 'Paul' rather than 'Hello'.

One morning, Sharif brings cake – a gooey, very sweet sponge cake. The best cake I've had for a long time! I try to find out what we are celebrating. Hassan, Senick and Ali Yeri are the only others in the compound; they join in but no one can tell me. I think it must be the birth of a child, but they don't let on.

The relatively amiable atmosphere continues, but translator Ali doesn't appear. I challenge Buggas again: 'Where Ali? Where contact lens solution?'

'Ali come soon. He search money; search aeroplane. Difficult.'

It looks like rain again. Buggas suggests I 'sleep *halkas* [inside house], day *halkan* [outside, in lean-to]'. This is a good idea. In the last hour before dawn, I have been getting wet from dew and waking up shivering; the humidity may be the lesser evil now the rainy season is approaching. I go back to the old routine, spending the day in the lean-to.

Ali has a few grumpy days. No learning – he just stands and stares. Then one morning he clutches his knee. 'Problem,' he says, grimacing. It looks swollen. I ask him what happened. I think I make sense of his story about an old injury. Five years ago he was at sea, in a fishing boat, caught out in a storm. They capsized, and Ali's knee was slit open by something. One man drowned. I can't help but sympathise with a fellow seafarer. I prescribe ibuprofen, give him four caplets with instructions, '*Lobo hadha, lobo habeen* [two now, two in the evening].'

Rotating three T-shirts and three pairs of pants, I need to do a clothes wash every four days. In between, on the second and fourth days, I wash my hair. On day three, I do special washing: a towel, sheet or flannel. Sweatbands and rags get rinsed as and when. In town, there are no bushes for the gangsters to throw things over, so those who don't have a wife or mother to look after them now use my line. Abbas is always polite. He's the only one who asks me if he can borrow the plastic bowl and makes sure I am not about to use the line, then grins, almost sheepishly, asking '*Peens?*' Unlike the others, his clothes never blow onto the dusty ground! I can rely on him to return the pegs.

The end of March draws near. Boredom sets in with the gangsters. Ali has a bad-head day, abandoning the dough balls before flattening them for chapatis. He just walks out! Four hungry men elect Sugal to take over. He manages, but cooking is not his forte.

For some days, I have been watching the birds. They're not afraid of me, and when the gangsters are away, they come down to eat the spilled rice. I take out the camera and snatch a few photos of an African starling, a pretty variant in bright blue, orange and white.

It's so sticky again. I sit outside at 8:15 p.m., managing for once to tune in the World Service for *Europe Today*. Ali Deri has other ideas. He comes over with his phone, sits next to me and proffers it. A movie is playing. Groaning fills the air. It must be the wounded in a war movie; that's their usual fare. Well, I thought it was . . . This is a hard-core blue movie! I feign interest for a few minutes, but Ali insists we watch it together – it runs for half an hour. 'England no!' I lie, much to his amusement.

Sunday, 28 March

I spoke too soon – of quiet days and boredom. This evening there's a massive gunfight: two hours of automatic fire, RPGs, mortars and the anti-aircraft gun. I can see the red tracer rounds cross the sky, from the ack-ack gun. The gangsters are agitated. They come and go but don't pose with the guns, not like last time. Silence, suddenly, then a couple of cars roar up, prompting much shouting and cheering. Ali tells me two 'militias' have had an argument, but it's over now, all good friends and no casualties. Perhaps I misunderstand; it sounds unlikely.

The next day, Buggas visits three times. He tells me, 'Ali no come. Too much fighting. Wait three days.' I ask to speak to Rachel and get another 'tomorrow'. Before dusk, an aeroplane flies close. 'House! House!' shouts Sharif.

For two more days, the sporadic shooting continues. I hear the big guns every few hours. Ali says militias are fighting 10 km away. He tells me Buggas has gone to fight, with six of our gang. In the evening, again before sunset, I hear a plane. Sharif too: 'House!' he yells. Surely they're not looking for us in the town? Perhaps this time it really is US drones, checking out the fighting.

Thursday, 1 April

All Fools' Day. In the tense circumstances, I don't think malarkey will go down well. The gang are very short-handed. Buggas is still away. Only Ali Yeri, Sugal and Deli are about. Deli insists I stay in the house, but he soon tires of keeping an eye on me and lets me do as I wish. By lunchtime, when there has been no fighting so far today, things calm down again. Mr F visits briefly, chats with the gangsters and leaves. Deli comes into the lean-to: 'You, Rachel, together *mante* [today],' he says.

A little later Sugal appears: 'Look Rachel *hadha* [now].'

Perhaps they do know about April Fools' Day!

At 5.30 p.m. Buggas and Omar arrive. Omar insists he's not working, just visiting family! They sit and Buggas tells stories, probably of the recent fighting. A few more of the gangsters turn up. Now there are eight or nine of them. I ask Buggas for a call to Rachel. He exchanges glances with Omar. Omar replies, 'There is no need. The family agree you will be with Rachel tomorrow, after tomorrow.'

I hope they realise that April foolery is allowed only before noon. They sound genuine. But what can I tell? I can hope, but dare not get too excited.

Friday, 2 April

A calm, clear morning. Ali is smiling as he holds out a handful of green chillies. *'Bes-bes* [chillies]. *Abbay* [father],' he says. They are from his father's garden. I get a more tasty breakfast than usual, as he throws a few, carefully de-seeded, into the liver. Again I am almost alone. In the afternoon Ali is preparing the *digir* earlier than normal. Deli comes out of the hut with his mat rolled up, a string around it. What's happening? Ali gives me a bowl of *digir*. He and Sugal sit next to me. At half past five I'm halfway through the *digir*. A car arrives, the gate opens and Buggas strolls in. He is grinning.

'We go Rachel's position. Pack. Quick!'

He needn't have said quick! I pack in record time. I don't worry about supervising the bags and all the paraphernalia but walk out and jump in the car. It may be a cruel joke, but I can't believe, for all his thuggishness, that even Buggas would be that nasty. Ten minutes' drive to another gate, another yard, and there, in the doorway to another house, is Rachel.

Three desperate months

Tuesday, 5 January

When Buggas orders us to separate, Paul and I are resolute. I don't focus on the gun Buggas is levelling at us. I no longer care what he does. We are resigned to die rather than be separated. This is the end.

Crack! Crack!

As Buggas fires, two of the gangsters grab him, pulling the barrel into the air. The gunfire challenges my resolve, but I soon realise neither of us is hurt. We wait for whatever comes next. We are still together. We remain silent, shaking with fear, while everyone around us is shouting incomprehensibly.

Mr F comes close and says, 'You crazy?' He tries to get us to separate. Baby Face is with him, making faces and signs to suggest the same. We shake our heads and insist 'No' again, in unison. In desperation, they pull on Paul, dragging both of us further from the shelter. Buggas pulls up a tree root and sharpens the end with his knife. He is shouting in the nervous high-pitched voice he uses when angry, and with a hissing flick of the root he whips us. I feel the pain from the whip slicing into my back but continue to cling on to Paul. I don't care. I won't be beaten into submission. Some men drag Paul away and I fall. Something heavy and solid whacks the side of my face as I crumple to the ground. I scream 'murderers' over and over again. Paul is gone . . . I lie on the ground where I'm left.

Men walk over me, to and fro; one kicking me as he

passes. They are collecting Paul's bags. I hear a vehicle move off, and the camp becomes quieter as darkness falls. I don't know what to do. My survival instinct says move back into the shelter and lie on the mat, but I stay where I am, uncomfortable on the bare earth, breathing heavily from the trauma. I can feel that my left eye tooth is broken and my cheekbone throbs with pain; a raw soreness tells me where the whip has marked my back and side. I begin to itch from imagined insects crawling over my exposed skin but stay lying down. I'm so angry and frustrated; I don't want to function normally. I hate these people so much. Why should I make it easy for them?

Time passes. Three of the guards come over and shout in my ear, '*Rijja! Rijja!* Up! Up!' I ignore them. They stand and mutter, then pick me up, one taking each arm, the other my legs, and carry me into the shelter, dropping me on my mattress. I lie there all night, hardly sleeping, my mind numb, confused, fraught with despair.

Before dawn, I go to the toilet. The guard hisses at me when I go one way. He wants me to go another way. How I hate the African habit of hissing! How I hate everything about these vile criminals!

I refuse breakfast. Sireet is worried. Samata and Oman come and urge me to eat. I refuse. Samata phones Omar and passes me the handset: 'Your situation is very difficult! The guards will beat you if you don't eat.'

I say I don't care and hand the phone back to Samata. More discussion, then I'm handed the phone again.

'If you don't eat, they will take your life.'

I tell Omar they're crazy. I'm ill and need paracetamol. Omar hesitates then says there are terrorists in the area and we'll be moving after lunch. That threat again! I continue lying down, not wanting to do anything, feeling desperate and lonely and miserable. What can I do?

Buggas comes back in the late afternoon but says nothing to me. He sits with the close guard, furtively watching me. Samata comes over with the phone. It's Omar saying he will arrange a conference call with Stephen. Some of the gangsters gather round to listen in, but nothing happens. Samata takes back his phone and they leave.

I wash my wounds. They're not bad: two weals around my side and back, only a little skin broken. I apply Savlon to soothe. My broken tooth is sensitive but bearable. I continue to refuse food. I have no appetite. You eat to live, and I have little will to live. I just lie on my mattress, letting the hours go by.

Another miserable day dawns. Oman tries to talk. He says, 'Buggas big thief.'

I reply, 'Buggas big problem.' I hear him repeating what I said, on the phone to Buggas, who arrives later with the Commander. I need to ask Buggas for more bottled water but dread him speaking to me. He settles himself on my chair and calmly asks how I am feeling. I mutter, 'Lonely, miserable. No Paul.'

Buggas sneers, 'Omar no here too much days. Militia. Problem.' I assume he's referring to the aeroplanes, which we've heard again today. Then he demands, 'No eat? Why?' I say I'm worried about Paul and that I need bottled water, not food. If I speak to Paul, then maybe I'll be able to eat. Buggas says, 'Eat. After speak Paul,' and leaves.

The cook brings rice, so I eat in the hope of getting a phone call to Paul. Afterwards, I ask Samata, 'Where's Buggas? He promised I could speak to Paul.' I've little idea how much Samata understands, but he replies, 'No Buggas. *Baree*.' I'm not surprised.

Friday, 8 January

I refuse breakfast. Same routine. I ask to speak to Paul but am told there's no signal. A new one! Samata says, 'Buggas, doctor, after.' So they've decided I need medical attention? I gather there are no local doctors and one will come from Mogadishu. Presumably one who's in cahoots with the gangsters. I lie and doze.

In the late afternoon the guards start packing up. Mr F appears and dismantles my shelter. Listlessly I pack – and discover some of Paul's things. I resolve to look after them. Mr F is in charge of the Toyota and guides me into the back seat next to a skinny gangster chewing *chad*. '*Chad*, good, ten dollar!' he boasts, showing me his bunch of green leaves. Buggas also gets in, so I'm squashed in the middle. I no longer notice their guns but squirm at their closeness.

We leave after dark and drive back through the village and onto a side track. I don't recognise the area where we stop. My bags are dumped by a nearby bush, and I'm told to sleep. Samata helps me tie up my mosquito net, and it's an effort to assemble my bed. It's windy, there are thorns everywhere and the net keeps getting caught up. The night is very cold, and my nerves are at breaking point.

Saturday, 9 January

Another new location to explore. Alone. At dawn Samata and the *chad*-chewing skinny gangster – who introduces himself as Haji Selbai – bring a tarp to make a shelter. Strong winds make it a challenge. They use strips of bark instead of line and don't bother to tighten it properly, so the tarp is flapping around a lot. Next, they stack some branches of brushwood against the tarp, to provide more cover. Job done, they sit under a nearby tree and ignore me.

When Sireet brings food, I refuse. Not long after, Buggas appears.

'No eat. Why?'

'I'll eat when I've spoken to Paul.'

'Eat! After speak Paul.'

'You told me that before. Two days ago you promised if I ate I could phone Paul. I ate, but you didn't let me phone Paul.'

Buggas sits and stares while I rant, then gets out his phone and calls someone. He hands me the phone. It's Paul! He sounds OK. He's coping and eating. He's spoken to Jill. I don't dare ask how that went. I don't want to raise their expectations by discussing it. We talk about how cruel they're being and ask each other why, why can't they understand we're not millionaires? We try to reassure one another but can't talk freely over the phone – it feels almost theatrical. It's better than nothing, even if we end up crying. Buggas soon demands we stop, but it's enough to give me hope.

I have rice for lunch and do a crossword. It's the first time I've been able to distract myself for four days. I just can't be bothered. I drift, letting the days go by.

I hate this place. It's windy, and dust and dirt blow into my tent, into everything. Sometimes we have a calm spell before the wind whips up. As it makes its way across the bush, it sounds like a helicopter approaching. When I first heard it, I got very excited! The men are camped out all around me and shout across me at night. There's no peace, no time to think. It's intensely cold at night and my hips become sore, making it even harder to sleep. My thin foam mattress, well compacted with sweat, provides little comfort. The tarp flaps a lot. I try to fix the problem, but Paul is so much better at it than me. The gangsters don't help.

I hear women passing by with their goats. Sometimes they banter with the men in a chiding way. The local environment is much the same, some bush and a field nearby, with a nomad house in the distance. I'm eating little. I accept what I'm given but throw most of it away. The guards are stand-offish, though Haji Selbai (who I nickname HSB) sometimes tries to talk. Mostly through sign language, he declares he wants to marry me. One forefinger is '*athiga*', the other is '*aniga*', and he brings them together. This skinny little wretch indicates that he wants to sleep with me, pointing to my bed mat! I tell him

I already have a husband, Paul. HSB is a good mimic and he picks up words quickly, though struggles with my name. He already knows numbers in English. He replies, 'You, two husband Paul, Haji Selbal.'

I manage to find out the names of the other gangsters guarding me. I have names for Sireet, Samata, Oman, Sayid and HSB. Now I learn that Fat Mohamed's 'real' nickname is Kalun – meaning fish in Somali. There's another cheeky youngster called Hamad and two older gangsters, Urday and Hamoud, who are both quiet and more disciplined than the rest.

After a few days I hear a plane, then another on the following day – but I no longer dream of rescue. I have lost hope. Fat Mohamed tells me, 'British militia, problem. No Paul.' Sometimes the men fire their guns close by without bothering to warn me. I'm always unnerved, especially when there's a burst of machine-gun fire. I struggle to develop or maintain any routine. Every day I wake up depressed and don't know what to do with myself. I feel so lonely and miserable. I can see no end in sight. Will I ever get out of here? Will I see Paul again?

Buggas comes and goes but says nothing for almost a week until one visit when he sits down in my chair, gun on his lap pointing at me, and asks how I'm feeling. 'Lonely and miserable' is my answer, but he doesn't understand those words.

He responds with, 'Paul, sick, problem.'

I guess he's goading me so I say, 'Me too.' I don't want to talk to him. The more lies he tells me, the more difficult it will be to ignore them. He asks, 'You. How much money?'

'You know how much. Paul told you: £130,000.' I know that Paul already told him this much – our joint cash savings – some time ago. He looks disgusted.

'No money. No Paul.'

I don't want to hear those words. They confirm his intention to keep us apart until money is handed over.

After he goes I try not to worry about the reference to Paul being sick, but I can't get it out of my mind. Fat Mohamed tries to taunt me about 'big money' and 'bank, London, money. No problem.' He's convinced it's simply a matter of time before I remember the phone number of my banker to call and order up the millions they want.

I get through another couple of days. The gangsters ignore me. Sireet delivers my food without a word. I struggle to say '*mahatsenit*'. Only HSB comes to 'talk', and all he says is 'Give me money' before the others call him away. Sometimes they used to teach me a few Somali words – *gil* for camel, *ari* for goat, etc. – but they've stopped doing that now. I've endured more than ten days in solitary, and I'm going mad. I can't stop worrying about Paul being ill. I can't sleep at night.

Saturday, 16 January

I wake, frantic. I have to do something. I join in the Allah choruses when the men are praying at dawn. I continue talking out loud, shouting for help, for Paul. I need to be free, away from these crazy people, away from this crazy place. I can't stand it any more. I don't know what to do. I don't know how to cope.

Buggas comes and grunts at me. I beg him to let me speak to Paul. He just asks again how much money I have. When I say, 'I've already told you,' he sneers and goes away.

I continue shouting. I need to do something. Buggas returns to bark, 'No shut up. Beat you!' I don't care and carry on until I'm exhausted. I doze fitfully for the rest of the morning, listening to Buggas and the gang chatting and laughing.

I decide to offload my emotions in my notepad. Under the title 'Despair':

11 days in solitary. No word from P since 'phone call, perhaps 6 or 7 days ago. Sick with worry about him, esp

since Buggas mentioned 'problem' two days ago. Can't bear the isolation. Despair at ever getting back to P. Feeling ready to die. No hope of getting out without ruining family. Military can do little, I guess, without risking much loss of life. Not worth it. Feeling desperate for P, to know that he's not suffering too much but knowing that he is.

The act of writing down my worst thoughts is a release. It helps me clear my mind. Claiming a tiny bit of control over my situation I feel better. I decide to give it another week. After all, what else can I do? There is no escape. I'm in the middle of a lawless country. I have no hope of finding someone who would be able to help. If I ran away in my flip-flops I would soon be caught! Even if I covered myself with my sheet (a floral pattern on black background) my white feet and hands would be a giveaway! I must assume Paul is OK. Even if he's not, he'll want me to survive. Our family will want us to survive. I must focus on survival. I must think rationally. It's stupid not eating: I might have less energy to use up, but it's clouding my judgement. I must get into a routine and keep hope of rescue.

Sunday, 17 January

Fat Mohamed sidles over and tells me Paul has gone to London. All I need is £2 million and I can go too. I do a crossword and tell myself it must be rubbish . . . but what if Paul has gone? Escaped or taken ill? Then I hear an aeroplane – another thing to worry about.

Hope?

Can I hope that Paul has been rescued? Or has he negotiated to go back and raise funds as Mohamed suggested? Or was he taken seriously ill and flown home for treatment, as indicated by Buggas's mention of him having 'problem' but not explaining because his English is so bad? And why did he take two bottles of water?

Possibly for the journey? Hope that P is OK & coping. At least no more stressed than I am!

Monday, 18 January

I start taking sugar in my tea, and eat as much as I can at breakfast, lunch and suppertime. I do yoga and feel so much better. I play Patience! I decide to think positively about Paul, about all the good times we've had together. I hear another plane, doing a circle. Perhaps it will see me. I make myself read John Gribben and immerse myself in the wonders of scientific discovery – thinking about how insignificant I am in the context of our world, our galaxy, the universe – before having another cry.

Escape Plan

Have to think of something to distract me from P. All the things we'd do together. All his irritating or endearing habits.

Helicopter will arrive soon and take me away. Lots of lovely Brit troops will soon overpower these idiots.

Mustn't forget my grab bag. Have I any warm clothes? Will soon be seeing you, P. Love you.

Tuesday, 19 January

I tick off another day. First thing, visiting the toilet bush, I scan the environment for my rescuers and listen hard for their whispered signal. Depressed – no sign of rescue – I dose myself up with sweet tea, ready for the morning challenge. How can I get through the next ten minutes, let alone ten hours or ten days?

Endurance

2 weeks of solitary. How do people cope? Am I just very weak? Must keep hoping of rescue. There was a plane yesterday, but how far away was it and would it cover this area? Keep hope of a solution. Paul is free and being looked after. We will see one another again soon. I must

keep going another few days. Someone must say something soon. Not Buggas of course! Rescue. Rescue. Rescue. Love you, Paul.

I force myself to eat and do things to distract myself. The guards are bored and demand my playing cards – one less option for me. I add sweeping out my tent to my daily chores. It doesn't always need sweeping, but it's something to do. Samata and HSB observe with approval that I'm behaving like a Somali woman. None of them, especially Sireet, likes the fact that they have to do things for me – such as cook and fetch water – but I'm their captive and they must keep me alive. My daily yoga session helps calm me.

Thinking of you, Paul.

Just finished yoga and remembering how well you did. So proud of you, even tho' you found it difficult. You made good progress for a 59 year old!

Remembering how you'd fix the tarp and find little projects to do in our tent. Hope you're finding plenty to do and are in loving hands.

R xxx

PS: We have everything to live for. We will re-invent our lives and carry on being gentle, kind, happy people. We have our minds and so much to offer the world, our family and friends.

By mid afternoon, I'm looking forward to my wash, hiding behind a bush, those precious few minutes away from camp chatter. I read and feel better as the evening approaches.

After dusk I sit in my chair and dig into my memory bank. What was the kitchen like in our cottage in Plawhatch? I can occupy myself for ages trying to remember the minute detail of somewhere we lived 12 years ago.

Talking to the World . . .

. . . about our plight + experiences, helps pass the time.

So does thinking about all our great friends and loving relations: Pa, Sarah, Stephen, Jill, many more. We love you all and miss you all.

Must not be bitter about these terrible events. Must think about a new future project with freedom – after escape and release.

I've had enough of sitting up by 7.30 p.m. so assemble my bedding and climb in, tucking my mosquito net around me. I lie there thinking, ignoring the guards' chatter and dozing when I can.

Thinking about the next onslaught . . .

Don't! What am I supposed to do? All I can do is wait and try to keep sane, assuming somebody is trying to help. I have no information, not any I can trust, so I am hopeless. But I have 'hope'? There is always 'hope' while I'm still alive. And faith in my family to do their best in a difficult situation. Perhaps if I think of the trauma they are going through I will have 'hope'. Perhaps not. Think of the good times & their love and kindness.

Wednesday, 20 January

Breaking Up the Day –

- 6 a.m. Wait until 6.30 to go out to pee
- 6.30–8 Tea + breakfast. Wash + chores. Perhaps laundry
- 8–10 More chores, diary, reading, occasional Patience
- 10–10.30 Yoga session
- 10.30–12 Lunch arrives. Reading. Patience
- 12–3 X-word + siesta. Patience?
- 3–6 Reading Gribben; reflecting, wash
- 6–7 Supper + bed preparation (after dark)

Banish thoughts of torment, suffering and endurance

Think of P and everyone in my life. Love you, Paul.

Thursday, 21 January

We will survive!

And grow stronger from our experiences. We have everything to live for: good friends and family. So many people we can help + love + care for. We can do so much to 'repay' the suffering, to recover from this ordeal. We will survive. Love you always. xxx

Another heartening yoga session. Surprising how fit I still feel despite the lack of aerobic exercise. Neck muscles have relaxed, esp on RHS. Good! Need to re-train them and keep standing tall. Problem of cowering when Buggas around + feeling down. Must stay UP UP UP!

After dark, guards come into my tent, shining torches on me. I'm startled and fearful. What can be happening? They pull at the mosquito net. '*Rijja! Rijja!*' Hamoud thrusts a mobile phone in my hand. Uday, Samata and others crouch nearby. I say, 'Hello.'

A man says, 'I am Somali man, Ali. How do you feel?'

I've no idea who this is. I say I'm lonely and miserable.

He says, 'OK. Listen to me. Your situation is very bad. I will put you through to someone. You must answer his questions. The pirates want money. Your family refuse to negotiate. The pirates say they will kill one of you if negotiations don't start in four or five days. Do you understand?'

I understand – noting that Ali's English is a lot better than Omar's. The threat to kill one of us is terrifying, but the fact that he speaks clearly is mildly reassuring. I've no time to think before another voice comes on the line and introduces himself as Angus Walker of ITN.

Angus: *Rachel. How are you? Do you know how far you are from Paul?*

Rachel: *Well, I'm all alone. I haven't seen Paul for over two weeks. I'm desperate. I don't know where he is, what they've done with him, and I'm terribly, terribly lonely.*

Angus: *Rachel, I spoke to Paul about 24 hours ago – he's physically fine, mentally in a similar state to you.*

Rachel: *That's a relief: to know that he's still mentally OK, well, still hanging on. That's what we're both trying to do – hang on [voice breaks].*

Angus: *What's their attitude towards you?*

Rachel: *Well, they have told me if they don't get the money within four or five days they will kill one of us.*

Angus: *Dreadful.*

Rachel: *We've been subject to torment and those kind of threats all the time. I suppose the video was the starting point, where they said – you know – we will kill you if we don't get what we want.*

Angus: *What keeps you going?*

Rachel: *What keeps me going is thinking of Paul, hanging on for him, and knowing the love of our family and wanting to see them again.*

Angus: *Do you wish the government to do anything, because their position has always been that they will not negotiate?*

Rachel: *Yes, I know their position and I don't know what to say. I mean, it leaves us here to die – that's all that I can say. I don't think anything I can say will change them, but it's a very hard position for individuals who are involved in this situation, just ordinary people like us.*

Angus: *When you say you are tormented, what do you mean by that?*

Rachel: *It's the daily aggression that I get especially from the gang leader whenever he's around. Also the fact that you have guards around laughing and joking, and you don't know what's happening. I don't know from day to day what's happening. I feel totally helpless and useless, and it's hard not to feel dying would be an easy way out. It's hard to explain, but when you're all on your own in a country and* *you've no idea where you are or when something might happen, or whether I'll see Paul again, it's just very, very despairing.*

Angus: *Well, I must tell you that Paul says he loves you and the message is 'Be strong'.*

Rachel: *Right. Yeah, and the message for him is hang on for me because my biggest hope is I will see him once before we die.*

I'm conscious of Ali listening in, and the fact that the conversation will be on TV, so struggle at times to know what to say. I *am* frightened by this latest threat to kill one of us. Is it credible? But I'm not so desperate as to plead and beg. I do my best to sound upset and grovel as they want me to, but I'm not really unhappy, because it's such a joy to be conversing with someone in English! Someone who understands what I say, who is not a gangster. I wish I could talk freely, to explain everything. It's so frustrating. I want to tell him that I don't want a huge ransom paid, that I would rather die, but I'm not brave enough. I want to tell him about the flights and our hopes of rescue, but of course I can't. The news that Paul is OK and sends his love is a boost to my morale! At the end of the call I hear Angus telling Ali that some video footage would be helpful. I guess that's what I should expect next: another video.

Afterwards, I think over things I said and would like to have said. I jot notes in my pad.

Angus asks about 'torment' + I try to explain about day to day suffering: enduring the loneliness, trying not to worry, fear of threats + aggression, taunting of guards laughing and chatting in Somali, sometimes mimicking English phrases, playing radio. Terror of never knowing what will happen next. Fear every time a vehicle approaches. Hopes always shattered.

Forgot to mention life as caged animal, though do

mention visits to toilet only time I'm not under close observation.

What next? Another week of waiting? Knowing P is still here leaves me in 2 minds. Thankful he's OK, sort of, if going crazy. More desperate about possible rescue mission. Mustn't give up hope of solution: someone to take pity on us.

Friday, 22 January

Buggas arrives with Omar and the Commander, strutting around, shouting as usual. He asks how I'm feeling and I say, 'Terrible.' Why does he bother? What does he expect? He doesn't understand, or care, and walks off.

Omar visits next and says, 'I can do nothing for you. Stephen and government refuse to find solution to your problem.'

I shrug my shoulders and say, 'Perhaps you should pray for me.'

'That won't help,' he sneers, walking off. I reflect on how he's now showing his true colours. At the start he was our 'friend', trying to help us, and referring to the gang as 'these men'. He's no better than the rest of them, just a pathetic, nasty, greedy criminal.

I'm worried about what they may be putting Paul through, pressurising him to beg for money.

Late at night, I'm woken for another phone call. It's Ali, putting me through to someone called Steven – not my brother. He says he's a negotiator and tries to be reassuring, talking a lot of code about 'chains of communication'. Steven says he'll speak to my brother. I tell him I'm desperate to be reunited with Paul, and he asks Ali to get us together again. Ali says, 'Tomorrow or after tomorrow, *insha'allah*.' I ponder this latest development. Who knows what this man can do. Maybe help Stephen? I cry a lot – a release of tension? I have a glimmer of hope that we will be reunited soon.

Putting on the act: numb with shock

Must explain that when in such dire circs the only way to survive is to try & shut it all out. That makes it hard to describe how it reall.y is. We're numb with shock + fear. If we let the reality into our minds we'd go insane. At some stage we'll have to let it all out again + come to terms with what has happened.

Days pass, often cold and windy. The guards say little.

Monday, 25 January

Dear Everyone,

Angus says there's hope. Negotiator Steven says lots of people are thinking of us. It's hard to hold on to this, hard to stay sane when living with such aggression, never knowing what awful threat will happen next. Not knowing whether P has any hope. Has he spoken to Steven? What will we have to face next? Can Ali bring any sense to Buggas? Why do they have to keep us here in this hostile place? Just to punish us! For being ordinary people, not rich British people, not ones with friends in high places. Our government will do nothing + nor will our family. How long should we wait? Long enough to see one another die at hands of Buggas in a fit of temper.

My darling Paul, I long for you with a passion + yearning that I've not exposed for many years. Oh, that we can be together again one more time. R xxxxxx

2.50 p.m. Worried my pen is running out!

Tuesday, 26 January

Another dawn move. Buggas arrives in the Land Rover, takes some things and leaves again. He's back in half an hour, and my bags and bedding are thrown in the back, with me hustled into the cab. Off we go in a different direction from our approach, bouncing along a new track.

I can see two tracks where the Land Rover has come and gone before. No other vehicle has been along here recently. Not much hope of seeing Paul yet. Maybe if we're to be reunited here they'll bring him later.

We don't go far and stop in a small valley. I'm told to sit in my chair under a tree. Sireet gets a fire going and unpacks his kitchen stuff. Early-morning sounds echo around the hollow: birds whistling and goats bleating as they start their daily munch through the bush. I hear the familiar noise of branches being chopped back and gangster activity. Buggas returns and takes me to my new shelter, on a ledge, under a group of bushes. The men laugh. 'New house,' they tease. How can they be so cruel?

It's hot and sticky, but I need to excavate the ground to make a flat surface to lie on. I'm allowed to walk up the side of the hollow to find a toilet bush, and I walk a bit further to the rim. I can see for miles all around. The bush is endless, like a sea. It's beautiful in the way that wild, isolated places are. I'm reminded of the awe-inspiring places we visited on the coasts of Northern Sudan and Southern Eritrea, great swathes of near wilderness. I can't help wishing for the claustrophobia of our little yacht, sitting in a tightly packed harbour, like the one on the Greek island of Idhra.

In the evening, a plane flies over, loud and low. I'm having a late supper, and it's almost dark. What can a plane be doing so late? The guards are spooked, and so am I. They get the machine gun out, shout a lot and make phone calls. Fat Mohamed comes and sits in my chair, pointing his gun at me and ordering me to 'sleep'. I leave my supper and go to bed anxious. I can't sleep.

At midnight they tell me to get up. I start packing, but no one knows what's happening. They are all running around, frantic, yelling. The Land Rover arrives with Buggas. He barks at the men, and they argue like a pack of wolves. Fat Mohamed comes back and tells me to sleep. I'm so frightened by the palpable nervousness in the air. I can't possibly sleep. I am terrified by these madmen. What next? How can I be more frightened than terrified?

Wednesday, 27 January

Everything is quiet again, but I'm on edge. I calm down with a session of yoga. Fat Mohamed comes to watch.

At midday I hear a vehicle arrive. Buggas appears with another man who introduces himself as Ali. He is not tall, a bit plump, smartly dressed and wears a gold watch. Dapper! His demeanour is altogether more confident than Omar, and he has a rasping voice, just like a movie gangster. He says he is trying to help us. He knows we are not wealthy people and he is trying to persuade 'the pirates' – as he calls them, rather than Omar's 'these people' – to accept less money, maybe 'as little as one million'. I swallow hard. Still crazy numbers. He wants me to ask Stephen to raise 500. What does he mean by 500? His English is better than Omar's, but he talks in code. I'm a newcomer to this business, and I don't understand. I'm frightened and can't think straight. Does he mean 500,000? Yes. He asks how much money I have. I tell him what I've always said, that Paul and I have £130,000 between us. He asks if I have any other accounts, and I say no. He mulls this over and to my relief doesn't press me. I firmly believe we should leave any negotiations to Stephen – and I hope he's getting good advice! Sarah, my sister, has power of attorney over our affairs so will be able to work out what money we might raise. There is nothing we can do ourselves.

Ali says Paul is trying to borrow money from his previous employer. My heart sinks at the thought. I know the business is struggling to survive, like so many in the current recession. How can they possibly help? How will we ever pay it back? Ali asks about my employer. No hope! I'm in a dilemma, because if I tell him I used to work for the government, will that raise their expectations? I tell him I've not been employed for many years and that it was a very small business so no hope of raising any money. I'm exasperated as well as frightened. Again he doesn't press me. He says he knows we sold our home to buy the yacht and asks me to think about any other way of raising money. He even has the gall to suggest I'll be able to write a 'history' about our experiences! I say I have no idea and rant about us being ordinary people, no big ship, no millions, just thousands.

Ali phones my brother Stephen. I'm so happy to hear his voice, but so miserable that I can't speak freely.

Rachel: *I'm in a terrible way, Stephen. I'm absolutely at my wits' end, and now they're very angry because there was an aeroplane flight over last night. They're really, really angry, and they say they will do bad things to us if there are more flights.*

Stephen: *Rachel, I've spoken to Paul earlier and I've passed on that you're good to him, and these planes . . . He mentioned it to me and I've spoken to the Foreign Office and they are American drone flights. They are not under our control at all. There's nothing we can do.*

Rachel: *They're American?*

Stephen: *Yes, but the Foreign Office are going to speak to the Americans today about it. You never know what the Americans are doing, I'm afraid.*

Rachel: *Yes, OK. I can but tell them that and . . . I hope they will accept that. The other thing is they are on to us about trying to raise some money . . . and Ali the interpreter says that they realise we don't have a lot of money, but they want us to try to find a way of borrowing £500,000. So if we can raise that much, maybe he can persuade the gang to release us.*

Stephen: *Yes, you see the trouble is up to now they haven't given us any sensible figures. If they're saying £500,000, that is a more sensible figure. You know they have been* *talking millions till now.*

Rachel: *I know and they still do keep talking millions, but Ali says that he will try, if we can find a way of tapping any source of money and try to find that money.*

Stephen: *Yes.*

Rachel: *Another guy I spoke to a few nights ago, called Steven, he might also be able to help. I don't know if you've heard of him, he's a lawyer.*

Stephen: *Yes, he's a friend of Ali's . . .*

Rachel: *Right, OK. Well, anyway, we're in a desperate situation here. Please do anything, anything you can, because it's just awful.*

Stephen: *I know it's hard.*

Rachel: *We're in the middle of absolutely nowhere, you know. It's not as if we were on a big ship and . . . I don't know, I don't know what to say.*

Stephen: *Don't worry, Rachel.*

Rachel: *Please, please do what you can and please, please try everything you can think of.*

Stephen: *We know we're going to see you home soon – you know we're looking forward to it.*

Rachel: *I hope so.*

Stephen: *And keep strong because it won't be long.*

Rachel: *And Paul's OK?*

Stephen: *Paul is OK. Don't worry, you're both OK. I know it's very cruel of them, and I don't understand why they've kept you separate, but you're both OK and they will look after you because you're valuable . . .*

Rachel: *Yes, it's just that they don't understand that we're ordinary people. They don't understand we don't have access to millions of pounds. You're not dealing with people that can understand. That's the problem – there's no way of making them understand.*

Stephen: *Yes, I don't understand it myself. I mean, obviously it's not like you're some big ship.*

Rachel: *No, we're just gentle people who . . . I don't understand how they can be so cruel.*

Stephen: *I promise you we're doing everything we can and we're all talking together and we're working together and that figure – I'm taking it back to speak to everyone and I'm going to ring them again tomorrow. We have been in regular contact, but it seems that they wanted to change the translator . . .*

Rachel: *Yes. I couldn't understand the previous person.*

Stephen: *No, that was our problem too.*

Rachel: *He was very difficult to understand; this man seems to speak more clearly.*

Stephen: *Good, good. I've had a long chat with him this morning. Don't worry, we'll have you out soon, as soon as they realise . . .*

Rachel: *I'm hanging on, I'm hanging on.*

Stephen: *I'm sure you will.*

Rachel: *I'm getting through every day and night . . . take care.*

Stephen: *You keep strong and we're thinking of you all of the time. We love you lots.*

Rachel: *I'm sure you are. My love too. Bye bye.*

I say £500,000 by mistake. I should have said dollars. I'm so confused and harassed by this pressure for money we don't have. Afterwards Ali says he'll try to get us back together again, before leaving.

I mull over the day's events, trying to find some hope, trying not to despair. Did Stephen sound more positive? Ali seems more realistic. His tactics are different from Omar's. How much influence does he have over Buggas? Can he make him accept what little we have, or at least as much as we can raise by selling everything we've got? I'm coming to terms with the idea of being penniless but still can't live with the idea that we'll owe more than we can ever pay back.

Dear Stephen,

Spoke to you today + so much I couldn't say! I don't

know how I'll ever thank you for all you're doing. I'm so proud of you and so happy that we have such a wonderful family. I wish I could have been more 'strong', but had to play the part. I know you'll do the right thing + I hope you continue to have good advice at hand. I can't imagine the anguish you must have been going through on our behalf + will continue to do so for some time to come. I'm realistic enough to know that we won't be out of here for some time. I'm looking forward to seeing you soon too. Love R

Friday, 28 January

I feel very confused this morning. Why didn't I ask Ali to let me speak to Paul? Will Ali phone today? What should I be prepared for?

I read a bit. A vehicle arrives, prompting the men to jump up, grab their guns and fire a few shots. Sayid grabs the machine gun and comes to my shelter. He sits outside, agitated, staring at the others as they rush off towards the car, out of my sight. Sireet brings my spaghetti lunch, his gun at the ready, and rushes off again. I can hear shouting at the Toyota. Some of the men rush back and Sayid stands up, shouting at them. He points the machine gun and yells some more. They stop in their tracks and scream back at him. He raises the gun and fires it in the air, then points it at them again and shouts even louder. They yell back. This goes on and on. Buggas stands in the background, watching.

I'm scared out of my wits. What on earth is going on? It's obviously about me. It's hard to breathe. I force myself to breathe. Then Buggas shouts something. Sayid and the others go off in the opposite direction and continue arguing. I don't know what to do other than pick at my lunch and keep my head down. I've not seen such behaviour before. It must be about me, but what? Buggas and the Commander remain at a distance. Why aren't they involved?

I don't notice three men approach. One comes straight into my shelter and takes off his shoes. He says he's a doctor. I put down my spaghetti and turn towards him. He squats on my mattress, opens his bag and brings out a stethoscope, then a blood-pressure testing kit and starts examining me. The second man introduces himself as Mohamed. He has a bag and brings out a small video camera. What *is* going on? The third man sits in my chair. I concentrate on the doctor. He checks my blood pressure, listens to my chest, and checks my glands. I don't like being handled without permission, doctor or no. He asks how I am. Isn't it obvious? I rant about being captive, separated from Paul, not sleeping, etc. What else does he expect? I'm suspicious of who he is and what his motives are. He must have come straight from having lunch, because his teeth are still covered with rice. Yuk! He asks if I have a message for the British people, and I'm taken aback. Then I realise that Mohamed is a journalist, and the video he is taking of me in this vulnerable state will be broadcast! Once again I feel utterly humiliated, abused. Is there nothing these people won't stoop to? Am I to be paraded on TV again, looking even more pathetic and helpless?

The doctor asks if I sleep at night and when I say no he asks what I do! I say I worry and find it difficult to stay sane. I tell him I don't have any sedatives, and he writes out a prescription for Diazepam, telling me to take one at night. I'll be happy to add it to my medicine chest – for emergencies – assuming Buggas gets it for me. Eventually, the doctor leaves. Mohamed says he will do everything he can to help us. What does he mean? And where's our new 'friend' Ali? I ask about Ali, then realise he's the third man, sitting in my chair. Ali says he's trying to help us, then follows the doctor.

Mohamed stays back a few moments to take some still photos. I know as they are taken that they will be heartbreaking for our family and friends to see. Mohamed tells me the big argument amongst the gangsters was because the men didn't want to let him in, so he's having to be discreet! He says he'd been tracking us for 24 days, that he's seen Paul, who's OK, that the UK Parliament is debating our situation and that the video will be on *Sky News*. I'm not sure whether to be grateful to him for coming or not. Can this publicity help or hinder our situation? I feel helpless. I'm not brave enough to refuse to cooperate. And it's so good to talk to someone civilised, to hear about the outside world. I long to know about what's going on, but Mohamed has to go. He packs away his cameras and rushes off.

Exhausted and confused, I don't know what to think. I sit, read fitfully, then offload in my notepad:

Freedom is . . .

- Not having a torch shone at you regularly during the night
- Not having armed delinquent guards around you 24 hours a day
- Being able to make your own breakfast, lunch + supper
- Not living in fear of the next onslaught from Buggas
- Not having to put up with inane chatter of guards, Somali music, mobile phones and radio
- Not having to endure guards' attempts to intimidate + joke at your expense
- Being able to smile and laugh with people who care
- Being with Paul, family and friends
- Not feeling that death would be a release
- Being able to phone, listen to music or the radio
- Generally knowing what's going to happen next!
- Knowing help is at hand if you need it
- Not having to beg for water, etc
- Not being treated like an animal!

I go through the motions: afternoon wash, sweet bean

supper, prepare for bed. After I've settled down for the night, Uday starts to dismantle the tent around me. I dress and assemble my things, finding Oman – who's already grabbed one bag and my chair – not far away. I complain about the rush, muttering to myself, not caring what they understand. 'Why rush? Me, old lady. Big problem.' Oman sneers and mimics my fraught 'big problem'. Buggas and Mr F arrive in a Toyota and Land Rover. As he grabs my two bags, Buggas tells me to 'follow'. I take my chair and walk out of the hollow to the waiting vehicles. Where to now? It's a squash in the car, and I'm hoping we won't go far. Just 20 minutes later, we arrive in the village and stop.

I can see little in the torchlight. Buggas leads me through a narrow door and across a small, rough yard, into a 'house'. It's a large room with some pine furniture. The floor is screeded. How civilised! On the bed there are even two thick foam mattresses, still in their plastic covers. My first thought is to look for signs of Paul. Nothing. Buggas says 'new house' and looks expectant. 'Thank you,' I say. I don't see the point of asking about Paul. I don't want to hear 'No money, no Paul'.

My bags and bedding arrive. I start to take off one of the plastic covers from a new mattress, but Buggas says, 'No,' and removes it, indicating that I must use my old, heavily compacted, thin foam mattress. What did I expect? At least I can use the bed base, which will be easier to keep clear of sand than the floor. I ask about the toilet and see, beside the hut, a small corrugated tin cubicle surrounding a crudely made squatter but with enough room to stand and wash. It has no roof, but at least the door has a bolt on it!

The men are setting down their mats in the yard. I request washing water, and Fat Mohamed kindly brings me a full container.

Time to settle in. I'm weary and long to lie down. I make my bed, not bothering with the mosquito net, as there's nothing to hang it from. Lying down, I realise how humid it is inside, even with the door open. There is only a narrow vent in the wall, firmly shut. I sweat heavily but can't sleep naked as I would on the boat.

Friday, 29 January

I wake before dawn. So many new sounds! The mosques are wailing their calls to prayer. Lorries hurtle through the village honking their horns. A cacophony of bird, animal and human noises arises from the surrounding huts and compounds – goats, chickens, cows, donkeys, camels, people, all rousing themselves and assembling for the daily trek around the bush to feed. Most noticeable is the sound of children. I've been used to a much quieter time in the bush.

My guards are uncharacteristically quiet. Perhaps they don't want to announce our presence in the village? The cook boils the kettle in the yard. Rather than an open fire, he now uses a *pochuko*. My box of household things was left behind, so I have none of my eating or drinking utensils. Oman gives me tea in his enamel mug. Fried liver appears in a new bowl, from which I eat with my fingers. Then my box of household stuff appears. Someone must have gone back to get it. I'm relieved and motivated to get organised and study my surroundings. The hut is 12 foot by 15, with wattle-and-daub walls and a corrugated tin roof. The door is a rough wooden frame with a flattened oil drum nailed to it. The vent is rough wood, ill-fitting so I can see a little outside through the cracks. I need to leave the door open for ventilation and light. Some of the gangsters wander in and out at will, fascinated by the furniture, especially a mirror on the cupboard door. They open it to see if there's anything inside, preen themselves in the mirror, look around the bed and check what's underneath.

I look in the mirror and see my face for the first time since the *Kota Wajar*. When Paul cut my hair, I could just about see the effect on the back of a spoon. Not that I wanted to! My eyebrows are straggly, so I pluck them. It occupies my time, but do I feel better? Hardly! My hair is growing fast, and I wonder how long it will be before Paul is able to cut it again. House flies are a problem, as are mosquitoes. Fat Mohamed helps me put up a line to a rafter, so I can hang up my bed net. In the middle of the day I lie underneath it to avoid the irritating flies, but I'm hot, sticky and restless. Uday is nervous when I go outside. I have to wash out my food bowl, but they won't tell me what to do. When I throw the dirty washing water in the hedge in the same way that Sireet does, I get told off. 'No! Inside!' All of a sudden, I feel very claustrophobic.

At dusk the village is alive with the sounds of goats and other animals returning from the bush. Doves scurry about on the tin roof. Gunfire is ever present in the background – more noticeable and worrying than before. After I've gone to bed the guards keep coming in to check on me, sometimes shining their mobile-phone torches in my face. At other times they come in to make their phone calls. When will I get any peace?

My dearest love,

I dare not imagine what you are suffering right now. I hope you are able to think through the gloom and continue hoping for my sake. I am trying to do the same for you and to banish all the fear that envelops me when B is around. We must deal with the worst and continue to hope for release. These people won't let us go without continuing to make us suffer for as long as they can. We will survive!

All my love, R xxx

How to endure the days on end when nobody says a kind word to you? Think of those you love and who love you.

I'm unsettled by this move to such a different environment.

237

The guards have their own hut, made of brushwood and integrated into the fence around the compound, but they spend a lot of time in the yard. If they speak to me it's incomprehensible or taunting, or both. They take my chair at night, and I have to beg to get it back in the morning. The wall of my hut is very thin, so I've no protection from their noise – which is soon back to high volume. Worst is when Buggas is here. They sit right outside in the afternoon and evening, chewing *chad*, shouting and arguing for hours on end, often firing a few shots – which make me jump out of my skin (or bed). Sometimes Buggas talks more authoritatively, as if recounting a story. It always ends in '*Bim! Bim! Bim!*' followed by sycophantic laughter. I imagine he is telling tales of how he shot down some poor victim.

After more than three months of captivity I can no longer drift off into a nice daydream and forget where I am. My subconscious has caught up with reality. In some ways that's good, because I no longer come out of my reverie to the shock of reality. I must exist as best I can and not worry, but I do.

Sunday, 31 January

100 days: time for a fresh start. Hope something will be resolved soon. Mustn't worry about P worrying about me. One day we'll be together again. One day we'll be free. We'll get there and find a way of holding our heads high again. BE POSITIVE + BANISH FEAR, DESPERATION AND HOPELESSNESS.

Another evening phone call. It's Steven, the negotiator, with Ali listening in the background of course. Steven says he's met my brother, who is doing all he can. Apparently I was on TV last night and everyone is concerned that I look thin. Did I get the medicines? I say, 'All I need is Paul.' He mentions that *Lynn Rival* is back in the UK. I don't want to hear this – not only will it raise the gang's expectations, but the idea that we'll somehow be able to pick up from where we left off is ridiculous. I tell him our lives are ruined and we will never recover our old life!

After the outburst I feel guilty about sounding so ungrateful. I apologise and ask to speak to Paul. To my surprise Ali arranges for Paul to join the conference call! It's so good to hear his voice. He sounds sane and remarkably calm. He's in a village hut and has the same problem as me of not being allowed out, not able to get any exercise. He asks Steven for help in getting contact lens fluid and says he has maybe four weeks' supply left. I rant about how cruel it is to keep us apart and ask to be allowed frequent calls to Paul. Ali cuts me off.

I reflect on yet another 'event' in a short space of time. I'm so grateful for the contact with Paul and the outside world but unsure about the point of the call with negotiator Steven. Clearly, Ali is trying to move things forward, but what is he up to? What's happened about the demand for 500,000 made to my brother? I dare not ask. I must keep hope.

Monday, 1 February

The days wear on, and I establish some routine. The guards don't like getting me water, so I get my own from the well, ignoring them as I walk across the yard. I do yoga at dawn then retrieve my chair from the yard. After breakfast I sit near the doorway to get as much light and ventilation as possible.

The guards who call in regularly to preen themselves in the mirror start hiding personal things in the cupboard and under the bed. Body butter is popular – the smellier the better. They sit and rub it over their bodies in front of me. If one has a pot, the others search it out. Sayid even brings in a small suitcase, in which he keeps spare clothing. On-watch they wear the traditional T-shirt and *ma'awiis*. Off-watch they dress Western-style. Haji Selbai keeps a close eye on me during his watch, always on the scrounge for things. Buggas checks on me once a day, if only a furtive glance into my room. Sometimes he comes in, strutting with his pistol in hand, barking questions about how I'm feeling and whether I'm eating. I say as little as I can. Since the beating I think of him only as a disgusting thug, evil to the core. I know he's looking to goad me, and I don't want to give him the opportunity. He is desperate for money, and he'll do anything for it. I imagine that he blames us for not being rich. He must be cursing his bad luck.

So very lonely. Silly hopes of something happening dashed. Dearest Paul, I love you lots. Dear Stephen, Sarah, Pa, Jill and all, we love you dearly too.

17.50. Congratulations on getting through another bad day. Just keep GOING.

Tuesday, 2 February

I'm very restless, lonely and unhappy. I pace up and down my room, just 20 paces each round, sometimes swatting the flies as I go. I talk to myself and the big fat gecko that lives on the wall just below the roof. It never moves. I desperately try to devise new forms of distraction. It's too hot to do yoga except at dawn. I've read all my books; I'm rationing the crosswords. In the afternoon I use cotton wool in my ears to dull the sounds of the yard. In the evening I take pleasure in killing a cockroach that dares to emerge from the toilet hole.

Reflect on abandoning Lynn Rival – end of dream. Grief sets in. Our lives will never be the same, if we have any left.

Reflect on becoming a public spectacle – what effect on family + friends? Hard to comprehend. Video 1 – humiliating + repulsive. ITN interview – more public exposure of our private lives. Doctor video – more humiliation, resorting to begging.

Is this one of the most public kidnap situations ever? Extent of publicity demonstrates what? Kidnappers' determination to make as much money as poss. They're used to getting what they want through intimidation. They don't understand. They're like children. It's not just Buggas, judging by the argument over doctor visit. They've all 'spent' the money they expect to get from us, having been told by Buggas in the first place that we're easy money. They will lose faith in him if they don't get what he promised. He faces a difficult climb-down. Can Ali sort this out?

Wednesday, 3 February

11.50 a.m. Thinking about the humiliation. Self-pity and begging is not attractive. Can I ever regain my dignity and strength?

3 p.m. Hanging on. At times it feels as if I'm hanging on to my sanity by a thread. The mid afternoon clammy heat in this airless room is stifling. When will it end?

As another week passes I become more and more depressed. The 'feel-good factor' of speaking to Paul wears off, and the daily struggle to occupy myself and ignore their taunts grinds me down. I want to know what's going on. I hate these cruel people. I'm angry and frustrated. I can see no end. Small problems irritate me: constipation and boils. What else is there to worry about?

Thursday, 4 February

What next? All I know is Stephen is trying to raise 500k, and P? Our 130k on top +? What will the handover arrangements be? How will we be delivered?

Starting to think about the next life. Is that confidence or what? The last few days have been so quiet + B less threatening. Is it just another calm before a . . . Should I think of starting our new life? Hard to know where to begin because the last one has not quite been extinguished! Love you, P. Everything is in the air. Not how we like it to be. Too many unknowns.

Friday, 5 February

3 p.m. Feeling very strange today. Am I going mad? Finding it hard to concentrate though eating what they give me. Don't feel I'm losing weight, but maybe lacking vitamins? Love you, P, and everyone out there in the real world.

Saturday, 6 February

No breakfast so far tho' saw signs of fresh meat and smelt bread earlier. Walk the walk around the room a few times. Good to be without indigestible bread. A lot of machine gun fire this morning. When will it all end?

Things to do when I'm free:

- Tidy up our former life. Thank everyone. Catch up on news
- Research Somalia, Google Earth, geography, politics, history, language
- Listen to music again. Learn to play an instrument. Learn to sing again
- Use library, free resources, recycle, etc.
- Make/sell things: market stall, car boot?
- Write, create, invent, knit!
- Do yoga every day. Find a way of being positive + staying so (w/o drugs, alcohol, etc!) Focus, don't drift
- Join in activities, live life to full.
- Put family and friends first. All those who've done so much to help
- Re-write my CV!

Dear Paul,

Five days since I spoke to you. Seems longer. Hope we can speak soon. Did you get Vit C tablets? Are you drinking milk powder, with added vitamins? Problem of no exercise. Pacing room is not enough! Love you.

Sunday, 7 February

My all-time favourite piece of music? Carmina Burana? More appropriate: 'I'm Going Slightly Mad' – Freddie Mercury.

11.40 a.m. Must think of positive things that can come out of this. We can help the authorities track down these criminals to understand how they operate, to galvanise international cooperation on action and determination to crack down on these people and bring them to justice, to restore proper law + order in Somalia, through legitimate government and aid.

We had a dream. And it came to a sticky end. How are you doing, my love? I wish I knew. How will it be when we meet again? So much to catch up on.

5 p.m. Who are these ruthless people who've imprisoned us for so long? Buggas: pirate gang leader and 'boss' of local militia. Typical gang leader? Shouts a lot for control. Knows how to intimidate w/o physical force (usually). Not esp large, but big shoulders. Flabby? Single-minded. Cunning, but not esp clever? Suspicious. Inveterate liar. Probably early 30s. Likes to dress up and show off. Thinks he's clever but has doubts. Really has inferiority complex. Omar: so-called 'translator' but English is poor. Pretends to be good guy but really a villain. Better educated. From Mogadishu. Are translators the Mr Bigs in this? Says Buggas has no elders, but B not organised so who looks after things, like the money? How does it get distributed?

Monday, 8 February

'English speak today, *insha'allah*,' says Samata. Perhaps a call from Ali?

A phone is thrust into my hand after breakfast. It's a

man from Somali TV UK. He asks how I am. I tell him the usual – physically OK but tormented, lonely, worried – and that I've not spoken to Paul for eight days. He's not allowed to say any more. The phone call lifts my spirits. As ever, I wonder about its purpose and what difference it will make, but the mere chance to speak to someone from the outside world gives me hope.

Buggas rarely comes to speak to me. The guards come and go, bored. When I ask about Paul, they ignore me or say, 'No Paul.' Fat Mohamed tries to tell me he's 400 km away, but I hold on to the hope that he's nearby. Ali Yeri and Hamad are attentive, asking about money and family. They surprise me by saying, 'London. Rachel, Paul, Hamad, Ali.' They want to come to London with us.

In the run-up to 14 February – our wedding anniversary – I'm once again fighting despair. We should be together. It's more than two weeks since I spoke to Stephen. Surely something must be happening?

Tuesday, 9 February

Pacing up and down in my stuffy room, talking to myself. What to make of latest 'interview'? Presumably Stephen and Ali still struggling to find solution. Thinking about my mental health. It changes from hour to hour. Have to keep thinking of P and everyone out there. Phone calls help even if people are just saying 'We're doing everything we can'. Why are these people so evil? What will happen next? Our lives are in their hands. We can do nothing but wait + listen to the gunshots, goats and chickens. Love you, Paul. Always will, whatever happens.

Wednesday, 10 February

Another long morning. 12.30 only . . . Sweaty. Pacing room, wishing away time. Started x-word too early. Finding Gribben hard – 20th-century stuff. When will it end?

3.30 p.m. Struggling. Feeling so depressed. No end in sight. Little Ali keeps standing and staring. Flies everywhere. Must be +ve.

Thursday, 11 February

How I wish to be out of here. BUT not at any cost. I don't want them to get a penny; but rescue now seems unlikely so what option do we have?

These wicked people have got it all worked out. Our family can sell their houses! We can borrow the money + get jobs to pay it back! How I hate them all, the smug, self-conceited b*****ds! Must maintain my dignity and not swear!

Friday, 12 February

I haven't given up hope of rescue/release without paying these awful people money, but it is a slim hope as is the hope that they will eventually be brought to account. I still struggle with the idea that we will be free but penniless and owing a lot of money all because of thieves. I shall not rest knowing that they have gained from us + will be continuing their evil ways in the future.

Dearest Paul, I love you lots + lots, and always will but I'm feeling very suicidal now and don't know how long I can carry on. I keep telling myself to give it another week but as the weeks go by it gets harder + harder. It's only three days since I spoke to Somali UK man, but it seems like a lifetime. Be strong without me. I'll always love you. R XXX

Saturday, 13 February

10 a.m. In limbo. I have to keep telling myself there's nothing I can do but wait. Whatever happens, there's a world out there with so much to do in it. Infinitely more than anyone can do in a lifetime. We will survive, if only subsist.

Buggas visits. The men have run out of shampoo, and I've told them I have none. Cunningly, they tell Buggas I need shampoo and he comes to quiz me. I confirm and beg to speak to Paul, expecting a rebuff. To my astonishment, he says, 'Tomorrow, Sunday, free day for Christa.' I have hope . . .

Sunday, 14 February

It's our 29th wedding anniversary.

Dear P, Can't wait to speak to you, assuming B keeps his promise. Can't help wondering what else might happen. Why has he decided we can speak now? As ever, we must be prepared for the worst. Can't say 'Happy Anniversary' because it's a reminder of all we've lost, the life that's gone + will never return, short of a miracle. We had a good life together so I'm still OK to face death if need be. Anything could happen + nothing is certain. We have to die sometime. Love you always.

True to Buggas's word for a change, I get a call. Paul sounds OK. He's struggling but hanging on. He says he's heard nothing since speaking to Stephen. Buggas has told him Ali is coming to visit any day and something about a minister in Nairobi. Despite the lack of information I'm boosted by the call. Our captors are still clutching at straws, and we must hope they tire of us soon. At least Paul is OK.

Samata brings me a piece of watermelon. Not very ripe but appreciated. How long since I've had any vitamin C?

For a few days I'm more relaxed, even enjoying a 'banter' with the guards. Samata wants to know how I colour my hair. He tells me in Somalia it's the men who dye their grey hair red. I tease him about all the preening and frequent applications of body butter, saying in Britain it's the women who do that. Haji Selbai is always asking for my body lotion, which he's seen me apply. He thinks it makes my skin white. When I give him some, he's disappointed that it doesn't work. The others laugh at his naivety. Fat Mohamed tries to scrounge biscuits, and I tease him about his paunch. The others say '*banjo* [fat]!'

Wednesday, 17 February

8.30 a.m. Pacing the room, 20 short ones. What to do next? Thinking about God and religion, and criminality, and fanaticism. What are the links, if any? If we didn't have religion, would there be more or less criminality, fanaticism, etc? What defines religion? Can anyone be religion-free?

Trying not to feel suicidal. If we get out, how will we ever describe what we've been through? The feeling of total helplessness, of frustration at being held by such callous people, the fear of their casual, easy-come, easy-go attitude and its consequences, the problem of communicating with uneducated thugs who have no powers of reason?

The Commander arrives as I'm sitting in my chair whiling away the time before bed. He hands me a phone and a man immediately asks how I am. I don't recognise him, so demand to know who he is. He replies, 'Mohamed from the Somali parliament,' and continues:

Mohamed: *How is your condition?*
Rachel: *I'm lonely, separated from my husband and don't know what's going on.*
Mohamed: *How is your condition?*
Rachel: *I'm physically OK but mentally unstable.*
Mohamed: *Do you have a complaint?*
Rachel: *Of course, I'm a hostage!*

Translator Ali butts in and cuts me off. The Commander takes the phone and leaves. I ponder the strange call, savouring the brief contact with civilisation.

Thursday, 18 February

Hoping for a miracle. Woke up depressed as usual but now managing to tell myself it's still possible some kind rich person may come to our rescue. Hang on, P. We'll find a way to come to terms with all that's happened, but it will take time. I guess it'll take the rest of our lives.

The heat and humidity is draining. I make myself a fan from a piece of cardboard packing case. It doubles as a fly-swatter. I walk up and down fanning myself to try to keep cool. If I lie on the bed, I'm soon drenched in sweat. I lie on my towel and use a cloth soaked in water to sponge my forehead, arms and chest. In the late afternoon I sit in the doorway, where there's often a little breeze. The men wash themselves frequently in the yard, splashing copious amounts of water over their faces, arms and legs. In the evening I put my mattress in the doorway and lie there until midnight, waiting for the humidity to drop.

Some days I hear unusual sounds. Through the crack beside the vent I spy a handcart going by. Its screeching wheel needs oiling. Another time I see a number of carts, piled high with brushwood, being pulled along by braying asses. Are they going to repair a roof or make a new fence? Often I hear children playing outside, and I watch them running along, trailing carts made from plastic oil containers cut in two with a piece of string attached. I don't know what they have inside, maybe just stones, but they race along having fun.

From the doorway I can see a mobile-phone mast – the only sign of modern technology in the village. And through the houses I can make out lorries passing on the track 100 yards away. Sometimes I see people sitting on top. The lorries must double up as public transport. Closer by there's a big goat pen and sometimes women there stand on something so they can look over our fence. They wave at me, sitting in the doorway, fascinated to see a white woman. But how sad they don't feel any shame for what is happening to me! Do they expect me to wave back? Perhaps they think I'm visiting under my own free will! I just look at them and feel despair.

Friday, 19 February

Ali Yeri, Hamad and HSB are frequent visitors. Today there is a mood of optimism in the air and they say, 'Twenty *malmod*, Rachel, Paul, Nairobi.' They want to come too! I've already told HSB that he can't be my second husband and suggested he comes as my 'baby', since he doesn't understand the word 'son'. Now we have three would-be 'babies'.

I try not to make anything of the mention of 20 days, but when Buggas comes later I muster the strength to ask to speak to Paul again. He mentions Sunday.

Birds in yard today. So nice to see some wildlife.

Saturday, 20 February

Hot sweaty day again. Guards all silly. Fed up of their stupid banter. So very, very lonely without you, my love. How many tears have I shed in the last four months? Enough for a lifetime, I think.

Buggas tells me Ali will come 'tomorrow, this evening'. I'm excited but fearful. What news will he bring? Bad or very bad? I've lost hope of release without payment.

Sunday, 21 February

Got carried away last night + imagined you were already gone + I would be going today. Didn't happen of course!

I'm on tenterhooks but no phone call to Paul, no visit from Ali. The guards say nothing. I'm dispirited again and afraid to go into the yard. I listen to their shouting and phone calls, but nothing makes sense. I find hope, then lose it, all in a few minutes. I hear gunshots and hope for rescue. How can I be rescued from a village where there are so many innocent people around?

Monday, 22 February

Four whole months. I should have known not to trust that cruel man when he said I'd be able to speak to you. We know these people are beyond comprehension. He enjoys the power he has over us + our discomfort. There is nothing we can do, but keep strong with our love. They don't understand love, only money.

Tuesday, 23 February

My watch says 6 a.m. when I wake, but the sun is well up. The battery must be running out. How will I manage without it? My coping routine depends on checking off the hours and doing certain things at certain times and not before. Crossword at midday, wash at 4.30, etc. I will be lost! HSB comes in. He has a ladies watch on his wrist. Stolen from somewhere? It's showing half an hour ahead of mine, confirming my fears. I show him my useless watch and say, 'Problem.' He smiles and offers me 'his' watch. Easy come, easy go.

Buggas comes with new provisions. I'm always downhearted when I see these deliveries – a sign that we're not going anywhere soon. When I think about Paul, I worry that something has happened to him. Why have I not been allowed to speak to him? I pace up and down, talking to myself, sounding like Golom in *Lord of the Rings*, only my mantra is 'freedom' not 'precious'. I am angry and frustrated. I need new ideas to occupy myself, to pass the time. I have read all the books twice over. The big fat gecko just sits there when I talk to it. I resolve to ask for a radio when I next speak to Ali. I wish I had my MP3 player. I crave music to drown everything out: the gang, the village, Somalia, everything. I sing as I pace, strong music, but I can't remember the words to many songs. 'God Save the Queen', 'Jerusalem', 'The Marseillaise', 'Swing Low Sweet Chariot'. I wish I had a strong voice. The gangsters think I'm crazy. I don't care. I hate hearing the call to prayer, reminding me of where I am and the hypocrisy of these people. I want to retaliate, and I recite the Lord's Prayer over and over again as I pace up and down my room. Forgive them their trespasses indeed! I'm no longer religious, but the familiar ritual helps dissipate my anger.

Wednesday, 24 February

Whenever a guard visits, I ask to speak to Paul. They just say, 'Tomorrow, Buggas' or 'Two *malmod*' or 'Tomorrow *insha'allah*'. Liars. I refuse my food. They laugh amongst themselves.

Thursday, 25 February

I must speak to Paul! Going mad last night worrying that P must be dead. Something happened Sat? Why did B mention Ali on Sat and why has he not spoken to me since? Even praying to God, who I don't believe in. Any god will do, but let me know that P is OK. Right?

Friday, 26 February

Suicidal. Lie around feeling dead. No hope. Want to end it all. Sorry, Paul, I know you are stronger. I'm finished. Sick, sick, sick of these vile people, laughing, joking, arguing at our expense. What did we do to deserve this fate? Suicide is justified. I need to be in peace and I will have peace.

Buggas comes but doesn't say anything to me, so I go in the yard and plead. He barks, 'Wait Ali, three days.' I am at the end of my tether. My only option is to kill myself. At least they wouldn't get any money from me. I have a razor blade. It would be easy to take some painkillers and cut my wrists when I go to bed. They would find me dead in a pool of blood in the morning. I would love to see the look on their faces!

But of course I wouldn't be able to. Am I stupid enough to do it simply to spite these gangsters? No. I couldn't do it to Paul, to Stephen, to everyone. I must stay strong.

One day Oman comes to preen and says, 'Paul good' and 'London 14 *malmod*'. He tells me to be happy and says that Buggas is a 'fucker' and a 'big thief'. Where did he learn such language? I remind myself of something that I thought of early on: it will be hard towards the end when they realise they won't make millions out of us. Some of them are bound to get nastier and pettier. Are we are getting near the end?

Tuesday, 2 March

At last I'm handed a phone. Can it be Paul or news of our release? No. It's Steven the negotiator. He says progress has been slow, but I must maintain hope. They've had 'difficulty' getting through. Apparently I was on TV last night, something to do with Nairobi. This is a mystery, as I've not spoken to anyone for two weeks. Steven asks whether I have tried persuading the gang to lower their expectations! I say it's impossible to communicate with them.

Another confusing call. What is Ali up to?

Wednesday, 3 March

The next day a phone is thrust into my hand again. I'm confused and don't recognise Stephen at first.

Stephen: *Hello, Rachel. How are you?*
Rachel: *Oh, hello. I'm very hot because it's the middle of the day.*
Stephen: *Yes, are you being fed properly?*
Rachel: *Everybody asks me that. They give me food three*

times a day and they give me water . . . I don't have any fruit so I don't get much vitamin C, but other than that . . . they're not being nasty to me.

Stephen: *We are making progress, Rachel . . . but it is slow.*

Rachel: *I do appreciate everything you're trying to do.*

Stephen: *Who rang you last night? Do you know?*

Rachel: *I spoke to Steven, the lawyer.*

Stephen: *Did you? Right, fine. Now the trouble is, Ali thinks a lot of these other people who are calling him will give him money. We know that lots of people are calling you, and it's causing problems because Ali thinks he can get more money from them . . .*

Rachel: *I've not had lots of phone calls. Before last night, the only phone call I had was from a member of the Somali parliament and that was two weeks ago.*

Stephen: *Right, now, are you together now, you and Paul?*

Rachel: *No, and I haven't spoken to Paul for, uh, almost three weeks.*

Stephen: *Oh. We believe that he's fine . . . Be as strong as you can and don't give up hope, Rachel. We're all waiting for you.*

Rachel: *Yes, I know, I know you're doing your best and . . . please try to speak to Paul and make sure he's OK, because I know he won't be able to see now because his contact lens fluid will have run out. He can't wear glasses, and he won't be able to read or do anything.*

Stephen: *Yes, I know people have attempted to get lens fluid to him . . . Now we're working hard to make a deal with the pirates, but they keep changing their demands and it's very hard to trust them.*

Rachel: *Of course, I know, and I do understand because they have very unrealistic expectations.*

Stephen: *That's right. We've got to be careful – we need to make a deal that will stick with them.*

Rachel: *I'm all on my own except for them. They mostly leave me alone. They come and look from time to time. I don't have any privacy of course, but they're not aggressive* *towards me. They're not threatening me – it's the boss who used to threaten, but he hasn't been threatening lately, he doesn't speak to me.*

Stephen: *That must be awful. Have you got anything to read?*

Rachel: *I'm re-reading a lot. I asked Ali yesterday if I could have a radio. A radio would be nice – I could listen to the English World Service. The guards have a radio and they listen to the Somali BBC.*

Stephen: *I'll see what I can do with Ali. He's not a bad guy. He's a nice chap but, um, it's difficult because he is obviously working with the others behind him and, until we can persuade them that it's only me who can make a deal, we won't get anywhere.*

Stephen tries to be reassuring, but he's obviously demoralised. I don't know how anyone can deal with criminals. The minute you offer them anything, there is nothing to stop them asking for more, and more, and more. I dread to think what Stephen must be going through.

Oman asks about 'news'. When I say, 'Money big problem,' he replies, 'Stephen big problem.' I try to explain that he's my brother, a farmer, not a big businessman. Oman says, 'Family house money. Somali diaspora money.' Where did he get that from? It's so depressing that they have been fed this nonsense and are so gullible, so easily depraved.

I'm given a radio and a new world opens up to me. Happiness is . . . listening to *Focus on Africa* on the BBC World Service. It's so good to hear English spoken, so reassuring to hear news of the outside world. I keep the radio close to my ear so it drowns out the gangsters' noise. I spend days searching all the frequencies, noting down the schedule. I find Radio France International and Voice of America as well as other English-speaking channels. Bliss.

Thursday, 4 March

Dear Stephen, once again so much we couldn't say, but I hope I made it clear how much we appreciate EVERYTHING you are doing. I wouldn't blame you for walking away from this situation. Why should you put up with it?

Heard on RFI this morning that another tanker, Greek flagged, with 14 crew, has been hijacked in Gulf of Aden. How depressing is that?

Mid afternoon, dozing in the doorway, I sense that something is happening. My guards start getting the weapons out, shouting and milling around the yard, coming and going through the gate. The machine guns and RPG launcher are stationed outside my hut. Some of the gang rush off with guns and spare magazines in hand. Mr F turns up and joins the few remaining in the yard. They sit tensely and chatter nervously amongst themselves. I hear sounds of fighting in the distance: lots of gunfire and even mortars. There are some shots fired nearby. It sounds like quite a battle. What is going on? I feel frightened and worry for Paul. Should I be excited about a possible rescue attempt?

No one says anything to me. After an hour or so, the sounds of fighting subside. HSB comes back with blood on his shoulder. Is he wounded? He takes off his shirt and washes off the blood. Only surface wounds. I suspect he was responsible for the local gunfire and is so incompetent that he's caught the recoil! The gang are subdued, preoccupied and melancholy.

Friday, 5 March

Occasional gunfire during the morning, then more in the afternoon. I'm on edge, but the guards are relaxed. I keep reminding myself that they need to keep us alive and they want rid of us as soon as possible. Fat Mohamed helps me get water, joking that I might fall down the well. I ask about Paul, but they ignore me. HSB brings an old man to look at me. I hate being on show, especially to this creepy old man. I cower and hope he will soon get bored of looking at me, which he does. On the radio, I hear about fighting in central Somalia, a clash between rival gangs, and 14 dead. Is that the fighting I heard yesterday? There is mention of elders intervening to resolve the dispute. What hope is there that they will intervene for us?

Saturday, 6 March

Over the last few days I've been trying not to think about my birthday. Paul and I are relaxed about celebrating them, depending on where we are. We rarely surprise each other with presents on the day. We like to have a celebratory meal but might postpone it until we are somewhere special. So today I convince myself that reaching 57 is no big deal. I get up and start pacing the room, trying not to think about my previous birthday, the day we arrived in the Maldives.

After breakfast Uday hands me his phone. It's Paul! He's OK, struggling with the heat, coping without more lens fluid and has enough reading for another ten days. He has compiled crosswords for me. Buggas has told him we'll be released in a week! His guards have said that Stephen is raising $1 million and the Somali community another $1 million. He also heard the fighting on Thursday, so we must be nearby! It's a long call, and we keep expecting to be cut off at any minute. We run out of things to say and start again. It's just wonderful to hear his voice, to hear that he's coping.

I sit in my chair and go over and over the call, trying to remember every line of conversation. My hope is restored: Paul is OK and surely we will be together soon. Despite the silly numbers talked about by the guards, time is running out. I've been thinking that if Buggas is a real pirate, he will want to go back to sea before the southwest winds set in. He's wasted a lot of time on us. If he wants to make big money this year, he will want to set out again in April. By then he will have spent six months failing to get what he wants. Surely he will decide to cut his losses soon? I'm hoping for release by the end of March . . .

My reverie is disturbed by a knock at the door. What on earth? Nobody has ever knocked on my door before. Equally formally, I say, 'Come in.' It's Ali Ad. I've not seen him for a long time. He politely hands me a small plastic bag and walks out again. It contains some notes from Paul and a Diana Gabaldon book! Amazing! 'Wait,' I cry, grabbing the empty plastic bag and Gribben's *Science* from my bag, before rushing out into the yard. Ali Ad is talking to some of my guards. I give him Gribben 'for Paul' and he leaves.

I read Paul's note: 'Be strong – every day is one day nearer release.' He has sent me his meticulous radio schedules – and two crosswords. Compiling them without a dictionary must have been difficult. I'm touched beyond belief and comforted by this sign of his resilience.

Later I hear a bad-tempered Buggas arrive, shouting a lot. When he's gone the men relax. HSB comes and reaffirms his 'baby' status. Obviously he thinks we'll soon be released. I bed down for the night in an optimistic mood. I think about Lynda and Helen, who share my birthday, and wonder what they are doing. March is a busy time for birthdays in our family. Can I hope to be home in time for any of them?

Sunday, 7 March

My spirits go up and down, usually low in the morning and brighter in the evening. Sometimes the sweltering humidity is relieved by gusty winds, blowing debris around in the yard. The gangsters are untidy, dropping litter everywhere. It ends up in the well, but they don't care. I suggest to Samata they should clear up. He indicates that it's women's work.

4 p.m. Feeling low again. Can't find strength to start P's x-word. Afraid it will be a long time before I see him again. Afraid of next development. Hard to believe there won't be more pain to go through. Must be prepared. (Let myself go a bit yesterday!)

I listen to my radio, especially when Buggas is here. I cheer up on hearing about the capture of a gang of pirates.

Monday, 8 March

Every time someone's mobile rings, I wonder is it relevant? What are they talking about? Is something happening? Ditto, every time there's a heated discussion.

2 p.m. Thinking about the role of the media in our situation. Is it good practice for media to play into hands of criminals, be used by criminals to help further their cause? Was the interview with Angus for ITN a step too far, knowing that we were not free to say what we really thought? Or is it no different from a video that is taken by the captors + shown by the media? How much did Angus hold back because some questions could have been harmful for us to answer, e.g. over attempted rescues, role of the navy? How did Stephen + others view media coverage?

Tuesday, 9 March

Buggas dumps a cardboard box in front of me. It's already opened and contains a jumble of books, medicines, toiletries, a postcard saying 'Be strong' and a packing list headed Ecoterra Survival. I ask if Paul has seen it and Buggas grunts, 'Look.'

He wants me to examine the contents, so I check everything off the packing list one-by-one. Some things are missing, so I assume Paul has had first pick. I can't see any contact lens fluid but hope that's the point. Once Buggas has gone I take pleasure in examining everything. The toiletries are very welcome, as are the multivitamins.

I read all the instructions on the medicines, mentally noting what they are for. It's reassuring to have them just in case. Then I choose one of the books to read. I don't think I'm desperate enough to read *Bridget Jones's Diary*, so pick a biography of Robert Maxwell.

2.30 p.m. Thinking about what negotiations might be going on. So very angry that we are being used as pawns. It makes me feel so very sick and suicidal. I don't want them to get any money from us, or from anyone.

I console myself that if Buggas hadn't got us, he would have got someone else and probably have made more money in less time.

This evening I hear news of the Somali 'transitional' president's visit to the UK, including mention of the 'elderly British couple' held hostage by pirates and rumours of release in two weeks. I balk at being called elderly but decide it's appropriate in the circumstances. I can live with the label if it means release is close.

I know there is a 'Transitional Federal Government' in Somalia, but I don't pin hopes on it. When Stephen told us back in November that he was appealing to the prime minister, I was more inclined to believe Omar's subsequent statement: 'There is no government.' Am I wrong?

Thursday, 11 March

20 weeks! Feeling impatient. Radio reception problems too. Mood up and down, or down and more down, or coping and down. Trying to find a state of mind that copes with the idea that we'll be here at least another week.

Friday, 12 March

Mustn't forget to thank Ecoterra. Really appreciate soap, toilet rolls, vitamins. Listening more to Network Africa and RFI – both provide more interesting topics than mainstream World Service? Striving to develop new interests for the coming weeks . . . African affairs, esp Somalia, and culture, even football (!) a good distraction. News of renewed fighting, deaths and injuries in Mogadishu of concern. Can't help feeling desperate at times. When will this end? And, how will it end? What will they do with us? How will we be transported?

Saturday, 13 March

Strange night. Intense debate in yard and on mobiles. Frequent activity these days — washing guns and holders for machine-gun bullets. Flies galore! They get worse every day. Very depressed this p.m. Just heard a burst of heavy gunfire nearby, always unsettling. No one tells me what's going on.

I must find a way of distracting myself. I have a fertile mind. Why am I being so pathetic? Why do I think I'm so hard up? At least I'm alive.

I remember the 30 or so people killed during the Iraqi elections. How sad that they got just a passing mention on the news. So many people die needlessly every day.

Sunday, 14 March

Dear Paul, Longing to speak to you again. Feeling less depressed today. Perhaps because there's a mood of anticipation. Maybe something will happen soon? Surely they want rid of us now? Love you.

The radio and new book are a help but no substitute for Paul's company. I'm so desperate to know what's going on. The big fat gecko has no answers.

Monday, 15 March

Buggas comes and asks the usual, 'How you feel?'

I respond as ever with 'lonely' followed by a request to speak to Paul.

Smirking, he says, 'Where Paul?'

I feel so desperate that I say, 'I don't know. Please let me speak to him.' He turns away and stands in front of the mirror, preening himself. He's in a mean mood.

Monday morning blues. Renewed intimidation from Buggas. Shouldn't be a surprise, knowing what a psycho he is. Unsure, as ever, how to interpret current situation. I hope it's a sign that he is recognising defeat, that he does now want rid of us as soon as possible. I must 'be strong' and face the prospect of enduring at least two more weeks. Hope for sting/rescue! Don't let them have a penny.

A bit later Fat Mohamed asks me if I'm happy. I say I'm not, because Buggas won't let me speak to Paul. Fat Mohamed repeats his taunting suggestion that Paul is 400 km away. I tell him he's a liar. He continues, 'Somali diaspora, big money.' Goaded, I respond that they are refugees and have little money. HSB joins in with, 'Three million.' Fat Mohamed is greedier: 'Six million – diaspora, Sheikh Sharif [TFG president], Gordon Brown, Stephen.' I tell them they are crazy but wonder what nonsense they're being told to keep them thinking this way. Has translator Ali done nothing to dampen their expectations?

We're all on tenterhooks. I get angry when the guards talk about raising millions from us. I know it's just chat, but I find their cruelty hard to stomach. Their greed is overwhelming. How sad that some human beings are reduced to this.

10.10 a.m. Once again I've resigned myself to dying here. I can see no reasonable way out. No one back home is to blame. It's simply that these people are impossible, including 'friendly' Ali, who is just leading them on. I can see now that his pretence at persuading Buggas to be realistic was just that. Of course Ali is on commission and they are all well experienced at playing this game of 'easy money'. They have nothing to lose, other than their lives. I don't know how long I can carry on but I'm resigned to death and know that I will be at peace in death. No one should feel sad, just remember the good times, love and happiness we've shared. Love you all. xxxx

Later. Turning anger into hope. Decide to live in hope that $2 million target reported by Paul last week is still a possibility, though where the money will come from is anyone's guess. Must not worry about moral implications, perhaps we'll be able to help identify + capture these villains. Thank goodness the French and German warships are on to them.

I remind myself that people are working hard to get us out. Ali will turn up soon to tell us it's all sorted. When is Easter, I wonder? Will we be home then? How nice it will be to have a game of Scrabble with Paul's father.

Tuesday, 16 March

Last night's radio report of an agreement between Somali TFG + Ahlu Sunna Wal Jam'a (a militia group with influence in central Somalia) has got my hopes up! But . . . another strange and troubling day, not helped by too much hope/expectation of good outcome from news of TFG/ASWJ accord. So frustrating not knowing what they are talking about and whether it is relevant.

Wednesday, 17 March

How are you, P, and what do you think of the latest non-developments, I wonder? My pipe dream yesterday burst with the usual bang. Silly to get excited when I don't know whether this ASWJ agreement will help us at all. More deliveries to yard confirms we won't be leaving tomorrow. I'm suffering a bit from IBS so must stop eating bread!

Thursday, 18 March

I've run out of batteries and am missing the radio. I use my torch batteries for the news, but I don't want the guards to know. They no longer have a radio so borrow mine. They always have it on full volume, using the batteries up in no time.

Five p.m. Out of the blue comes a call from Paul! It's a terrible line, and we're soon told to finish. We discuss the mysterious parcel. He knows no more about it than I, and it didn't contain contact lens fluid, so he's struggling. Buggas has told him they're expecting Sheikh Sharif to help us, but he's had no other news from the outside world.

Friday, 19 March

Feeling confident of political solution soon. Beginning to dream again of what might be: return to UK and re-building our lives. Can't wait to get back to the cold! Ha ha.

When I ask for batteries I'm told, 'No money.' Sayid comes and demands '*trrup*', wanting my playing cards, which they like to borrow. I respond, 'No batteries. No *trrup*.' He looks affronted but goes away. I make a point of playing Patience all morning. The cards are in use. In the afternoon, Sayid comes with two batteries and holds out his hand. Happily, I give him the cards.

Buggas comes and says, 'Yesterday, speak Paul.'

What do I say to this statement of fact? 'Yes. Thank you.'

He seems to ponder my response, then leaves. His demeanour is almost civil. I'm worried. Surely if the end is near he would be angry, pissed off? It's probably the *chad*.

Saturday, 20 March

The yard is busy and it's hair-cutting time for some of the gangsters. I sit in the doorway hoping for a breeze. Haji Selbai comes up to me and rants, 'No money. Give me 20 *senna*.' For a small man he has a very loud, deep voice. I don't know what *senna* means but gather he is unhappy. I ask about Sheikh Sharif and he snorts, 'Five hundred. No money. Fucking Stephen. No money. Somali people hungry, no food.'

I'm furious when they talk about Stephen like that. It reminds me of what he must be going through, but I bite my tongue and say, 'Me old lady, Stephen old man, what can I do?'

Oman comes into the yard in a bad mood. He comes close to where I'm sitting and talks loudly and pointedly to the others, all the time looking at me, threateningly. I sense he wants to hit me but knows he can't. Hamoud, who normally keeps his distance, stares at me. Later, when I'm sitting on my mattress in the doorway, he comes up and shouts, 'Money, money! Dollar, dollar!'

I repeat, 'No money.' I'm uncomfortable but not threatened by this behaviour. They are behaving like pathetic children who can't get what they want. Dare I hope that some realism is creeping in?

Tuesday, 23 March

We've been captive for five months. The guards keep their distance, but I'm being well fed, often with nice and tender meat on the bone. I have no one to talk to but the gecko, a couple of doves, flies galore and the occasional cockroach at night.

I've found proper earplugs from *Lynn Rival*'s first-aid kit. When I'm not listening to the radio, they're blissfully effective at shutting out the irritating chatter of the guards. They stop me speculating or worrying about what they're talking about.

I am glad they're not happy – and not getting what they want.

Wednesday, 24 March

Oman comes in to preen, then points to the bone I'm

gnawing and asks for the English word, telling me the Somali in exchange. HSB comes in while I'm lying down and announces that he's my 'friend'. He takes my cardboard fan and flaps it furiously for a short while. The Commander comes for a visit and the gangsters are calmer afterwards. Then Ali Yeri turns up. I've not seen him for a while. He stands and stares, then whispers, 'Look, Paul, *insha'allah.*' Samata also says something to get my hopes up, but HSB sticks to his standard 'Twenty *malmod*'.

I must ignore them, but it's hard not to clutch at straws. The big fat gecko moves tentatively down the wall, scurries along the floor and disappears. It's the first time I've seen it move. Is this an omen?

Thursday, 25 March

My anxiety rises again. We're all bored and waiting for the end. The men play cards and listen to the radio. Sometimes they have *chad* but not every day. When Buggas turns up with more supplies I tell myself it's only another week's worth. When I ask for *Omo* and Sayid gives me enough for a month, I know they'll soon run out and be taking it back! When HSB rambles on about Paul, money, Sheikh Sharif and so on, I tell myself to ignore him. The others are often moody and miserable. Surely that's a good sign? This can't go on for much longer.

Friday, 26 March

Auntie May's birthday. Just another miserable Friday here. Trying to be patient. And philosophical.

Miss you so much, my love. I just want to hold you tight. I don't think I'll ever want to let you go. These people are so wrapped up in themselves. They simply don't understand how cruel they are being to us. Those that perhaps do, presumably enjoy it.

Sunday, 28 March

9.30 a.m. Lying on bed listening to tribute repeat of Charlie Gillet's World Music playing 'Seven Seconds' (I'll be Waiting – poignant lyrics!), Youssou N'Dour and Neneh Cherry's hit single, tears running down the sides of my face.

Monday, 29 March

10 a.m. Feeling so depressed. Don't know what to do with myself. Mornings are always bad: so sweaty and frustrating, knowing I have so many hours ahead to kill before dark. Last night I heard news of another lot of pirates being thwarted in their 'expedition': a Dutch warship chased them + they dumped their arms. Long may the warships keep up the good work and eliminate the lot of them! Meanwhile B + Co. go on and on, but must keep hope that President Sharif will prevail and find solution. Every day here is one more day that they don't get any money from us!

4 p.m. Got my act together, convincing myself it's just a matter of time!

Tuesday, 30 March

10.30 a.m. Twelve weeks without you, my love. How will we ever catch up? Heard on radio last night that pirates had captured ship just 20 nm off Aden. Oh dear!

2.30 p.m. Reading depressing part of Fiery X: battle with regulators. It doesn't help my mood. Must keep finding nice things to think about. Springtime in UK?

3.45 p.m. Have to keep convincing myself that these goons really don't want to keep going, day in, day out, for weeks and months more, without the prospect of more money on the table. And surely the possibility that one or both of us will fall ill must be a concern?

Wednesday, 31 March

End of March! Get through morning OK. HSB just came

to see me + said confusing things about Paul, Somalia, London, money, Sharif, finish, etc. Assume he was having another go (as my 'friend') at taunting me. Problem is, he's got my hopes up again.

Thursday, 1 April

The men are behaving strangely. Ignoring my requests for more bottled water and batteries is not unusual, but to have groups of them coming into my room for quiet discussions is odd. I hear muted discussions going on in their hut too. Unsettling, or am I being paranoid? They're 'on alert' and snarl at me when I venture out to the loo.

5 p.m. What a day! So much argument, presumably over our release (or not) terms. Hostility from some; kindness from others. Never know who is on which side. Quieter now. They've calmed down + are playing cards. Feeling surprisingly 'resigned'. At least something must be happening?

Friday, 2 April

The gangsters are notably relaxed today. HSB comes in early and says 'London' and 'Paul' in the nasal voice he produces – feigning a conspiratorial kinship with me – when not at full volume. Samata comes in with his mobile phone, sits in my chair and proceeds to show me footage from the film *Black Hawk Down*. Others come and go, amused that Samata is entertaining me. Out of the blue, Samata says, 'Paul, here, two days *insha'allah*.'

I allow myself to become a little bit optimistic. In the afternoon, something even stranger happens. Oman takes my chair and tells me to follow him into their hut, where he puts it down and tells me to sit! It's cooler in their traditional brushwood hut, so I perch there watching him and Sayid play cards. Despite the cool, I'm not comfortable, and when they start saying their prayers I leave. I'm glad I did, because Buggas comes shortly afterwards and shouts at them for half an hour. At dusk, Buggas returns and tells me Paul will come here 'after this evening'. Like the others who are hanging around, he looks expectant of a reaction. I find it hard to believe. I'm so afraid of being disappointed, and quietly say, 'Thank you.'

Six-thirty p.m. A vehicle arrives, the gate opens and there is Paul.

I hardly see Buggas and the rest of the gang bustling in as well . . . All I take in is the sight of Paul walking across the yard towards me. He looks so much older and thinner, but his engaging smile tells me he's still the same Paul. We hug chastely in front of our audience. Buggas seems almost human as he demands, 'Happy?'

'Yes! We are.' We hurriedly reorganise my bedding to make room for Paul's and then sit out in the yard and catch up on each other's ordeals. We race to talk about and share our experiences but are guarded about discussing our hopes for release. After all, the yard is full of gangsters and we never know how much they understand. At least they are in good humour.

Whilst we were apart, I sometimes worried about how reunion would feel. Would our long separation and different experiences be difficult to come to terms with? We are so unused to being apart. At reunion all that matters is: we're together and we survived!

Unbeknownst to
Paul and Rachel . . .

Sunday, 14 February, London

It's Paul and Rachel's wedding anniversary and, coincidentally, the date on which prominent Somali organisations in London hold a 'Release Paul and Rachel' demonstration in Camden.

The Somali community, keenly feeling the stigma on their national identity caused by the pirates, rally to try to bring about an end to the Chandler's ordeal. More than 1,000 people attend the emotionally charged event. Speaker after speaker declares the pirates' actions to be against all the moral and religious codes of the Somali people and calls for the elders in the community of Harardheere, one of the pirates' strongholds, to 'stand tall in their leadership roles' and influence the pirates to release the couple without further delay.

The demo fuelled further outrage among the Somali community of all generations. Yusuf Kadiye came home from school in East London and appealed to his father Dahir, a Somali-born businessman who had brought his family to live in the United Kingdom in 1997. 'Dad, I can't play football with my mates at school any more. I feel such shame. Why don't you go out there and do something?'

On 25 February Dahir, who belongs to the same clan as the pirates and knows the region well, responded to the teenager's plea and flew first to Nairobi, then Mogadishu, to re-establish links and see what he could do . . .

False hopes

Friday, 2 April continued

We talk, and hug discreetly, for hours. We have much to catch up on, and then we wonder, and hope, about the immediate future. The gangsters leave us in peace that night and the next day. Only Ali Yeri enquires – as soon as Rachel has gone out to the privy – 'How many? *Habeen* [the night]?' His gestures make it clear that he is asking about intimate matters!

The two 'sub-gangs' have combined, making the compound crowded, and it's difficult to find a free time to use the privy. I have to get to know the new faces. Rachel has names for them, which I find difficult to learn. Now Rachel and I can pass the time together, I feel no need to develop a rapport with them. I notice immediately that the men who have guarded her are aggressive, intrusive and unfeeling. They come in to the house frequently and stare at their reflections in the mirror, preening themselves like teenagers. These men form the bulk of the evening sit-arounds, when Buggas and Omar join in for a couple of hours, sitting outside our doorway. Omar, stripped of translator duties, seems to have become part of the furniture. What can be going on?

Over the next few days we read each other's diaries and talk through what happened. It's uncomfortable to read and hear what pressure Paul was put under. He is such a kind and gentle person, not used to dealing with criminals, let alone kidnappers. I know it was easier for me.

Another thing I find unsettling is the relationship Paul has established with his guards. He seems almost to like them. He admires those who have some soldiering skills. He recounts unquestioningly some of the things they've told him about their lives, families and clan. I'm more inclined to think of them as thugs and be sceptical about anything they tell us. I could never feel any rapport with mine, none of whom show any compassion or shame for what they are doing to us.

Our reunion is surely a precursor to release? Buggas has always said we wouldn't be brought together until he gets the money he wants. Omar is here 'just visiting', he says, but I interpret it as another positive sign. No doubt he doesn't want to miss the payout! It can't be long now.

The gangsters are mostly good humoured. Paul's are relatively friendly and helpful. Mine are more demanding, but now we're together again I'm more assertive with them. When they clamour for the radio, I hand over our spare (we now have two between us). When they try to claim our playing cards, I refuse. It's our last pack and they're precious: a Detroit Red Wings souvenir, given to us by friends in America.

On our third afternoon together a skinny, young, loud-mouthed gangster comes through the doorway and yells, '*Trrup!*' He wants the playing cards. He stands over Rachel to intimidate, his demands becoming more aggressive. I ask him precisely which syllable of '*maia*' he doesn't understand. We all three have a shouting match. Deli comes over from the hut, pulls HSB – as Rachel calls him – from the doorway and pushes him away from us. A bad mood envelops the yard. Several of Rachel's guards are heckling; one storms up to harangue me.

'*Maia, maia, maia!*' I shout back.

Abbas joins Deli, and the two of them face down the nasty guys. It begins to sink in what a hard time Rachel has been having. I am sure there is more to the differing attitudes than the fact of Rachel's sex. Maybe there are two factions within the gang. I hope 'my' faction will stay around.

Omar is still here most days. One evening the Commander also appears while Omar sets up a short phone call from an officer in AMISOM, the African Union force supporting the TFG. I'm allowed only to confirm who I am and that we are both OK; he says that they will try to get us out. Omar explains that AMISOM are conferring with the president and the prime minister; this call is to establish that they're speaking to the right people. But surely things are going well? Perhaps AMISOM is getting involved in the practicalities of our release? We hope, and wait.

Thursday, 8 April

Translator Ali visits at last. We've not seen him since the end of January, but we consider him our lifeline, our hope of release. He's clearly a step above Omar and he understands our predicament, but he's elusive. We are utterly at his mercy. Unannounced, he saunters into the house and remarks that we look comfortable playing cards, then – in his distinctive rasping voice – informs us the negotiations have concluded. The money will be paid partly by the government and partly by Stephen. We'll be taken to the airport in a week!

I'm afraid to ask how much money. I both do and don't want to know how much we'll owe. I simply want to be happy that we'll soon regain our freedom, but I fret about what the future will hold. Smugly, Ali tells us not to sail near the Seychelles again. As if we could afford to now – without a boat and probably no savings left! He says the pirates are targeting those islands.

In the afternoon we have another confrontation over the playing cards. This time Ali Ad, with his loud, commanding voice, comes up close and shouts, '*Trrup!*' I refuse to hand them over. He is stunned, like a spoilt child used to getting his own way. Ali Yeri is sent in to threaten us with '*Maia cadu!*' (no lunch). I laugh and still refuse. Then – third attempt now – Ali Deri brings over a can of hot ashes and threatens to put a bullet in it. To blow up in my face? Momentarily I'm scared – Ali Deri, the 40-something-year-old father of four, who speaks a bit of English and sometimes calls me 'my sister' is, after all, a fighter, a sharp-shooter, a killer. The others pull him away. We shout, 'Get Buggas,' and they disperse. I let out my breath and sit down again. I win.

The next day Ali comes and again comments on how comfortable we look reading our books and listening to the radio. Worried that he thinks we're in no hurry to leave, I tell him every day is TORTURE. We would like to be home before the end of April, thank you very much! The weather continues to be extremely hot and sticky, making everyone irritable. We complain to Ali about the guards demanding our pack of playing cards. Later, Buggas and the gangsters play dominoes. Probably Ali bought them to help keep the peace. They play with great gusto, like ten year olds, squabbling over whose turn it is, but at least they're occupied.

On Saturday Ali is back to tell us that Stephen has raised '440' and the Somali government is 'contributing'. It's merely a matter of bringing it all together. He's expecting a call today.

I start pondering again the problem of the physical handover of a ransom for us. How will they get us out of here? We're not on a pirated ship, where the money is dropped and the pirates melt away into the background once they've counted the loot.

On the radio we hear about the impending UK election and the prospect of a change of regime. We're worried that whoever is advising the gang will clutch at another straw: the possibility of a change of UK government policy towards negotiating for our release.

The weather is the only notable event: overcast, with violent electric storms around, but no rain. When the rain does come, it pours down hard, but only for an hour – or even less – around lunchtime, and only for a few days. The freshness lasts an hour after each shower, and then the relentless humidity is back. The blustery wind soon returns, picking up the quickly dried sand and flinging it in our eyes. Paul gives up wearing lenses. He has to grope his way to the privy and, although he can see enough to play crib, reading is out of the question.

We exist, grumpily maintaining our routine. Rachel's fed up with eating stodgy bread and spaghetti, both of which make her constipated. She pleads with the cooks to give us rice but is rarely successful. They're all so bored, hanging around like us, waiting. They have their own daily routine, but it soon palls when there are no 'events' to amuse them. Buggas comes and goes, occasionally sitting down in our doorway for a loud, intimidating phone call. We suspect he's hearing bad news about us. The Commander still visits, but Omar has gone. The gangsters say the same old familiar things: Fat Mohamed with the occasional request for 'news?' followed up with the comment: 'Stephen problem!' Samata mutters about 'satellites, planes, militia', but with no great hostility.

The radio news is now full of the chaos being created by the volcanic ash cloud covering Europe, prompting concern about the problem of getting home.

Thursday, 22 April

Six months in captivity. We are patient, but the gangsters are restless again. They have a pow-wow in the evening, but Buggas is not here. Have negotiations fallen apart? We can do nothing; only enjoy watching the lightning as it circles around the village in the evening. Better than television!

We're all so bored with waiting. HSB rambles on about 'seven *bilod* [months]' and 'Sheikh Sharif three million dollar'. Samata says, 'Stephen, before, big money, yes. After, no.'

We go through the same old routine of trying to explain

that neither we nor Stephen have big money, but it's futile. We complain about being in prison, using the crossed-hands gesture for emphasis. Samata simply sneers, 'Rachel Paul together, every day food, no problem.'

Since reunion we've been less concerned about keeping ourselves occupied. We have each other to talk to, but now two weeks have gone by with no sign of Ali and no more news of our release. The gang's mood is more hostile. The men have broken the radio we gave them and demand our remaining one. Rachel hides it under her dress. Ali Yeri looks on in disgust. Clearly he doesn't want to handle it after it's been there! They back off but vent their anger by throwing stones at the tin roof above us and later, still peeved, they throw a stone over the top of the toilet cubicle, narrowly missing Rachel as she has her evening wash. It's unnerving, but we're determined not to give in.

We're finding it hard to remain optimistic and occupied. The crosswords are finished, and we haven't much mileage left in the extra books from the Ecoterra parcel. We only have one pen and worry about it running out. Paul is unable to wear his lenses, so can hardly see. An ear infection makes him miserable. Humid, thundery, wet weather continues, and when we ask about Ali we're told the rain is making driving difficult.

The Commander and Fat Boy are here, also Land Rover Man – a sign that some event might be imminent? They have abundant *chad* sessions and sometimes conspicuous group prayer sessions in the yard. Who are they trying to impress? There's also another regular visitor, an older grey-bearded man, wearing sunglasses. Is he important?

Tuesday, 27 April

I look out of the doorway and see a sea! I laugh at Urday, one of the quieter ones from Rachel's faction. Yesterday, he built a tarp shelter, carefully erecting a frame of tree branches in the middle of the yard, to protect himself from the expected rainfall in the night. But he built his house at the lowest point in the yard – which is now a foot deep in water. No Boy Scout's badge for him!

Thursday, 29 April

Ali appears. 'It's OK. Just arranging some money from Nairobi for these guys. No problem.'

Paul pleads for contact lens solution. 'We could be here for months.'

'No,' says Ali. 'Not months. Days only.'

We're fighting off the doubts. Setbacks are expected, and we still want to believe Ali is sorting things out. But Paul's ear infection is worrying us both. He starts antibiotic drops in his left ear. The right one has recovered, but the infection is bouncing from one ear to the other.

Saturday, 1 May
Rachel's diary

> Sit outside at dusk. Fat Mohamed asks usual question about BBC News. Tell him we heard about bomb in Mogadishu. 30 killed in mosque.
>
> Sayid is very aggressive, saying, 'Stephen no money. Al-Shabaab. You dead,' indicating decapitation for me and 'Bim!' shooting for Paul.
>
> We reply usual 'We know nothing'. Eat supper and go to bed at 8 p.m. Guards noisy and argumentative. Hear anti-aircraft gunfire.

Sunday, 2 May

One a.m. 'UP! UP! Go another where!' Buggas shouts. 'Al-Shabaab come.'

Half awake, we turn on a torch and rush to dress. It's been a long time since we've had a night move. We're both excited and anxious. Is this the beginning of the end? We scramble to pack our belongings before we're bundled into the back of a Toyota.

We travel through the night for an hour, heading south-west, before turning off the dusty track, bouncing across the scrub for a few minutes and lurching to a halt, followed by another Toyota. We're ordered to get out. They put a mat and our thin mattresses down on the rough scrub ground, more or less next to the car, and tell us to lie down and sleep. Sleep to order, like a dog? We've learnt to do that now.

A sense of trauma returns. For the last month we've been held in the same place, living in hope that the end is near. All along we have coped when together by shutting down our emotions, by not allowing ourselves to get agitated about things beyond our control. We have recited the mantra 'We're the good guys, they're the bad guys' to prevent ourselves agonising about the pressure to raise money that has been put on our families. We have long since suppressed the instinct that makes you flinch when a gun is pointed at you. Our minds have switched to some sort of psychological survival mode. To see the gang panic, prodding us to up sticks so suddenly, reminds us we are in a lawless land and our lives depend on the whims of the evil Buggas and his gun-toting henchmen.

This evacuation into the bush is not an organised move. There's no effort to make a camp. They are concerned that we bed down quickly and stay quiet. Buggas takes the second Toyota and we are left with Land Rover Man, Ali Yeri, Deli, Fat Mohamed and Oman.

The guards wake us at first light. They're all standing around, jumpy, apparently confused about what to do next. They tell us to follow Oman. Fat Mohamed and Deli grab our mat and a mattress, and hustle us along a track into the bush at gunpoint. Anxiety gnaws again. This is unusual. Normally they carry our stuff, as well as tarps and cooking gear to make camp. If we don't need our things . . . what can they be planning for us?

We walk for ten minutes into thicker and thicker bush. They follow tracks, quietly conferring at times; they try their phones but can get no signal. They seem lost. Without Buggas, they don't know what they're doing. They give up and point to a thorn tree, ordering us to 'sleep'. For how long? Oman says three hours.

We clear an area to lie down on. We know from experience that the thorns are vicious, penetrating the thin mat, digging deep into our flesh and devils to remove. One of our bags appears, then another, bringing some peace of mind. The guards settle down 20 or 30 yards away and leave us to our own devices. They sit with their guns at their sides and don't bother about securing the area. It's quiet apart from the sounds of the bush – the hissing-chirping of the cicadas, the scurrying of insects, small wildlife scuttling over scrubby vegetation, occasional bird calls and the faint sound of goats and camels grazing.

The sun soon becomes intolerable. We've been used to the full shade of a house for more than three months. Paul approaches the guards: 'Too much sun. We need shade. Where's Buggas? What's happening?'

They shrug, but Oman finds us a shadier spot and we hang our blankets under a denser thorn tree to protect against the harsh sun. Ali Yeri comes with bread and hot water, but we have no *alen*, no mugs or sugar. We have become accustomed to having around us our bags and the boxes of household basics we've been allowed to accumulate . . . the small trappings of 'our normal life' to cling on to. When our routine is interrupted, we are rocked and anxiety sets in. This situation feels chaotic.

Paul is struggling without his contact lenses. He's got used to shuffling about in the confines of the compound, but he trips and stumbles in the inhospitable thick bush with scrub on the ground, thorns everywhere. Even our heads are covered with scratches and thorny splinters. We are on edge, irritated, restless and ill at ease. And hungry.

At 2 p.m. we hear some shouting. It's Buggas coming from a new direction. He takes one bag, and we struggle to follow him through the bush with the other bag and mattress. Minutes later, we're crossing the wadi where we camped at Christmas. There is some comfort in the familiarity. Up the other side, we see the two Toyotas. As we approach, we recognise more members of the gang standing around. Some are eating bananas! We haven't seen a banana since November. We are given one each – a great treat. They taste like nectar. It's a high point for the gangsters too. When Rachel says, 'Ooohh bananas!', Sayid mimics her and they all laugh. When they mimic us in good humour, we are sometimes tempted to join in their fun. It is a strange moment, a small pleasure universally shared.

Returning through the village in daylight, our guards hold up scarves to stop anyone seeing us through the windows. Why bother? Surely everyone in the village knows we are here?

We're soon back at the same familiar house we left in the middle of the night. The gangsters say al-Shabaab came through the village that morning. It's a reminder there is always a chance that al-Shabaab, the Islamist terrorist group controlling much of southern Somalia, will seize us. We have become used to the gangsters using the name as a threat, and it now seems real. They'd been tipped off and able to hide us away. Lucky for us?

Later, we hear a radio report that Hizbul Islam (another Islamist terrorist group) have made an assault on Harardheere – to evict the pirates who operate from there, 110 km south-west of Hobyo. If our village, Amaara, is on the way, that would explain today's events.

With that understanding comes a little relief. We are exhausted and downhearted from another unsettling event. Rachel has sunburn on her neck and shoulders. Once again we pick ourselves up, saying, 'We'll survive, we won't let them beat us.' Surprisingly, nothing has gone missing from our bags, boxes and bedding, so we set up home again and settle down to a game of crib. The gangsters are attentive, so we demand bottled water and batteries. They come pronto, and also bananas and biscuits – a feast!

Another week passes with no news. I wonder if I am falling apart. As soon as my ears are better, my gout flares up again. I stop the antibiotic ear drops and start Diclofen, with the occasional ibuprofen for good measure. And I grope my way around without lenses.

Ali Ad rejoins the resident group after a spell away. The hardliners lose no time in getting him to ask for 'his' radio. '*Shun daqika* [five minutes],' he says. He looks uncomfortable, as am I, but we don't give in.

The weather is still sticky, often stormy, and occasionally breezy. The fly population appears to have doubled. Paul compiles 'new' crosswords for Rachel, using the clues from ones in a book completed so long ago that they're forgotten. We listen to the radio, searching out coverage of the UK general election. Some of the gangsters know the name Gordon Brown and understand that we're in for a change.

One evening Buggas turns up with a shovel. By now the yard is full of rubbish and litter. He huffs and puffs, even chopping down small bushes and creeping weeds that have been flourishing in the rain. He badgers the others to join in with the clear-up. Soon there is a big heap on one side of the yard and the compound is a little tidier. Is this a sign that we may be leaving soon? Are they expecting an important visitor? Then new supplies arrive: sacks of charcoal, rice, sugar and flour, milk powder and *Omo*. Are we in for another month?

Wednesday, 12 May

Paul is still suffering without contact lens fluid. For three and a half months he was using only one lens to conserve solution; for almost a month now, he's worn no lenses. We're sitting in the yard listening to the evening RFI slot. Buggas is lounging nearby, chewing *chad*. He calls across, 'Britain new government.' What can you say to that? Paul responds by reminding Buggas that he needs more contact lens fluid. 'Now,' says Buggas, laughing, adding that he will give us some camel milk! Our disjointed exchange peters out with none of us any the wiser.

Ten-thirty p.m. Someone has taught HSB to shout, 'Wake up.' He is standing at the door, gesticulating for us to get up and pack. Excitedly, we scramble to dress. Buggas comes to check on us: 'Run! Run! We go!'

We leave in a convoy of three Toyotas. No Land Rovers. Ali Deri is in the front passenger seat with a machine gun. It's a squash in the back with four people, plus two AKs and a rocket launcher. Deli and Hassan squirm in discomfort at being so close to us and having to have their weapons ready to fire. We drive west through the night, passing occasional villages. Unusually, we see traffic coming the other way: convoys like ours on two occasions.

Thursday, 13 May

At 4.30 a.m. we reach a village. Another Toyota joins us and leads the way to an open, flat area by a lake. We are allowed out to stretch our legs. Our bodies are tired, stiff and sore, but no camp is made. Some of the men roll up in their blankets on the damp ground, completely cocooned from head to toe. The area is desolate and inhospitable. Ali Deri tells us we are waiting for dawn. We get back in the car and wait, hoping this is the beginning of the end. There's no point in trying to sleep.

At first light we set off again, just two cars travelling across sparse scrubland. We pass a small group of people who stare at us as if they've not seen a vehicle for some time. We turn onto a long, straight, rocky track and make very slow progress. The countryside is incredibly bleak but dotted with large wind-sculpted earth mounds made by termites. We seem unusually short-handed. We're still hoping – dreaming? – that we're on the way to a rendezvous for our release.

We continue for another slow-moving hour, stopping and starting as the gang looks for a particular location. Eventually, we pull off the road and arrive at a large group of trees bordering a shallow lake of fresh rainwater. A third Toyota joins us, ferrying more of the men and Fat Boy, who distributes a vitamin C feast for breakfast – *ambi* (mango), *lin bombelmo* (grapefruit) and *lin* (limes). Also tins of tuna. We all eat hungrily and the atmosphere is like a Sunday picnic, with Fat Boy playing the bountiful host.

We wash in the lake and go exploring for a toilet bush, discovering among the termite mounds a variety of eye-catching cacti and small gourds growing wild. Then the white Land Rover arrives with freshly fried bread for everyone. After our extended feast we lie down and rest. We keep hoping something momentous will happen soon.

At 1.30 p.m. we move on, travelling in the same excruciating discomfort. An extra passenger squeezes in – a local guide to show us the way? We now leave the rocky road, passing through an oasis where we see many animals but no fixed settlements. It has rained a lot in this area and for a while the bush is thicker and greener. Swarms of butterflies take flight as we brush by.

After another hour we turn off and stop near an African hut. Everyone gets out and starts milling around. There's no sign of Buggas, and they don't know what to do. After a few mobile phone calls we are ordered inside again. A short distance further down the track, we find the third Toyota already parked with Buggas and Omar. Where are we now?

The tree cover is sparse compared to other bush locations we've been in. Buggas selects one for us and rigs up a shelter. It has branches in all the wrong places, and he uses only one 12 foot by 15 tarpaulin. It's his usual dog's breakfast, but we're both too tired, physically and emotionally, to do anything about it. We sit in the cooling breeze until sunset and go to bed early, wondering what tomorrow will bring.

The camp mood is unsettled, and we're disturbed again. The gangsters, including Buggas and Omar, are itching and want mosquito repellent. Wearily, we give them some of our Deet, warning them not to get it in their eyes. The wind is now strengthening, and the tarpaulin flaps madly. In the early hours it collapses on top of us. We should have known better than to trust gangster knots.

Friday, 14 May

The white Land Rover arrives with Ali Yeri and Sireet and their cooking paraphernalia. Clearly, we are to be here a while. So much for our hopes that we were close to release. Maybe, just maybe, we'll be home for Paul's father's 99th birthday on 6 June.

The daytime guards sit under a nearby tree. In the afternoon we watch the Commander arrive with a big delivery of *chad*. Omar comes over to us with a small box. It's Paul's lens solution, plus mosquito repellent, sunscreen, vitamin pills and hand wash. Thank you! It's come from Nairobi, and the box is addressed to 'Nur Galaxof, c/o Toyota, Adaado'. We deduce that the local Toyota dealer acts as a posting box for the gang. Paul can see once again!

Omar also gives us bananas, grapefruit and tinned tuna galore. So many treats! We ask him for news of our release. He denies knowing anything but informs us that we're near the town of Adaado, which has an airport and flights to Nairobi. We're optimistic again. It's refreshing to be back in the open after three and a half months cooped up in the village house. The environment is fascinating, with many different types of tree and bush, and all sorts of birds, insects and butterflies to admire.

Over the next few days we hear the reassuring sound of aeroplanes. The camp is often busy with visitors – the usual goats and goatherds and also men who we guess are local gangsters. Rachel thinks Buggas is having to buy off our presence here. They come to look us over. Sometimes we are given goats' milk – especially delicious as we've not had fresh milk for more than seven months.

When there are no visitors the gangsters usually sleep, their guns hanging in the tree above them, along with the black plastic bags containing their *ma'awiis*. The machine guns are left strewn on the ground, often covered with a jacket or spare blanket.

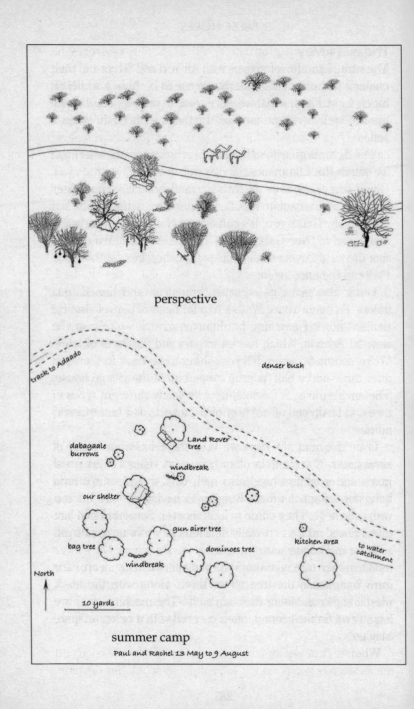

perspective

track to Adaado

denser bush

dabagaale
burrows

Land Rover
tree

windbreak

our shelter

gun airer tree

bag tree

dominoes tree

kitchen area

windbreak

to water
catchment

North

10 yards

summer camp

Paul and Rachel 13 May to 9 August

The gangsters are soon bored with their new environment. Most of them are idle buggers. Oman rants, 'Hungry, want money,' so we rant back about 'lazy militia'. Abbas and HSB have a fight. Later, HSB comes for treatment and sympathy: he has rope burns and a bump on the back of his skull. Buggas had tied him up as punishment. The next day, Senick and Sayid have a fight. Both are hogtied and left to sweat in the hot sun for half an hour. They laugh it off afterwards.

Our first week back in the bush is very stormy. It's better than being confined to the hot, sticky house in the village but poses a new set of problems. Torrential rain falls during the fourth night. The wind backs from its usual daytime direction and drives the rain straight through the open side of our shelter. We move the bags and boxes further under the tarp, then huddle miserably on our stacked-up mattresses. Buggas drives a Toyota right up to the shelter, headlights shining straight at us. He opens the door, 'Inside. Sleep.' We get in and sit, damp and depressed, while the storm rages for a few hours. Buggas reclines the front seat, puts his feet on the dash and snores. As the rain eases off, he orders, 'Go your position.' We are not sorry to get back into our 'home'; damp it may be, but we regain our tiny, tiny amount of control and independence.

In the morning the sun and wind help us dry out. There is similar activity around the camp. The nearest big tree is turned into an airer for machine guns and AK-47s! Guns and ammo belts are hung from the lower branches. Bushes are littered with drying T-shirts. During the storm the gangsters had just crawled under tarps. Now fortification-like walls are appearing all around. The battle for the nearest stones is over; the slower thinkers have to go a long way to find suitable rocks. Tarps are thrown carelessly over thorny bushes and left to the ravages of wind and thorn. Maybe the gangsters don't expect to be here long; or perhaps they're just being careless in their easy come, easy go way.

When it's not raining at night we often get sandblasted and the mosquito net provides little protection. In the daytime,

Rachel has to be careful of sunburn, having been so long inside. It's difficult to find somewhere private to wash, so Rachel is disgruntled but manages to wash under her dress, which has a convenient zip up the side.

Wednesday, 19 May

We're getting used to the weather: torrential rain most nights.

In the afternoon Ali and Omar turn up together. Ali tells us that big problems in the TFG have prevented them from completing the deal and that Stephen has agreed to pay 440 (meaning $440,000 – Ali never says dollar or thousand), that a church in Nairobi has offered 400, but that they still need another 660. Apparently the gang will settle for $1.5 million. Ali says they have spent 200 so far just on guarding us. He is continuing to talk with the TFG, pressing them hard, but he seems to have accepted that there won't be any more money from our family. We wonder why on earth a Kenyan church would give money for us. Just another straw for the gang to clutch at?

Omar says we have a new government in Britain – which the gangsters think will pay for our release – so we must make another video and interview. We tell them it won't make any difference. The new British government won't pay ransoms. Ali responds with a story of a British hostage who has been held by al-Shabaab for two years. He says al-Shabaab was after us at the village house, arriving the next day! They want the money. He also tells us this area is the heartland of the pirate clan, so we are safe. Is he trying to wind us up but also not worry us too much?

We ask Ali for batteries, toilet paper, soap, needles and thread. He and Omar discuss the merits of Dettol soap as opposed to Lux. Deli raids the Land Rover toolbox and brings Rachel some very large needles, big enough for sack-making, but they'll do to repair her dress, which is getting full of holes. She fills many hours unpicking thread from unused clothing.

We hear aeroplanes every day; Ali Deri says the *chad* plane comes daily.

Thursday, 20 May

Ali picks us up in his Toyota, a much smarter and better-looked-after vehicle than any of the gangsters' cars. The white Land Rover follows with the guard detail. We travel northwards for 20 minutes and then walk a short distance to the shelter of a large tree. Our chairs are already there. A man who is setting up a video camera on a tripod introduces himself as Jamal Osman. He is a quietly spoken UK-based Somali journalist, professional and friendly. He tells us how sorry he is about our situation and takes us through a list of questions.

I don't want our families and friends to worry any more than they must be already, so I don't stress the negatives. I talk of our routines and our minor health problems, loss of weight and fitness, but explain we have adequate food and medicines. I say we've been captive for 210 days, of which 97 have been in solitary confinement; that we haven't been treated violently – except for the beating when we were separated.

Ali has told us to make an appeal to the government. I ask the new prime minister to issue a formal statement confirming their policy on ransom. I enquire whether there's a lottery winner who doesn't know what to do with the money? Perhaps he could help us?

Jamal asks what we think of the naval inaction when we were transferred to the *Kota Wajar*. I tell him that the warships are an absolute laughing stock, regarded as a complete joke by the pirates.

I stress that this is not piracy but kidnapping, extortion and even torture.

When he picked us up, Ali suggested we ask our family once more to get money from our accounts. I'm exasperated but don't sense any strong pressure to beg. The bigwigs are all here, hovering at a distance behind the camera, but the mood seems very different from our first video. We are going through the motions – to eliminate this latest straw the gangsters are clutching on to.

Before he started Jamal asked us to confirm that we are giving this interview of our own free will. What a bizarre question. Of course we are not! I say as little as possible and try to be reassuring without risking the wrath of Buggas and the others. I hate the thought that this will be shown on national TV but no longer worry about what the world thinks. It's almost three months since we've spoken to our family. I hope they take comfort from seeing that we're still alive.

Jamal packs up and we chat with him before he films us walking back to the car. He generously gives us all he can from his bag: pens, batteries, tissues, wipes, four English newspapers and *The Economist*. We welcome this contact with the civilised world. He is the first decent Somali we have been able to converse with. He tries to be reassuring, saying that maybe the clan elders will come to our rescue; that the UK Somali diaspora are disgusted and holding rallies. But, really, there's no new ground for hope. We have to wait, to survive, and hope that within a few weeks Mr Cameron will respond to extinguish the gangsters' renewed expectations of British government money. Perhaps then a deal will be done.

I fight back tears as we return to Ali's car, back to isolation after such a brief period of communication with the outside world. It's the same bittersweet emotion I get every time we have contact: 'our world' feels so close, yet is far beyond reach.

We know that it will take time for this latest 'event' to come to nothing, so resign ourselves to another few weeks. At least we now have plenty to entertain ourselves with. We're absorbed in our first newspapers for seven months. They're full of the post-election coverage and news of the coalition government. We study them from cover to cover, relishing every word and taking in every mention of all the different names and faces. We see pictures of the Gulf of Mexico oil spill. Radio can't do justice to an environmental disaster like that. We cherish the crosswords.

Despite the rains and sandblasting, we enjoy the open environment. The area has suffered from serious drought, so many of the trees are circles of dead wood on the ground around where a trunk used to be. No shortage of firewood! The trees that have survived are often pathetic trunks with just a few branches, which now sprout growth direct from the stem. The recent rains have brought on a mass of ground plants. We compete to find the most colourful flowers. There are lizards, beetles, butterflies and dragonflies galore. We spot a big stick insect on one of the stones holding down our tarpaulin. Birds soon realise we're here and come looking for scraps: the ubiquitous doves, which find us wherever we are; also colourful starlings, bossy bulbuls, timid flycatchers, and many more. In the afternoons, two pairs of large birds of prey descend from height to impose their superiority. We have *dabagaale* nearby. If we sit still, they scamper up close, grab a piece of scrap bread and scurry away.

Buggas is cheerful, and so are the other gangsters. Fat Boy is around and always laughing. They often sit under their tree, playing dominoes. At night some of the guards warn us about al-Shabaab and not to go far when we go to the toilet, but they're otherwise relaxed. They now have more tarps, courtesy of UNHCR, so fix up some better shelter.

Buggas brings us more bananas, with instructions not to give them to his men! We welcome the addition to our diet, both as an energy and a morale boost. But there are far too many for us and they don't keep long in the tropical heat. As soon as Buggas's back is turned, the men are pleading for them, if not helping themselves. Rachel makes it easier for them to steal the riper ones. As stocks dwindle, we hide away the last few and eat them surreptitiously.

One niggle is water for washing. The water catchment is some distance away, and the cooks get fed up with us taking their water. The others don't care. We're not allowed to go to the well ourselves and have to nag them to get enough to do our laundry. When Ali Deri is around he's willing – telling us he knows about 'human rights'!

Another problem is the radio, which the guards keep demanding. After one refusal Samata gives me the phone and says, 'Buggas.' A voice on the end says, 'Here Buggas. Give radio to man.' I know it's not Buggas, not the gruff voice I know so well. It's Fat Boy, who is standing just a short distance away, speaking into his phone. The men are all giggling and chuckle even more when I tell them crossly they are all liars! They try to look indignant but accept defeat.

Up to now we've been treating the gangsters' ailments: scratches and scrapes, head and backaches. For the first time I see something serious. Deli has a nasty parasite infestation on the base of his hand. The next day he comes back to show me some Parazole tablets and antibiotic cream. We learn that there's a medical centre in Adaado, which is good to know. If something serious happened to one of us, would they take us there?

After another stormy week, we experience a minor flood. We manage to stay out of the rain, but the run-off funnels around our tree trunk, straight into our mattresses. In the morning, it's time for a major reconstruction. It's difficult to make one 12 foot by 15 tarp provide enough shelter from the sun, wind and rain. It's windy all the time, the tarp flapping wildly, with what seems like tons of windblown sand being dropped on us frequently. And the wind direction sometimes changes, swinging through 90 degrees. As it is mid summer, the sun is well to the north and intrudes from the opposite side; the minute the wind drops, we roast! I venture further into the scrub, scavenging for stones the right shape and size to hold down the edge of the tarp. I manage to rearrange new lines to suspend it lower and more centrally. Then I weight down one end and pull the windward side down to within a foot of the ground, using a row of ties to yet more large stones that I've retrieved from the bush. We form a wind/sand break under this lower edge with our bags and boxes. On the other side, I dig a drainage channel and build a dam to divert the run-off water. Our headroom is now much diminished, but there is an area outside the open end of the shelter where we put our chairs and hang a blanket from the thorny branches above for sun protection. We call this 'the patio'. We sit there with our backs to the gangsters and put them out of our minds.

Many of the gangsters have gone away; we are down to 14. Some evenings we hear whispers of 'al-Shabaab'. The machine guns are taken out every day, set up in outposts maybe half a mile from the camp, covering the two access tracks. Buggas now disappears for three or four days at a time, leaving the Commander or Fat Boy in charge. The gangsters are noticeably more tense when Buggas is around, so we welcome his absence. Perhaps he is negotiating the deal?

The intense sunlight continues to be a problem. Paul has been experimenting with tying a blanket over the top of the tarp to provide more protection for daytime activities. With this extra shade, we are comfortable enough to play Scrabble. Prompted by the Scrabble puzzle in one of the papers – showing a quarter of the board and many of the letter values – Paul has made a set of tiles. He's marked the letters on pieces of old playing card and cut them up using a discarded razor blade. We keep the 'tiles' in a small plastic container, safe from the wind. The 'board' is laboriously drawn on a piece of paper. As the game proceeds, we pick out our tiles then write in our chosen word, setting aside the used tiles. We play Scrabble for at least two hours every day, often getting engrossed in long debates about spelling. Another welcome chore for Paul's daily routine is the construction of new 'boards'.

We have many wet, stormy nights. Even after Paul's efforts, we still get damp from water coming in through holes in the tarp. A few of the men are now coughing, including Buggas, probably from chest infections. The mood in the camp is subdued, if not aggressive. We're almost out of bottled water, and no one seems to care. Then Ali Yeri arrives with a fresh supply, followed by another box of bananas. Where did that come from?

> Buggas is sitting under a tree surrounded by a few of the gangsters. He doesn't look well. Beckoning me over, he rasps, 'Rachel, here.' He points to his chest, coughing and wheezing, and, as I approach, shows me some phials of Chloramphenicol. I read the instructions, and they look at me expectantly. Buggas also has sachets of vitamin B in powder form. He adds one to a phial of Chloramphenicol and shakes it up. Then he picks up a syringe and starts filling it up. He offers it to me and wants me to inject it for him! Even though he's suffering, I can't think of anything more repugnant. It's one thing to treat the pathetic members of his gang who don't comprehend what they are doing, but do I really want to help this brute who's destroyed our lives, who's caused untold misery to our family and friends? I say I don't know how to give injections and retreat.

In the evening Buggas leaves to 'go hospital Mogadishu', according to Ali Deri. We wonder what would happen were Buggas to die. Would there be an obvious successor as gang leader? More likely a fight. Where would that leave us?

Sunday, 1 June
Ali Deri shoots a *sagara*. We have a little for supper and the gang entertains visiting goatherds – they talk noisily well into the night.

The next morning a baby deer wanders around the camp. Did Ali Deri shoot its mother? The gangsters make a fuss of it. Ali Yeri warms up some milk and feeds it. How long will his caring last?

> At 11.30 a.m. I get a phone call. It's Ali telling me that Stephen is refusing to negotiate further unless he's allowed to speak to us. Ali says he'll call at 1 p.m., and I must ask Stephen for a further 60 (thousand), then maybe then the pirates will settle.
>
> It's exactly three months since we've spoken to Stephen, so I'm deliriously happy at the thought of hearing his voice. Are we finally getting close?

We wait in anticipation for the rest of the day – but there's no call. Our guards know something is happening and keep asking for news. Is that a good sign? At night we're restless, not helped by our nagging hips, which are suffering from the damp weather. Our mattresses provide little comfort.

Tuesday, 3 June

Rachel mopes, waiting for a call. At dusk Buggas turns up with Omar and croakily demands paper and pen. He sits down in Rachel's chair and starts writing, frequently shouting to the men. Paul can see that Buggas is writing two lists, as if they are going to split us up again. We are now expecting a move, if not separation. One of the men is packing up a tarp. Some men have already gone, including Ali Yeri. We get no supper; when we ask for it, our bowl is found on the ground near the kitchen area, filled but forgotten.

Another day passes, and we are still here. Maybe Buggas was just changing the guard. But the general mood is unsettling, and we are very apprehensive.

Saturday, 6 June

> Father is 99 today. Happy birthday, Pa! I can't bear to think of what he is going through. Although frail, he is mentally

strong. I am sure he will be making the best of it and celebrating his birthday with Jill and his friends in Dartmouth.

Sunday, 7 June

Buggas returns from his sick bed and we receive yet more fruit: mangoes, grapefruit and bananas. After dark I'm lying under the mosquito net listening to the radio when I hear Buggas calling my name. It takes me a while to wrap something around my shoulders and extract myself. 'Quick!' croaks Buggas impatiently. He hands me a phone and it's Stephen! It's so good to hear his voice. I struggle not to cry with joy. Thank goodness he's calm and businesslike.

Stephen: *How are you?*

Rachel: *We're both OK, though not getting much exercise, so we're a bit stiff these days.*

Stephen: *I don't know how much time I've got, Rachel, so I need to speak to you fairly quickly. Has Ali told you we have made a final arrangement with him?*

Rachel: *No, he hasn't.*

Stephen: *Right. We've made a final agreement for a ransom. Don't worry about this money. Do not talk to them about it. We've made an agreement for a ransom of 440,000 US dollars.*

Rachel: *OK, and thank you so much for everything you've done.*

Stephen: *We're going to send a fax and you must sign this fax with Ali and send it back. It's got to come back to me. Do you follow me?*

Rachel: *Yes.*

Stephen: *We saw your interview with that Somali journalist last week. You both looked in good shape. Are there any medical problems I need to know about?*

Rachel: *No. Please send our love to Paul's father for his 99th birthday last Sunday.*

Stephen: *Yes, that was all passed on to him, don't worry. We're working for you and we want things to go smoothly, so it's very important, Rachel, that you cooperate 100 per cent with the pirates. Do you both still have your passports?*

Rachel: *Yes.*

Stephen: *Good. It's not 100 per cent critical. Is there anything else?*

Rachel: *When I last spoke to Ali a week ago he told me to ask you for another 60,000.*

Stephen: *That's been sorted. Don't worry about that.*

Ali: *Yeah, we stopped that for some quick action.*

Rachel: *Thank you, Ali. I just wanted to do everything that you say, Ali, because I know you are working very hard for us.*

Stephen: *All of us are very proud of you, and we will work with the pirates to get you home as fast as we can, but it depends on how safely we can make the payment and how quickly we can arrange to make the payment to come out to Ali. As you can understand, it's difficult. We're working as hard as we can to get money through the banks and into Kenya, but it all takes several days.*

Rachel: *We do understand.*

Stephen: *Ali has told me there has been fighting locally. Have you had any problems with it? It's not striking you as being dangerous where you are at the moment?*

Rachel: *As you know, Stephen, this is a very dangerous country.*

Stephen: *We've said to Ali it might take ten days, but we're working very, very hard to get it a lot quicker than that.*

Rachel: *We know it's very, very difficult for you, Stephen, and we know you're making tremendous sacrifices. We appreciate everything the family and everybody have done for us.*

Stephen: *We're very proud of you. You know, in that video, if you see the headlines, it was very good. I'm sure Ali would like to get his money. As soon as he can get me* *his fax, the sooner we can get it all going. How to get you out is the problem, because it's not going to be an easy trip, I am sure. Ali's got ideas on how it's to be done, and we will work with him, but communications have been difficult in that area in the last few days. I don't know what happened. People have cut the communications.*

Rachel: *It's always very difficult, so you can but do your best. I know Ali's trying to do his best, and we will just stay strong.*

Stephen: *I'm sure you will, and while the two of you are together you can help each other and it makes life easier. Are you moving about much?*

Rachel: *We haven't, but I wouldn't be surprised if they move us after this phone conversation. Thank Ali for letting us speak to you – it's really appreciated, thank you.*

Stephen: *I very much appreciate speaking to you now. And there's nothing else you want to say?*

Rachel: *Nothing we can say, Stephen, just our love to everybody who is thinking about us. We hope to see you as soon as possible.*

Stephen: *I'm sure it won't be long now. A while ago, I thought we got agreement, but that fell apart. People outside, who haven't got any money, have raised expectations, and that's been part of the problem. But anyway we've got this final agreement for 440,000 dollars, and I know that Ali wants to get it sorted as quickly as he possibly can, so we will work very, very hard towards that. It's lovely to speak to you again.*

When I hand the phone back to Buggas, he asks what was said. I tell him Stephen has reached an agreement with Ali. Buggas croaks, '500?'

I say, '440.'

He replies gruffly, 'We'll see' and leaves us.

Paul and I can't sleep for excitement, surprised by how quickly things seem to have moved on.

Monday, 8 June

Ali comes and shows us the fax from Stephen. It's a jumble of statements, saying that the pirates and family agree on our release, together and unharmed, in exchange for payment of $440,000 and that neither side will tell the media beforehand. There are spaces for each of us and Ali to sign. We sign it and hand it back to Ali, who immediately puts it into his car and leaves soon after. We wonder why on earth Stephen wants such a document. How can there be any formal contract, enforceable anywhere? Perhaps to be sure that we know how much money is being handed over for our release? Later, Buggas asks about the fax and we confirm that we've signed it. We're conscious that if he's accepting $440,000, it's a big defeat for him, so we need to tread more carefully than ever. He tells us that local groups in the area are a problem. He's probably having to pay them a lot.

The level of activity suggests this must be a serious development – at one time today there were six cars on camp. Do we dare hope? Now we can only wait. Release seems so close. Oman and HSB ask about Stephen and money. We say we know nothing. Oman says, 'Seven days.' How often have we heard that before? We still worry about the problem of handover. Our family won't want to deliver all that money without being sure we'll be released. But with these people, how can they ever be sure?

Tuesday, 9 June

The rains seem to have stopped. The days are partly overcast, which is welcome, but strong gusty winds blow in the afternoons and through the nights. Windblown sand is the biggest problem; Paul's left eye is very sore, and he can only wear the right lens until about 4 p.m. most days. Buggas goes out every day. Does he go to Adaado hospital for injections?

Ali Yeri comes back, and Paul welcomes his return. The battles for food when Afieri is in charge are trying. It's hard to explain why it is such a struggle to do something simple like ask for supper, but every little confrontation requires a build-up of mental strength, preparation for what the response may be.

Our only luxury is a daily all-over wash. Rachel walks out into the bush to escape from the camp, whereas Paul likes to wash after dark, on our 'patio', having taken his lenses out. On the rare occasions when he goes alone to the toilet area after dark, he still finds it difficult to navigate his way back. There's an irony there!

Life goes on while we wait. HSB comes over one morning with a swollen arm. Hassan explains, by drawing in the sand with a stick, that HSB has been stung by a scorpion. We've no idea how to help, so he goes off in a Toyota, presumably to the Adaado hospital. Is that the last we'll see of him?

We pass the days expectantly: killing time with all the chores and entertainments of our daily life, sometimes being ogled by passing visitors. The environment is a continuing source of interest, with birds large and small, a friendly lizard, big flying insects that dig holes and bury their caterpillars, scurrying beetles of all shapes, colours and sizes, including dung beetles with their acute sense of smell and ability to push large balls of dung backwards, unerringly, to their burrows, plus the occasional scorpion or snake. The guards pester us for fruit and, if we have spare, we dole out the odd mango or grapefruit for good behaviour, such as fetching us water. Sometimes we're disturbed by their chatter at night, especially if they catch a small deer and cook it on a fire close by. Rachel is mystified one night by the smell of roast pork only to find porcupine quills scattered nearby the next day. Not *haram*?

Friday, 11 June

It's the start of the World Cup, and there's no avoiding it on the radio. Although not soccer fans, we decide to make the most of it, making sure we know who's playing who and taking note of the scores. If there's anything that provides a topic for discussion across the world, it's football. Surely they are aware that the World Cup is being hosted in South Africa?

When they ask us for news we say, 'South Africa 1, Mexico 1.' They're not in the least bit interested! How sad is that?!

Buggas goes away for a few days, and we're left with Abdullah. He's a rank above most of the gangsters because he has charge of one of the Toyotas, a clapped-out one with dodgy suspension, which he's always tinkering with. The fact that he has control of a car suggests that he's been on a successful pirate raid before. He has boundless energy and is always laughing and noisy, but he doesn't speak English and usually keeps his distance. He and Oman decide to show us some coins. 'Money?' they ask, as if for explanation. The coins look oriental, maybe Chinese.

We say, 'Little money.'

Abdullah laughs and says, '*Kota Wajar.*' Maybe he was one of the pirates who attacked the ship?

The gangsters are desperately bored. The wind is strong and everyone is finding the continual sandblasting very trying. Buggas comes back for a short visit, to deliver some *chad* to keep his boys happy, and goes again. At least that settles them down.

Wednesday, 16 June

Two p.m. Ali Ad brings the phone. Hope! Rachel speaks to Stephen, then passes the phone to me:

Stephen: *Hello, Paul, how are you?*
Paul: *I'm fine, thank you.*
Stephen: *Good. Now I need to give you some instructions for tomorrow. We have made arrangements, Paul, to deliver the money by plane to a town called Adaado tomorrow at 11 o'clock. Now, the logistics for this are a bit awkward, because the pirates say they need four hours to count the money, so the plane will probably need to fly back to Kenya and then come back to collect you on Friday morning.*
Paul: *Right.*
Stephen: *Do you understand that?*

Paul: *Understood, yes. We are not far from Adaado, and we hear the plane coming in late morning and usually leaving in the afternoon.*

Stephen: *Now, I know this will be difficult for you, Paul, to see the plane and then for it to leave again, but we want the pirates to take you to the airfield tomorrow so the pilot can see you and identify you both from the air. Do you understand?*

Paul: *Yes.*

Stephen: *They will take you up to the airfield at 11 o'clock so when the pilot comes in to deliver the money he can see you first before he drops the money.*

Paul: *Right.*

Stephen: *Now, I will also call you tomorrow at eight o'clock in the morning to speak with both of you.*

Paul: *Is that local time?*

Stephen: *Yes, before the delivery of the money. We have given the pirates instruction by fax today, so they should know all this.*

Paul: *OK.*

Stephen: *Now, Paul, maybe, and this is a very big maybe – so please don't expect it to work – we may be lucky and the pirates might count their money very quickly and the plane have enough time and fuel to land again and collect you tomorrow, but we only have a very small chance of that happening because it's a long haul from Kenya. Do you understand?*

Paul: *I understand and I appreciate that it will take a long time to count the money because they're not terribly clued up.*

Stephen: *Now, if the plane cannot land again to collect you, then you will stay with a Mr Mohamed Aden tomorrow night in Adaado.*

Paul: *Mohamed Aden.*

Stephen: *Yes. Mohamed Aden is the District Governor who lives in Adaado and he is not a pirate. I repeat, he is not a pirate.*

Paul: *OK, yes, that's good.*

Stephen: *We have been working with Mohamed Aden to arrange the airport logistics for delivery of the money and your flight out. He is working on our side. He is a good man and you can trust him.*

Paul: *OK, so we should expect to spend tomorrow night with him unless we're very lucky and the plane manages to make a second trip tomorrow.*

Stephen: *That's right.*

Paul: *OK, I understand that.*

Stephen: *You must stay calm and do everything that the pirates or Mohamed ask you to do. You must cooperate with them. Now, there may be other changes and delays to this plan. So be prepared for that. I will talk to you again if there are any changes.*

Paul: *OK, thank you very much, Stephen.*

Stephen: *Everything is looking good at the moment for tomorrow and Friday.*

Paul: *Fantastic, fantastic. Thank you.*

Stephen: *Do you have anything you need to say to me?*

Paul: *Well, no, I don't think so. We will say everything when we see you in due course and say thank you.*

Stephen: *Good. I'll talk to you again at eight o'clock tomorrow, Paul.*

Paul: *Eight o'clock our time?*

Stephen: *Eight o'clock your time tomorrow morning, yes. Can I talk to Ali now, please? I assume he's listening . . .*

Ali: *Yes, yes, I'm here, Paul. I'm on the phone.*

Is this it? We think it must be! My mind races. Will Stephen be in Nairobi? We'll need to go to Dartmouth to see Father as soon as we can. Our car should be OK; I left it insured and MOT'd. But we will need to get to Tunbridge Wells to pick it up. How will we manage for spending money? I dare to hope that tomorrow or Friday we will be free, and I allow my mind to fill with the practicalities.

Then I wonder how it will be in Adaado. What is this Mohamed Aden's house like? Will we meet his wife? Will she cook supper for us?

I go through my bags, making sure I have the most important things organised in case we are not allowed to take much. I wash my hair and use my one remaining disposable razor to shave my legs. I don't have a problem choosing what to wear for travelling: my favourite, if well-worn, three-quarter-length trousers and sleeveless mauve top. And a bra! I've not worn one since the first day. I only have one pair of shoes: Paul's trusty flip-flops that have lasted all this time. That's sorted; can I now allow myself to dream about freedom?

The gangsters are solicitous and inquisitive. Ali Deri and HSB give us their mobile-phone numbers. They want us to call them when we get back home. HSB mimics me calling him from London: 'Hello, Haji Selbai. Richer here. London, good!'

There's so much to think about. It will be wonderful to see everyone, to be able to talk freely to our family and friends. There will be so much to sort out, but it's no good worrying about that. Will there be medical checks and debriefing? It's all so uncertain, but at least we'll soon be able to take back control of our lives.

Relief and excitement; no sleep!

Thursday, 17 June

In the morning, we are up early, sitting, waiting, bags as ever more or less packed. At eight o'clock, Ali Ad and Sharif come over. 'No fly *mante*,' they say. 'Go *baree*.' It's not unexpected. We try to stay calm, eat our chapati and have a cup of tea. At 8.15 a.m. there's a call. It's Stephen. He speaks to Rachel, then me.

Stephen: *Hello, Paul, I have to speak to both of you. That's the thing now.*

Paul: *Good morning.*

Stephen: *Our plane is delivering the money and is flying towards you at Adaado and will arrive at . . .*

Paul: *I can't understand you, Stephen.*

Stephen: *Do you want to pass me back to Rachel?*

Paul: *That's OK now . . .*

Stephen: *Oh, good.*

Paul: *It's just all the traffic going on around.*

Stephen: *Yes, I can hear. OK, now the plane is flying towards you. It will arrive in about three hours, delivering the money at 11 o'clock local time.*

Paul: *Yes.*

Stephen: *Now, this is just a short call to confirm that you are still both safe and well before we make final payment.*

Paul: *Yes, we are both safe and well.*

Stephen: *We've been told that the pirates will take you to the airfield today – no, probably NOT take you – sorry – to the airfield today. They MAY not take you. They will not take you. But don't worry about that . . .*

Paul: *OK. They have just told us we won't be going anywhere today.*

Stephen: *Fine, good. You will be passed into the safe custody of Mohamed Aden later . . .*

Paul: *Yes, later today?*

Stephen: *We believe so, yes. The aeroplane will come back for you tomorrow morning.*

Paul: *Right, OK. I understand all that.*

Stephen: *Now, I will call you again tonight, Paul, to talk with you about arrangements for tomorrow. Stay calm . .*

.

Paul: *Thank you.*

Stephen: *Stay calm and cooperate with the pirates today. Is there anything else you need to say to me now? Any questions?*

Paul: *No, we're fine. We'll just wait for events to happen and do what we are told. Thank you.*

Stephen: *Well done. That's it, keep calm and cooperate.*

Keep strong, because it's very close now, so take care.
Paul: *OK.*
Stephen: *We'll talk with you tonight with Mohamed Aden.*
Paul: *OK. Thank you. We'll look forward to it.*
Stephen: *Thank you, Paul.*
Ali: *OK*
Stephen: *Thanks a lot. Goodbye.*

And that's the last we hear.

The long haul

Friday, 18 June
Rachel's diary

> Sleepless night. Wound up & worrying about what will
> happen. Up 6.30. Early liver, then chapati. Blustery again.

Over breakfast we ask ourselves over and over again: why
didn't Stephen phone last night? Why is nothing happening?
What's gone wrong? If the money was dropped according to
the plan, why aren't we in the safe custody of Mohamed
Aden? We sit in our chairs, struggling to shelter from the
blustery winds, and wait on tenterhooks.

Ali Deri wanders over and says, 'Buggas here after one
hour. News flight. After two weeks.'

What does he mean, two weeks? We're supposed to be
leaving NOW. We don't want to wait two weeks. Why doesn't
translator Ali speak to us? We don't want to see Buggas. Two
of the evil creatures, HSB and Ali Yeri, come over to where
we are sitting with our backs to the camp. Ali says, 'News?'

Paul stands up and lets off steam: 'You're all lying bastards!
Fuck off and leave us alone!'

He shouts with utmost sincerity, although he's in tears.
They go away.

We brood a while, then calm down and begin a game of
Scrabble to pass the time. There really is nothing we can do
but wait – and hope.

Cars arrive with Ali, Buggas and Fat Boy. Maybe now we'll
hear some news. They talk in a group but say nothing to us.
Are they avoiding us? Ali leaves, but there are still five

vehicles in the camp, so something must be going on? We watch intently – hoping for a sign of action.

Another blustery day goes by. Something must have gone terribly wrong. Our family have paid the money, yet Buggas won't let us go. Our worst nightmare has come true. What can we do now? Hope that Stephen pulled out at the last minute! Maybe it's just a question of waiting a bit longer . . .

By the following day the bigwigs are gone with the extra vehicles. There's no sign of any money.

Since Paul's outburst the men have been wary of us. Now they are back to their old ways – scrounging medicines and asking for 'news'. Buggas is patently ignoring us, but that's nothing new. We try not to fret, to keep ourselves occupied, but a sense of powerlessness is inescapable. It's no good trying to talk to Buggas. Translator Ali is our only lifeline, but no doubt he is chasing yet another red herring and we have to wait another week – or probably three. They seem to wait three weeks after an 'event' before getting wound up again.

Monday, 21 June
Paul's diary

Another day like yesterday. No meat.

Tuesday, 22 June

Cloudy start, cooler than usual. No lunch. Less windy p.m.

Wednesday, 23 June

Sunny spells in morning. Some wind & clouding over. Blustery evening. No meat.

Thursday, 24 June

Mostly overcast. Very blustery all day.

Friday, 25 June

Windy but mainly overcast. Quiet day in camp. Buggas away.

One week on and the waiting is intense. The sun rises and sets, the wind blows and calms, we eat the same old food, play the same old games, and we exist. No contact, no news from anyone, anywhere. This is the reality – a painful and prolonged bang following our eve-of-release high. What is going on? All we know is that we are still here. We keep talking through the possibilities. Either the bastards have the money or they don't. We want to believe that Stephen aborted the money drop and we are in some sort of stand-off scenario, awaiting the re-start of discussions over how to make the exchange. We won't admit that the money has been handed over to the bad guys. If that were true, they might as well kill us.

Tuesday, 29 June
Paul's diary

> Day 250. And absolutely no sign of anything happening. We focus on the act of existing. Live the routines. My mantra, last thing before sleep: 'I love you. Another day nearer release. X – 250 days to go.'

It's hard not to fret. The weather is cooler, but the wind is often blustery, the conditions exhausting. When one of us has a bad day, the other finds the strength to stay calm. We are lucky to have each other.

I no longer take solace in thinking about family and friends. Sometimes the radio is a hindrance. The start of Wimbledon is a reminder that it's summertime in Britain, triggering thoughts of what everyone might be up to. I sink into an abyss. I fear we will never get out of here. My head feels like it's boiling with frustration. I can't cope with the despair, the feeling of powerlessness. I sit quietly, consumed by my own thoughts. I know Paul has no answers. I tell him I'm having a bad day. We hold hands but say nothing. I know I can get out of it. I've been here before. It's just a matter of finding some hope to cling on to. I keep churning things over in my mind. Eventually I find some hope and stop, too exhausted to counter it with despair. I squeeze Paul's hand and smile, then do something practical, like washing my towel. I'm OK again – until the next time.

At the end of June Omar visits for a few days but leaves without speaking to us. He and Buggas chew *chad* every afternoon. Both Mr F and Land Rover Man are here, two men who do show signs of concern for our welfare, ensuring we get enough food and washing water. Mr F brings two specimens for our inspection: a small baby rat-like animal, dead, and a yellow scorpion, about three inches long, also thankfully dead. A sting from such a scorpion would almost certainly be fatal. It's a reminder that every day we face significant risks.

Monday, 5 July
Paul's diary

Heavy overcast all day – cool, less humid, but very windy.

Tuesday, 6 July; Wednesday, 7 July; Thursday, 8 July; Friday, 9 July

Much the same as Monday!

Yet another uneventful week passes. One day Ali Deri says quietly, 'No problem. Find more money from TFG. 440 small money.' He doesn't want the others to hear; there hasn't been any sign that the gangsters know any more than we do. Ali Deri does appear to be trusted by Buggas, so now I know they do have the money Stephen raised. They are holding us in the hope that the ineffectual TFG, which is not transitional, or federal, or a government, will come up with more money. No hope. I won't tell Rachel; we had almost convinced ourselves that the money hadn't been dropped.

We're both feeling irritable and desperate for news. Neither of us is sleeping well, and the lack of exercise is taking its toll on Rachel's knees. We wake up stiff every morning – with weak and painful joints – and struggle to maintain our routine. How much longer can we put up with this? It's three weeks since we spoke to Stephen and nothing has happened.

Fat Boy visits for a few days and the camp numbers increase, but the men are not cheerful. They don't like the wind and rain. The temperature plummets at night and some are now wearing ladies' pyjamas. Imagine – self-respecting AK-47-wielding gangsters in pastel-pink nightwear! They build themselves ever more elaborate windshields, using the cars as well. They are as frustrated as we are. Ali Deri and HSB rant about 'big money' and 'fucking Stephen'. When we insist Stephen is a good man, HSB sneers and relays 'Stephen good man' to Buggas.

Any unusual gangster activity becomes a focus of interest. A new youngster starts doing vehicle maintenance. He spends many hours tinkering with the white Land Rover, including removing and refixing the bonnet. He appears to be a competent fitter; certainly he gets the engine running smoothly. We call him 'Son of Land Rover Man'.

Sunday, 11 July

Almost everybody who's anybody is here again: Buggas, the Commander, Fat Boy and Omar. But no Ali. The gangsters hold a pow-wow, which descends into the usual argument. It's impossible to ignore them or block out their din. We find it hard not to wonder what they are saying about our fate. The top brass depart again, and everyone else relaxes, sitting under trees enjoying their *chad*.

After breakfast the next day, we are told to pack. Apparently, Ali is coming. Our hearts race as we start organising our bags. Another move! Where to now? Is this our release at last? Then Ali Deri informs us that we will 'look Ali, after back'. So no release. But what instead?

Land Rover Man drives up in a Toyota and signals us to get in. Ali Deri and Ali Ad clamber in too. The white Land Rover follows behind full of cheerful boys dressed up in their gangster gear – shirts and trousers – wrapping scarves around their heads, happy to be on an outing.

We're driven past the spot where we had the interview with Jamal Osman. Then on – through sparse and undulating scrub with few trees – for half an hour. At a village, we join a major track and head south-west, accompanied by high-decibel chatter and phone calls. Soon we meet a vehicle coming in the other direction. It veers off the track in front of us and we follow, towards a large open area with a cluster of trees. There's a car already here. Is it Ali's?

It feels a familiar routine: we are led to a tree and told to sit on a mat. No chairs this time. Translator Ali comes over and starts rasping his usual confusing mix of information and incomprehensible negotiator-speak. The problem is not Stephen's money; it's the 'Somali community' money. They need 'proof of life'. And in a minute we will speak to a man who has come to get this evidence. We must ask for help and say our conditions are bad. On cue, Ivarr produces dirty cooking pots to prove it!

A man approaches. Rachel recognises Mohamed, who came with the doctor in January. Another journalist! What use is that? He sets up his camera and tells us he's sorry about our situation and that he's been in the bush for 30 days waiting to see us. We are furious. We've been through all this before. What good can he do? So much for proof of life: this is merely another attempt to raise public sympathy for our plight. Will these people never give up?

Mohamed asks us the usual questions about our conditions. We try to play our part, but we're poor actors. In Rachel's unenthusiastic efforts to ham it up, she says the food is 'quite tiresome'! It's such a farce. Mohamed asks about the ransom payment and confirms our fear that the pirates do have the money our family raised.

Hearing that, we turn to translator Ali and accuse him of betraying us. Paul tells him that the pirates will never be trusted again if they renege on their agreements. Ali, uncomfortable, says the money is 'in Nairobi' but 'they haven't used it' and that the gang are trying to get the 'second half' from the Somali community. What does that mean? We are spitting blood, so angry, so frustrated, and totally outraged.

The leaders stand around, joking at our expense. Omar comments that we will soon be back in our home, enjoying a luxury lifestyle. Buggas just smirks. The other gangsters come and go, off camera. Clearly they think this is going to help their quest for more money. Mohamed tries to involve the gangsters. He translates our responses to his questions and asks them for a reaction. We're even more infuriated by this. How can he imagine we can engage in a civilised debate with these despicable people? Paul tries to reason with them initially but ends up incensed.

We both rant on various themes. Paul complains that we receive no respect even though we're old enough to be their grandparents. He even tells Mohamed that the UN should send in troops to shoot 'the bastards'. Rachel keeps calling them the 'devil's children' and going on about how they've ruined our lives. Mohamed gives up and stops filming, but Ali complains that we've not begged enough for help, so we have to have another go! Then Mohamed persuades Fat Boy to stand in front of the camera and answer questions in Somali. He wraps his scarf around his head and answers a few questions amid much laughter from Buggas. Fat Boy calls Buggas *tuk wain* (big thief). That's all we understand.

At the end of this theatre, Mohamed tells us quietly he was the one who arranged the parcel with contact lens solution. Despite our reservations about his interviewing techniques we are very grateful. We seize the chance to appeal for more supplies. As we walk back with Mohamed to his car, we tell him as much as we can about our location, that we've been there two months and that we think we've reached the last stand. The gang has nowhere else to take us now. While the gangsters finish packing up, Mohamed returns with his still camera and plays the paparazzo, taking photos of us sitting in the Toyota.

Driving back to the camp, we stare at the desolate landscape that matches our mood. We can't see how this latest contact with the outside world will do any good. The gang is still clutching at straws for further extortion, and we'll have to wait another few weeks while this latest publicity runs its course. Ali Ad, sitting next to us, cheerily taunts us with, 'Money, money, money.'

Rachel is so frustrated that she responds, '*Maia, maia, maia*' – and immediately regrets rising to the bait. It's so demeaning when we allow ourselves to behave like them.

For the rest of the day we're both occupied by our own thoughts. We don't want, or need, conversation. It's no good going over what was said. There's nothing either of us can say that will help. We determine to hang on to what little hope we have: that they must give up soon.

The gangsters are irritatingly buoyant, even jesting about Paul's request for the UN to send in troops to shoot them all! Then Ali Deri asks us about news of the suicide bombings in Kampala – killing and maiming crowds watching the World Cup final. We hear on the radio that al-Shabaab has claimed responsibility for the attacks – their first beyond the borders of Somalia – as retaliation for Ugandan involvement in AMISOM. Another 74 needless, innocent deaths. We're lucky to be alive.

The next morning one of the gangsters brings a phone. What on earth now? Ali puts through a man who says he is Jarma, a Somali negotiator in Nairobi. He speaks to us both, asks a series of questions to establish identity and says he hopes to sort things out within a few days! We don't bat an eyelid. We've heard that before. The call is an irritant – no longer are all phone calls a welcome contact with the outside world. Maybe there is some truth in Ali's references to another source of ransom money, but we remain sceptical.

Slowly we adapt back into survival mode. Buggas is away and the Commander is in charge. There are lots of visitors to entertain the gangsters, and the mood in camp is upbeat. We even have calmer, less wearing weather.

Abdullah is now a regular feature at the camp. Most days he drives off in the morning and returns in the afternoon, often with *chad*. One afternoon he returns to the camp with Hamoud. They jump out of the Toyota, visibly excited, and walk over to us, clutching something. We're apprehensive as they present it to us. We're wary of Hamoud, who can be very moody and aggressive, but they're both laughing and delighted at our surprised looks. It's a massive egg, about eight inches long. We think it must be an ostrich egg, but we had no idea there are ostriches in Somalia. We draw an ostrich in the sand and they laugh even more. Next thing they mime us eating it. They build a fire and then boil the egg for about 30 minutes in a large empty powdered-milk tin filled with water. Everyone is standing around in anticipation. They crack the shell with a rock and carefully break it off. The boiled egg is very hot, so it's a difficult operation. Eventually they present us with a portion, served in a piece of shell. Ali Ad has a lime and sprinkles a little juice over it for us. We have our first egg in over eight months. Not only is it delicious but the whole event is a rare moment of fun for all. For the next few days we are given the same afternoon treat. The poor ostrich has lost its whole nest!

The next week passes as slowly as ever. Buggas returns and tension fills the camp. He says nothing to us, but some of the gangsters become more aggressive. Ivarr, normally restrained, taunts us about money, pointing to each of us in turn and saying, '*Hal million* [one million].' We try to take comfort in their aggression as a sign that realisation is sinking in – once more reminding ourselves that it will be hard at the end. But it's not easy to stay calm, and we keep succumbing to minor ailments. Paul has a sore throat and cough, on top of the ongoing problem of sore eyes. Rachel's stiff joints, if not painful, make her feel vulnerable.

Sometimes we get small insights into the lives of the gangsters, especially Ali Deri. He has now established a regular night spot not far away from our 'patio'. Though irritatingly noisy at times, he occasionally talks to us about his family. We learn his father is Somali and went to fight in Yemen in the 1960s. There, in Sana'a, he met the girl who was to become Ali's mother. Ali's own wife is apparently serving a four-year prison sentence in Mogadishu, guilty of shooting dead a fourteen-year-old girl. She expects to be released soon, so Ali will go away for a few days.

Tuesday, 20 July

It is Stephen's 59th birthday. Not likely to be a happy one! It's more than a month since we last spoke to him. How we wish to tell him not to worry about us today. What will he have made of the last video? Despite our hammed-up complaints, we can't have looked that bad. What does he know about what Ali is up to? We've had no further word from the mysterious Jarma – another one-minute wonder!

In the afternoon Fat Mohamed stands by us talking loudly on his phone. Does he do that to taunt us? Then Ali Yeri jeers at us with 'No money, no flight.' However much we try to ignore him, it still hits home.

Two days later a large box arrives with a Nairobi address. It must have been sent by Mohamed Dahir as it contains many of the things we asked him for: *The Economist* (four issues); *New African*, a glossy weekly; vitamin pills; Wordplay (an Indian copy of Scrabble); playing cards; books, including Adam Williams's *The Emperor's Bones*; moisturising cream, sunscreen, mosquito repellents, wipes, pens, toothbrushes, nuts and more, but no contact lens solution. Poor Paul must continue wearing only one lens to eke out his remaining supply.

We should be excited to receive a parcel, but we're depressed. Buggas is here again, and the camp resounds with the gangster soundtrack of boisterousness and smug laughter. They've held on to us for nine long months now, and we're afraid they are still far from giving up hope of millions. How long can we go on? We're feeling unfit and useless. Our mood changes when we start reading the news and find ourselves absorbed in the stories behind the headlines. Even the most obscure topics transport us away from our petty, self-centred worries. There are so many interesting things going on in the world to contemplate. In one of *The Economist*s we find a scribbled note: 'Your father is OK.' The best news in a long time.

We have plenty to occupy ourselves, but the men are getting bored and restless again. Ali Yeri annoys us with his talk of joining al-Shabaab and fighting the Ugandans. As he's the cook, we humour him. In the next breath, he tells us his wife has just had a baby boy, but he seems in no rush to go back to Amaara to play the family man. Oman and Hassan are interested in our magazines. They like to look at the photos, especially in the *New African* magazine. They want to know the names of all the different faces. They alight with comic incredulity on a picture of female troops in an article about the Cameroons. It's a revelation to them to see women in fatigues, carrying arms!

The end of July is marked by the return of Omar, who comes over and asks how we are. We look at him with pure exasperation. Why waste breath on him? He, if anyone, is responsible for prolonging our agony. Then he gives us bananas, mangoes and grapefruit. We could kiss his feet. It's pathetic how grateful we are. We know the fruit will give us a lift, if only a temporary one.

Omar stays a few days, overseeing many dominoes tournaments. Bored members of the gang sit around watching, sometimes chanting monotonously in a way that rankles. Another month draws to a close, and we are both feeling tetchy. Will it never end?

Wednesday, 4 August

Translator Ali turns up with Fat Boy. He waves at us but says nothing. Fat Boy scowls – an unusual expression for him. They join Buggas and Omar under 'the' tree and have a pow-wow. Can we afford to raise our hopes? For some time we've been wondering if we might be released before the beginning of the fasting month of Ramadan. It can't be far off now. The group moves away, and the pow-wow turns into the customary shouting match involving other gang members. Some peel off and squabble in smaller groups. Ali Deri approaches us and suggests they should send Paul to London to raise money, leaving Rachel behind. This rings alarm bells. We tell him we must speak to translator Ali, and we wait, feeling deeply unsettled. The suggestion that one of us is freed, to raise the money they want, has been made before. Although not credible, we're disturbed that they persist in harping on about it.

Translator Ali leaves without enlightening us. The camp

settles down again. We glean some more bizarre snippets over the next day or so. Ali Yeri tells us we fly in 30 days. Ali Deri talks bitterly in broken English: something to do with telling Stephen '440 small money'. It's hard to believe he has influence, but his behaviour is disquieting. Oman is also agitated. He sidles over and asks us about 'Church, *mahwille*, Rome'.

We respond, 'Pope?'

He says, 'Pope give militia money.'

We say we're nothing to do with the Pope. Oman then rants and rages about 'Fax, Stephen, no money'. We try to ignore him but can't help wondering what they've been told.

Saturday, 7 August

Ali Deri shouts, 'Yesterday go house Amaara.' We look blank. He repeats the sentence, but we are perplexed. 'You know house? House in town?' he persists.

'Yes, *guri*,' Paul replies, using the Somali word. We realise he means tomorrow, not yesterday. Ali Deri is angry, not with us but because he prefers to be in the bush. We've no idea whether it's a threat or reality. After almost three months in one place we've become quite settled. The thought of returning to the village is depressing – so much for this being the last stand.

Sunday, 8 August

Rachel's diary

Three cars on site. The gangsters have a big chad session.

The following afternoon, they've got over their hangovers and start packing up. We realise we're moving when they start dismantling our tarp. It's strange seeing our 'home' disappear in an instant. We liked this place with its fascinating environment and its proximity to Adaado, despite the regular sandblasting. We don't want to uproot and go back to the village.

We're put in Abdullah's rattling banger, in a convoy of three. Abbas gets in the front with a machine gun. They take a more northerly route, thankfully missing the rough stony track used on our approach almost three months ago. The terrain is very sparse, but we see goats, camels and encampments, plenty of people wandering about, seemingly in the middle of nowhere. For a few miles, we have a young guest with us in the back, until he is dropped off near a settlement. Then we have the relative comfort of the back seat to ourselves. Abdullah is a surprisingly steady driver, which is just as well. As he handles the steering wheel, he alternates smoking with chewing *chad* and drinking tea, while making occasional phone calls and keeping up a one-sided conversation with Abbas, whose main contribution is '*mhhmm*'.

After an hour we suddenly stop. Abdullah gets out and consults with Buggas. They open the back door and start pulling out our bags. Buggas points at two, 'Rachel's,' he says. They are taken to the other car and pushed into the back.

'What?' we exclaim.

'No problem,' replies Abbas.

Abdullah jumps back in and off we go. We grasp each other's hand. Are we to be separated again? What other reason can there be?

We already knew the suspension on Abdullah's car was knackered and even with the lighter load it is bottoming frequently. This must be the reason for the baggage transfer. We hope that Abbas is right to say, 'No problem.' Even so, we are stressed; this journey is unusual. They are all chewing *chad* and none of the calmer senior figures is here. Whatever his faults, we miss Omar's presence.

We have several short toilet and prayer stops, and pass through three villages. One is the town where we spent our first night in Somalia, all those months ago. We see lights, shops and a hotel/bar on the main street. It's the first time we've registered such a cluster of commercial activity. We stop on the outskirts for dusk prayers and see that Oman leaves here and Hamoud joins. This must be their home town. Not all the gangsters are from Amaara.

Finally, we arrive at our destination – the house we left on 12 May.

Buggas takes us inside, smirking. He's mellow from chewing

chad. Our hut is now empty of furniture, but inside we find Hamad, a young gangster who was shot in the lower leg in March and is still recovering on crutches. We've seen him occasionally, but it appears he's been based here. He's turfed out and we settle back in. The rest of the place is as we left it. The yard is still full of heaps of mess. We hang up our mosquito net and bed down on the floor. No supper is cooked, but at least we are still together. We put aside our disappointment at this backward step and focus on the here and now. We are happy to collapse onto our stale and compacted mattresses in the familiar house after the long journey. Thinking can wait until daylight. We are so relieved not to be separated.

In the morning Buggas strides in and declares, 'We go big home, after three days.' We don't know what to expect, but hope it's an improvement. Ramadan is about to start; perhaps it's related to that. In the afternoon, Deli comes over and says, '*Sadambe guri wain* [After tomorrow big house].' He mimes turning on a tap and showering, '*Ell maia* [No well].' A house with a shower and piped water supply? Wow.

A minor sandstorm envelops the village; in the evening it's so murky we breathe sand.

Thursday, 12 August

At 4 a.m. we hear the sounds of early breakfast. Ramadan must have started. Hamad comes in, banging his aluminium crutch on the floor. Otherwise we are undisturbed; no breakfast cuppa.

Buggas comes and sits proprietorially in one of our chairs. He informs us that Muslims don't eat during the day. He gives us a bag of dates and tells us he's searching for 'fishes'. Why is he now so chatty? Has he decided to play the genial hostage host during Ramadan?

It's very windy, so we sit inside to avoid being sandblasted, but it's sticky in our room. We miss our well-ventilated bush shelter! We resign ourselves to staying uncomfortably captive for Ramadan. Perhaps release will come at Eid, the festival at the end of the month.

On Friday Paul announces he has a note in his (mental) appointment book: Rachel's haircut. It's amazing how one 'task' can be turned into a day's highlight.

Again Deli tells us we will move tomorrow. He's excited about the plumbing!

Saturday, 14 August

At 8 a.m. we're on the move – without a big convoy or any attempt at concealment. Buggas drives us a short distance through town to a part where several mature trees shelter two or three large houses. We stop outside a pair of steel gates in a substantial concrete block wall – the entrance to a newly built house within a high-walled compound. Buggas leads us in.

The house is single storey but quite tall, with rendered concrete-block walls. The yard isn't finished – it's a building site strewn with rubble – and we soon discover that the house isn't completed either. Buggas shows us into a room off the entrance hall. His first action is to close the steel window, shoot the bolts and tell us not to open it. The room is now dingy, lit only by a grilled vent above the window and light from the open door. There is a second door, through to another room. Gangsters trek through our room as they come and go, excited at this apparent increase in their status. Our paraphernalia arrives, but the floor is unfinished. How will we cope with the dirt and builder's dust?

Paul goes out into the yard and grabs a tarpaulin. Some of the men object, but he persists. It's 'every man for himself' at such times. The tarp covers most of the floor in our room. Then we put our mat and mattresses on top. We shut and bolt the second door; the gangsters will be able to get into their room via the hall and passage. It looks as if we'll have more privacy here, but it will be dark most of the time. At least there is a false ceiling of plywood, which will improve the micro-climate – preventing convection of heat from the crinkly tin roof.

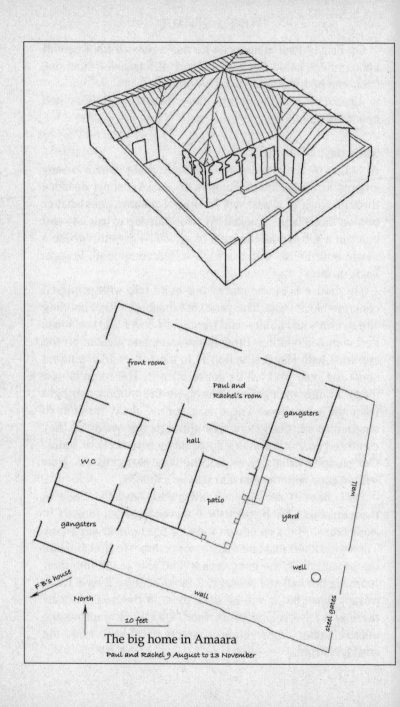

front room

Paul and
Rachel's room

gangsters

hall

W C

patio

yard

gangsters

wall

wall

F B's house

North

well

steel gates

10 feet

The big home in Amaara

Paul and Rachel 9 August to 13 November

The house is much bigger than those we have seen before. It must be under construction for someone important, or perhaps a wealthy pirate. The entrance hall and passage lead to the largest room and a WC, which has tiled walls and floor, complete with porcelain squatter. The tiler certainly wouldn't get a job in Western Europe! Deli will be disappointed – the plumbing is, as ever, a well in the yard and the usual plastic oil containers. The big room has a walk-in cupboard, in which the gangsters put the RPG launchers. There are two other rooms, each with access from the yard, where some gangsters settle. The front door doesn't open, so entry is via a covered and half-walled 'patio' area. We complain to Buggas that it is too dark in our room to read, so he tells us to sit in the hall. We spot three leftover concrete blocks and use them to make a table. Now we can play Scrabble and crib in relative comfort.

For all the distraction of a new place, the prospect of another four weeks cooped up here with this lot is daunting. The men are ratty – no doubt from the fasting. We too are ravenous and dying for some tea. We keep searching our minds for ideas, for some reason to be philosophical. Perhaps the builders have taken Ramadan off and that's why Buggas can use the house. Once Eid is over they'll have to move us somewhere else. Surely they must give up on us then?

Over the first week of Ramadan we muddle into a new routine. Although many of the gangsters pray regularly, there are quite a few who don't. Ivarr and Afieri are non-fasters; they continue to smoke, eat, drink and chew *chad* openly. HSB is the same, though he prefers chewing tobacco to smoking.

Rachel masters the mysteries of the *pochuko* to boil water for morning tea. If it is no longer warm from the pre-dawn cooking, the hardest part is finding a smoker to provide a lighter. When the watch changes, around 9 a.m., Ivarr cooks rice for our 'brunch'. After midday a boy brings a bag of meat from the village butcher. Afieri starts cooking the evening *ashok* around 4 p.m., when we get a flask of hot water for tea, followed by fried liver.

Fifteen or more gangsters gather in the yard every evening in anticipation of food and drink. Usually a few visitors come. A bucket of squash is mixed, using sachets of powder, lots of sugar and well water. At 6 p.m. they all tuck in to dates and squash, then wash before praying and squatting in groups for *ashok* – goat stew and chapati. We are offered the same, but our teeth struggle on the chewy meat, so we ask for just stock. Most of the gangsters dress up and go out afterwards, presumably to visit friends and family. How lucky they are!

We don't expect any 'events' during Ramadan. As we knuckle down, we take comfort in the relative privacy of our room. The temperature and humidity are tolerable. The toilet is convenient and more spacious, but we have a new skill to learn. The outlet from the hole is trapped and paper will not pass. Up to now we've been humoured in our strange Western habit of using toilet paper. But now there is nothing for it. We must remember which hand to use for what! It takes some getting used to.

The biggest downside to the house is the lack of space to exercise in. The yard is impossible – too small, too bumpy, too much sun – so we are reduced to pacing around the room in the dark. But at least it is comfortable to do half an hour or more of yoga before getting up every day.

> It's two months since we spoke to Stephen. My anger keeps creeping to the surface. I don't know what to do with myself. The gangsters are extremely irritable, bored with Ramadan, tired of being in the 'big home'. They are noisy both night and day. We never get any peace, either in our room or sitting in the corridor. HSB is forever on the scrounge. Ali Yeri keeps asking for news and money. Then he complains when I cut Paul's hair in the yard and insists I do it in the toilet! Sharif blames us when the toilet gets blocked. The gang are too lazy to bring in enough water to flush it properly. Fat Mohamed yells at me for going into the yard when they are washing for prayers. It goes on and on.

Buggas comes and goes. When he sits on the patio 'holding court', his presence is unbearable, but we have nowhere to go, except our dark room. One day he watches us play Scrabble. He is bemused by how slow it is. The gang's latest game is dice. It's very animated, because of the bets they put on – hundreds of dollars according to Ali Yeri. They don't understand quiet games. Or quiet anything for that matter. Buggas walks by and demands to look at Rachel's yoga book, which she is studying. The gangsters are mesmerised by the pictures of men and women doing the poses. 'Exercise,' explains Rachel, to which Buggas announces, 'Somali men no exercise!' He is so fat we can believe it.

Paul, suffering with a tummy bug, retires to his bed. The gangsters show their usual concern when they realise he's not eating. Abdullah turns up with a bottle of contact lens solution and some Well Woman tablets. Where did they come from?

Some of the gangsters are semi-comatose during the day, but there are now more of them moving around. Throwing rocks onto the roof is the new game. The guards on duty inside the compound hide away playing dice and ignore the pounding at the gates from anyone returning from a trip, even Buggas. There are usually one or two off duty, lounging around, but they won't open the gates either. Hence the rock throwing. Mature!

Sunday, 22 August
Paul's diary

Day 304. Ten months in captivity. No celebration.

Buggas has a clear-up in the yard, levelling off the ground to make an area for group prayers outside. Ali Deri and Ivarr help, then start digging a new hole for rubbish. Momentarily lost in wonderment at this burst of activity, we almost miss some incredible news on the radio – contact has been made with the trapped Chilean miners. Miraculously, they're OK, but it could take four months to get them out. How must they feel? Trapped like us but almost a kilometre underground in the dark? We can imagine only too well that they are experiencing the same feelings of vulnerability, frustration and helplessness, struggling to find hope.

Tension continues over food during Ramadan. By late Wednesday morning there's no sign of brunch, so Rachel asks the men playing dice on the patio: '*Maia cadu?*'

Sayid gives her the piece of liver from the meat delivery that arrived early. We decide to cook some rice, potato and onion to go with it. Paul does the chopping. When Rachel adds the rice to the pan, Sayid gesticulates for her to add more. They all watch us closely. When the food is ready, Ivarr appears. He and Ali Deri eat our leftovers. Ali Deri is another '*maia son*' (not fasting) even though he's a keen prayer. The others look on, uneasy. Later, we hear Ali Ad complaining to Buggas about '*behr*' and '*briis*', but hear no more about it.

Buggas visits again that same afternoon. He stands staring at us for a few moments, then says, 'Satellite. You like?'

We look blank, so he sketches out a box with his hands, points up at the wall, 'TV– satellite. Understand?'

We nod to humour him and Rachel questions the power source: 'Electricity?'

Buggas shrugs and walks out.

During Ramadan the gang has been operating – at best – on amber alert. We can't see what's happening outside the compound, but inside it's been rare for more than two or three of the gangsters to have their AKs in hand. The machine guns are kept inside, and there's been surprisingly little gunfire, for practice or otherwise. Now that changes. The machine guns are brought out and cleaned. Heavy firing practice follows. Buggas struts about in his usual self-important manner, shouting orders, before taking the machine guns away with some of the men. Ali Yeri is entrusted with the pistol and proudly parades around with it. He tells us there is inter-family fighting going on. The others that remain are subdued and tense. These people are not warriors. They have no cause.

Monday, 30 August

Buggas arrives with a large satellite dish, receiver, TV and generator, together with two new faces. One of them assembles the kit and starts the generator. We've not heard one being run in the village or seen signs of electricity being used. The TV sits on the ground in the 'patio', the dish and generator in the middle of the yard. Buggas turns to Paul expectantly and says, 'Search satellite,' so Paul laboriously rotates and tilts the dish, trying to find the direction of a satellite. Oh well, we don't have any pressing engagements!

The hangers-on are distracted, chatting to the gangsters, so Rachel's job is to watch the signal indicator on the screen. It's getting hot; the windblown sand is getting to Paul's eyes. We get a signal momentarily but can't latch on to it again. The generator runs out of fuel. That's a good excuse to stop. We're all disappointed. '*Baree*,' we agree.

By now it's sunset: time for drinks, dates, prayer and supper. We retreat for the night, happy with our radio. It's a lot less complicated.

The two 'TV men' come back the next morning with another generator and get it going. Paul is again sent out in the yard while it's up to Rachel to watch the screen. The men are a local tailor and his son. That would explain the generator – for a sewing machine. He speaks some English and offers to make Rachel clothes. When she tells him we have no money, HSB chips in, 'Money no problem. Buggas money.' While this conversation is going on, Paul has disappeared from the yard. He's been handed a phone and speaks to a man called Frans Barnard, a humanitarian worker who visits Adaado from time to time. He tells Paul that there is nothing he can do for us, but he will report to the British High Commission in Nairobi. We're upset by this. It's our first contact with the outside world for six weeks and another dead end. Calls like this are not helpful. To dismiss him as another interfering do-gooder who means well sounds churlish, but we now realise that such interventions merely muddy the waters and prolong our captivity. All they do is raise the expectations of the gangsters. We decide that if anyone else calls we'll tell them up front that if they have no concrete proposals they should stop interfering and leave us alone.

Samata asks us for a 'report'. Others, including the tailor, are standing around keen to know what's going on. We tell them this man can do nothing. They respond with the usual 'Stephen problem'. That's all they know. We are 'on the edge' emotionally. We rant at the tailor about how we've been captive for almost a year, about how despicable these people are, about how we should be with Paul's father, who is 99 years old. Of course he doesn't understand, but we are so furious, we need to let off steam at somebody, anybody, who might show some compassion. He looks embarrassed.

When brunch is offered, we refuse it. We need time to regain our composure.

Buggas appears, no doubt told of our outburst and refusal to eat. 'Problem?' he innocently asks, with the men looking on.

We have to respond, but what is the point? We say, 'Prison' – that sums it all up!

Buggas immediately replies, 'You free two weeks.'

We let it sink in. This is the first time he's predicted our release for some time. Do we believe it? Of course we want to believe it. Two weeks will be the end of Ramadan, so why not? It's credible, but we're beyond belief: we've heard such promises before . . .

Buggas moves back to the patio and sits with the others, joking and laughing, with the occasional mimicking reference to 'no money'. When they disperse, Rachel is openly crying in frustration. Some of the men notice. Abbas comes over and whispers, 'No problem.' Hamad gesticulates in a kind way as he stomps by. Then Buggas reappears and asks if Rachel wants a dress made. It seems a good idea. She changes into a T-shirt and long shorts, and gives the tailor her comfortable but tattered blue dress as a template.

We retreat to our room, listening to the radio and having a siesta, but are soon disturbed by the sound of the generator starting up. Paul is expected to go out in the yard again to try to find the satellite. Every now and then we get a weak signal, but it soon goes.

The tailor comes back. He's already made a new dress. Rachel tries it on, but it's too tight – and diaphanous! She gives it back to him, explaining the problem.

Afieri brings Paul the liver and kitchen knife. We turn our attention to preparing 'high tea'.

I'm sitting in my chair cutting up the liver. The kitchen knife is an aluminium-handled eight-inch steel blade with a good edge and a point. We are well organised, using a leftover glazed tile for a chopping board. Rachel is in the other chair, supervising, but she is being taunted. Samata is a devious, nasty piece of work, flaunting my diver's watch, which has found its way to him. He gives me the creeps and always has something malevolent to say. He stands over Rachel, staring, then shouting about the cost of liver.

'Fifty dollar!' he declaims. 'Every day FIFTY dollar!'

Rachel tries to ignore him, but he keeps repeating it. She picks up the bowl and thrusts it towards Samata: 'You have it. We don't want it. We didn't ask to be here.'

Samata winces and says, 'No,' and continues heckling, 'Every day fifty dollar.'

I've had enough of him. I jump to my feet, remaining piece of liver in my left hand, knife in my right, and shout back at him, 'Go away! Don't shout at my wife! GO AWAY!'

Samata turns towards me, and I automatically bring up the knife. I'm not genuinely threatening him. Or am I? Samata is shaking and shouting at me now. I thrust the liver towards him, 'You take it if it's so bloody important to you. Leave my wife alone!'

He knocks it out of my hand, onto the floor. Abbas

pulls him away; with Hamad and Deli, Abbas drags Samata onto the patio. No one else sees me as a threat; they leave me with the knife, but I don't want to carry on preparing liver. Samata continues to shout at us. Rachel picks up the bowl again and thrusts it towards Samata. He knocks it out of her hand, scattering the contents over the patio. We give up and I sit down again. We have not been 'good hostages' and we must wait for the consequences. Rachel retires to our room.

After an hour, Buggas turns up. He goes to one of the outer rooms, talks to Samata, then stalks into the hall. He rants in his horrible high-pitched angry voice, 'Rachel knife, MAKE KILL MAN!' He is salivating, drooling with anger.

Rachel comes out of our room and shouts back at him. I try to out-shout them both: 'I had the knife, NOT Rachel!'

We trade shouts for some time. He steps back and picks up a shoe, one of the men's slip-ons. He raises his arm. He's not close enough to hit either of us. Rachel repeats in a more measured way, 'I DID NOT have the knife.'

Buggas calms down, drops his arm, speaks with more control, a less high-pitched, 'You make knife. Kill you,' and slinks off.

It takes a while for my blood pressure to come down. Did we win? Or are we just lucky? It shows how easy it would be for a disaster to happen. And how short our fuses are getting. I know we must be careful to avoid confrontations like that. Thank goodness Abbas, Hamad and Deli were not far away. Some of the others might have egged Samata on rather than restraining him. I hate him.

We retreat to our room. After a while I sit out in the chair again. Afieri decides to be nice. He has picked up the liver and washed it. He sits in the other chair. '*Sahibki* [friend],' he says. '*Aniga, athiga sahibki.*' He points at himself and says, *'Behr, brr* for you.' I manage to eat; it would serve no purpose to refuse.

Later Hamad hobbles by and gesticulates with his spare hand – a downward movement of the palm meaning to stay calm. He puts his finger to his temple and says *'militiou'*, indicating they are crazy. Although Hamad can be disturbingly vocal in gang arguments, he does seem to have the capacity to think rationally. Most of the time he is serious and calm, though his monotonic religious chanting gets on our nerves. He has no English but makes the effort to say slowly, *'Insha'allah* London *wahir cabadi* [little later].' He looks sympathetic. Does he know something? He isn't one who has teased us before, and he doesn't seem the sort to mindlessly repeat things.

It's the last day of August and there is yet more entertainment. The tailor comes and starts the generator, but it breaks down. The noise is a pain, so we are happy. No sooner have we settled down for a siesta than it's started up again and the fumes are coming into the house. We still haven't found a satellite signal, so the tailor brings along a DVD player and a handful of films. The younger gangsters gather round and watch a fantasy movie in some strange language. They are mesmerised.

After sunset Buggas turns up with the tailor and they have another go. Men gather around the TV expectantly. We are sitting in the corridor listening to the radio. Buggas calls to us, 'Look, film.'

The tailor flips through the menus. We don't recognise anything until we see *The Day of the Jackal*. Buggas picks up on our interest and says, 'Jackal.' He likes the word. The film is selected.

The men make room for us to sit on the mat; it's a bizarre situation, all huddled together watching TV. When the film starts, we realise it's dubbed in an East European language. Luckily we remember the plot, as Buggas demands a commentary. While the gangsters enjoy the noisy, bungled shootout at the beginning, we do our best to explain that it's about an assassination attempt on Charles de Gaulle. It's surprising how much can be conveyed in simple terms and gestures. We confer before trying to explain the plot to Buggas, who then translates for the others. It must seem so strange to them. How can they comprehend the sophisticated world of 1960s France portrayed here? Some have visited Mogadishu, but we doubt even Buggas has been outside Somalia.

For once they are almost silent. When it comes to the end, Buggas is confused. He's missed the vital bit where de Gaulle moves his head so doesn't get killed. We explain that the assassin 'Jackal' fails, and he's very disappointed.

TV viewing continues for a few more days. When Buggas is here, we watch 'Jackal' again. Second time round we remember more of the plot and anticipate the bits the gang will be interested in, like when the Jackal kills someone. Rachel laughs at the rather slapstick scene where he kills an elderly woman who gets in his way. Ali Ad is surprised by her amusement at a killing. At the end we make them all watch very carefully to see the bit where de Gaulle moves his head and avoids the carefully placed bullet.

Wednesday, 1 September

Finally the tailor succeeds in finding the satellite. We are excited about the prospect of being able to catch up on global current affairs. Ever since hearing on the radio about the devastating floods in Pakistan we've come to realise how difficult it is to visualise the enormity of such events. We wonder what we'll see. Some channels are in English, but they turn out to be God slots. We glimpse a Vietnamese news station, more religious shows and a channel dedicated to go-go dancing. The men sit around watching each channel in turn for a few minutes before moving on to the next. They are fascinated as much by the US evangelists as they are with the Vietnamese news. Senick rushes in to join the throng and hails us with, 'Richer! Paw! TV gooood!', his face split by a huge grin. We can't help but smile at his boyish delight. The younger ones can't get enough of the go-go dancers, but the older men disapprove.

We are now into the final week of Ramadan. Some missing faces have come back – though not Samata – and the house is full. We are both feeling under the weather with colds and sore throats but muddle along, taking pleasure in small kindnesses or treats. Sayid has bought some yeast and sometimes makes leavened bread – the first we've had in almost a year. Rachel receives a modicum of praise from Sireet when she solves the problem of the cooking oil container. No one can open it. In turn they apply brute force to the top, but it stays stubbornly on. Rachel works out it must have been near the fire, as the plastic threads have welded together. Using a knife, she frees it up. They marvel at her ingenuity.

Paul has another ear infection, and it's making him grumpy. He's preparing potatoes and onions to cook with rice when Ali Yeri tells us to cook for six people. Will we be cooking for the lot of them once Ramadan is over? Actually, we don't mind, as it's something to do.

One morning our culinary efforts are disturbed by heavy gunfire nearby. The gangsters go into headless-chicken mode. They get out the guns and order us inside. Ali Ad calls Buggas, and they calm down a bit. We listen to the gunfire and watch the men's behaviour. It's probably a small local fracas. We no longer hope of rescue when this happens. Soon we go back to preparing lunch.

Thursday, 9 September

At sunset the builder's ladder is put up against the wall. Sireet and others climb up and stand on top, looking expectantly towards the west. They have sighted the first crescent of the new moon. Ramadan is over! Gunfire booms around the village in celebration. Eid-al-Fitr, the feast that marks the end of Ramadan, has begun. In the morning, breakfast begins with special bread: finger rolls that look 'shop-bought'. The gangsters relish their goat stew and we have liver. 'Life' is back to normal.

After breakfast, almost everyone gets dressed up in their best clothes and goes out. Hostages excepted! The house is peaceful for an hour. We've been pinning our hopes on getting released at Eid. This is a time of goodwill for Muslim people. Surely there will be pressure on Buggas to release us now? How can this community tolerate our prolonged captivity? Also, we've not seen any of the bigwigs – Ali, Omar, Fat Boy or the Commander – since before Ramadan. Have they given up on us?

Monday, 13 September

We're still here, sitting in the corridor, listening out for sounds of 'release' talk. Buggas is on the patio with his henchmen around him. At first he talks quietly, then the usual arguments break out, and the occasional burst of nervous laughter. Some of the men glance at us from time to time. It's unnerving – we know they are discussing our fate, but we have no idea what's going on. When they break up, Rachel starts crying. Paul tries to offer comfort, to no avail. Abdullah comes over and says, 'Flight, London, *hal tadobaad* [one week].' It's the first time Abdullah has said anything like that.

Later, Ali Ad asks how we are. When we shrug our shoulders, he says, 'London *tadobo malmod* [seven days] *insha'allah*.'

We reply *'insha'allah'* and find a small hope.

But days pass with no news. It's calmer because Buggas is away. The men are resigned, like us, just waiting. Paul is still a bit crook. His back is now twingeing. He can only walk stiffly, and yoga is impossible. Both his ears are oozing and itching like mad. He gives up an experiment using palm oil and starts using hydrocortisone eardrops to get on top of the eczema.

We settle into a new post-Ramadan mindset, holding onto the belief that something will happen soon. Another week passes. A new food and cooking regime emerges. We're given chapati and a bowl of tasty meat stock when the gangsters have breakfast. Afterwards we cook our liver. It all helps to fill the time and amuse us with little challenges. Every few days Paul crushes some of the local salt crystals, using the flat of the knife on the ceramic tile, so we can regulate the seasoning more effectively. We are not given a midday meal, so sometimes we cook rice. Supper is always *digir*.

Our hardest routine challenge is the daily battle for the chairs. At night the on-duty guards take them away; they like to sit on the 'patio' and later out in the yard, smoking if not chewing *chad*! When I get up in the morning, I psych myself up and go out, bleary-eyed, to recover my chair. It's become a game. There are 12 or more men, often with Buggas in attendance, sitting in the shade of the yard wall. One is in the chair. I make my way over, avoiding eye contact; I don't want to look at them at that time of day. I get close then ask, '*Kursi, fadlun* [chair, please]?' If it is Abbas, or Deli, or any of the youngsters in 'my' faction, they stand up and pass me the chair. But if it is Hamoud, Fat Mohamed or Sharif, they ignore me. Then Ali Yeri or Deli eggs me on, pointing, laughing and gesticulating that I should pull the chair away from whoever is sitting in it. If any of the nastier men are there, like Samata, they take up an aggressive stance; perhaps they chant, 'No money, no chair.' It's so difficult, but I know that it's a fight I will always win. They will give the chair up to me eventually. They have their orders.

I make my way back to the hall and join Rachel for our first cup of tea. Rachel has already been through the same process, but with a slightly different approach. Why do we find this so much of a struggle every day?

A week later Buggas reappears late morning and enquires about our water stocks. He asks if the food is good. He must have been told that we've stopped bothering to cook lunch.

We tell him breakfast and supper is enough. Later Ali Yeri cooks lunch for the first time since before Ramadan: spaghetti and vegetable sauce. He insists we get up from our siesta to eat it. Buggas's orders?

In the evening Buggas tells us he is waiting for a call; he's been negotiating with the man we spoke to. We presume he means Frans Barnard. Probably another red herring, but maybe, just maybe, something is going on. He also says that Stephen wants a new 'letter'. Intriguing!

I'm careful not to get my hopes up, to maintain a steady equilibrium, keep up my night-time mantra: 'I love you. Another day nearer release. X – 333 days to go. We'll beat these bastards.' Yes, it really is day 333.

It's Sunday, 19 September. I am half listening to the World Service and catch '. . . International Talk Like a Pirate Day . . .' They can't be serious? I listen on. Apparently they are. It has caught on, enough to warrant a five-minute slot on *Newshour*. The rolling of 'r's is appropriate, but there's not much 'Yo ho ho and a bottle of rum' or 'Heave ho, me hearties' here. A lighter moment, but how I do wish that the BBC had taken the opportunity to add a rider: that modern piracy is no laughing matter and that hundreds of hostages are held captive in appalling conditions.

Friday, 24 September

Hamad is now saying '*hal sano* [one year]', a reference to our anniversary of captivity in a month's time. I don't want to be reminded we could be here yet another month. It's all the same to them, just as long as they get fed. I've had enough of their nonsense and our fruitless discussions with them. I'm angry. I feel like picking up a gun and shooting my way out of here, regardless of the consequences. But I don't know how to use an AK-47.

Tuesday, 28 September

It's Paul's 60th birthday – we agree to postpone our celebration! Paul says he doesn't feel a day over 28, though he's not in perfect order. We usually go out for a meal to mark our birthdays, and we try not to think about the pizza we enjoyed last year at Sam's in Port Victoria.

Abbas hovers, so Paul explains. He doesn't know the word for birthday, although he's tried to find out on several occasions. He says in his best Somali that yesterday he was 59 and today he is 60. Abbas smiles; he tries to lift our spirits, but no one brings Paul a card!

Later we hear on the radio that the Puntland authorities have sentenced to death a pirate who killed the captain of a ship. We also hear mention of a hijacking that has been thwarted by using a citadel (safe room). It's some comfort to hear news that the pirates don't always win. The next day, we hear news of another ship hijacked off Tanzania. Gloom.

At the end of September they have another clear-up in the yard and fill in the waste pit. Is this housekeeping a sign? Abbas keeps saying, 'No problem, be happy, *hal sano.*' He means well, but he's said it so many times.

Soon they dig a new rubbish hole. It's a good idea to bury the rubbish, but to bury it in a ten-foot-deep hole within twelve feet of the well doesn't seem too bright. Oh well, we haven't died so far.

A month has passed since the 'knife confrontation', and we haven't seen Samata since – another indication that Buggas is not entirely daft.

It's now three weeks since the end of Ramadan – and we're desperately searching for signs of activity, anticipation, expectancy. Our ailments linger and wear us down. We exist, often irritable. Sometimes we bicker but quickly call a truce. Every moment together is precious – too precious to waste arguing. We have enough antagonism around us. There is so little hope to cling on to – no sign of any of the bigwigs for two months. We feel abandoned. Our only hope is that our one-year anniversary will generate some new activity.

Thursday, 7 October
Rachel's diary

> Still struggling with aftermath of cold. Not sleeping
> well. Weird dreams about life with the gang. My sub-
> conscious has well and truly accepted this as reality!

Buggas has been around this last week but has said nothing to us. We hear his voice but hardly see him until one evening he sits on the step blowing his nose on a pink rag. Quite a few of the gangsters have colds. When the men blow their noses, they close one nostril and let the snot fly out the other. Buggas is more refined. Paul asks him for more bottled water and is told 'tomorrow'.

Paul announces he's decided he hates Buggas. This is not a new topic of conversation. We often occupy ourselves discussing what we'd do to Buggas in the unlikely event that we get the opportunity to punish him for what he's done to us. Our ideas are unprintable.

There are only six or seven gangsters around, and the off-duty men go out for most of the day. On Friday afternoon Buggas delivers a bag of 'uniforms'. There are several sets of matching jackets and trousers in a buff-coloured cotton. Sireet dresses up for war; his jacket even has pouches for the RPGs. He is shy, with the gangsters as well as with us, takes his religion seriously (three-quarter Muslim) and has always been much happier with pots and pans than carrying a gun. But he is inordinately proud of the new uniform.

Ali Yeri has a go at Rachel for not cleaning the pan she used to cook rice. Talk about the pot calling the kettle black! The yard is a tip already, even though they had a tidy-up last week. When we ignore Ali, we know he'll find a way to get his own back. Usually it's to tear off a piece of our breakfast chapati as he hands it to us, then to stuff the piece into his mouth and chew as he watches us. Ali Yeri is a thinker. He's intelligent enough to feel trapped in his situation. When we say we're in prison, he says he's in prison too. He wants more than just guns and the oblivion that comes from *chad*, but what hope has he?

We get excited when Oman, Ali Yeri and HSB bring us a mobile phone. They are looking at a video. To our horror, we realise it's footage from our first video, taken last November with armed gangsters in the background. They laugh at our reaction. We're reminded of how pathetic and despicable they are.

On the evening of 9 October, we hear the sad news of Linda Norgrove's death and reflect on how lucky we are to be alive. Four days later comes news of a breakthrough for the Chilean miners. We listen to the news reports with fingers crossed as they emerge one by one. How happy we are for them to be rescued and reunited with their families! We can't help but feel an affinity to other people in similar situations to us around the world, whether hostage or trapped by some disaster. Surely it will be our turn for release some day?

Ali Yeri has taken to asking us for news updates every day. On three consecutive days, he asks, 'Speak Ali?' There must be something behind this questioning. Has he heard from someone that translator Ali is making progress? We dare not let our spirits rise; we must just keep healthy and hopeful.

After a day away, Buggas comes back with Samata – who stares at us but keeps his distance. We're given a box of grapefruit and bananas and enjoy our first fruit for some time. We also note with dismay that Buggas has stocked up on supplies for another month. So much for the idea that we'd have to vacate this house after Ramadan! We tell ourselves we'll be here until Christmas but secretly hope our one-year anniversary will be significant. We're finding it hard to conjure up reasons why Buggas should give up now. He's dug himself in so deep.

Ali Yeri and HSB keep asking Paul about BBC news, so we listen in to the World Service and hear about another kidnapping. A man working for Save the Children has been kidnapped by an armed militia in Adaado. Radio France International gives more detail – they say he is a security consultant working for the charity and that he has dual British and Zimbabwean citizenship. The gangsters learn of it by phone from their mates.

We also hear on the World Service that there has been fighting in Adaado between al-Shabaab and Ahlu Sunna Wal Jama'a. We tell Ali Yeri the BBC news about Adaado. He says Adaado is 'al-Shabaab no Ahlu Sunna Wal Jama'a'. What does this mean for us? Another British hostage in the area can only complicate things. And, if Adaado is unstable, what does that mean for our exit route? It's all very confusing. Ali Yeri also mentions that Ali Deri was in Adaado and was killed by a shell. We ask others about Ali Deri. We haven't seen him for a long time. '*Mort*,' is the stark reply. There is no emotion. We could have been talking about the football results for all they care.

Later in the week Paul gets trapped in a fruitless exchange with Ali Yeri and others about money. He tells Ali Yeri we'll be here for years and it annoys him. He has a more intelligent perspective than the others and struggles to maintain his confidence that we'll produce millions. We argue over how to handle Ali Yeri: Paul advocates keeping on his good side whereas Rachel won't pander to him, knowing his moods and pathetic threats are only ever temporary.

Wednesday, 20 October

'Our' region of Somalia – almost next-door, in fact – makes global news again. We wake up to a flurry of activity before sunrise. When we get up HSB is sitting atop the southern wall. 'Militia,' explains Ali Yeri, with plenty of gestures. 'Too much *nin, ah kay,* machine gun*, toban yr shun* Toyota, Zimbabwe *nin* free.' We question Ali further and establish that just before dawn 15 carloads of men, armed with AK-47s and machine guns, surrounded a house nearby. The occupiers did not resist and released a white man, who was promptly driven off. Ali is sure it was 'Zimbabwe' – released six days after his capture it seems. Other gangsters tell Paul that 'Zimbabwe' has been rescued by 'government'. Sounds intriguing . . . a successful rescue of a hostage held in the same village . . .

A few hours later, we hear on RFI that the kidnapped Zimbabwean has been released for a possible ransom of $100,000. The BBC also report the release, identifying him as Frans Barnard – the man who called Paul at the end of September – and mentioning Mohamed Aden, the District Governor in Adaado who was to have played a part in our release in June.

Ali Yeri and Senick tell us that 'Zimbabwe' had been brought to Amaara. Mohamed Aden's militia of 100 men came this morning to free him. He was released because 'Zimbabwe' – as they call him – is in control of World Food Programme money. They say definitely no money was paid! So much to think about. Who kidnapped him? Why? Presumably another Amaara gang. How many are there? At least he's now free. If Mohamed Aden can free him, why can't he free us?

Amongst all this intrigue, Buggas arrives. We're in our room. 'Rachel!' he calls. He only uses our first names on rare occasions. Usually it's – at best – a gruff 'hello'. Buggas hands over a black canvas bag containing medicines, books, toiletries, a compendium of games, pens and – contact lens solution (six months' supply!). The gang have already rifled through it, but there's still plenty for us. Some of the medicines have London pharmacy labels; others are in Boots plastic bags. There must have been some family input, at least some suggestions as to what we would appreciate. Rachel is intrigued by the prescription medicines, including Buccastem. Someone must have checked her medical records, as she was prescribed it five years ago for vertigo. Some of the medical equipment worries us. A chest-wound sealer – in case one of us gets shot? A strap and instructions for its use as a tourniquet – no good as Buggas has taken the vital metal bit. Did he think Paul might use it as a lethal weapon against Samata?

The books include at least two Dickens – well, they will be a last resort, as neither of us can cope with small print – and four very welcome books of *Telegraph* crosswords. The games compendium has been 'inspected' by the gangsters – the playing cards and dice are missing! Inside the bag is an airline tag, passenger name Mohamed Dahir, flying from London to Nairobi, via Dubai. Thank you, Mohamed! Paul is so pleased to have the lens solution. We don't dwell on the time it will take us to finish 960 cryptic crosswords.

After claiming a small first-aid kit-bag for himself, Buggas disappears for the night but returns the next morning, smiling most unusually and waving a small Somali–English phrasebook. 'Book good?' he asks. He turns to some phrases and tries to read the English. He finds a random word in Somali, says it, then slowly reads the English translation: 'river estuary'.

Rachel says, 'Yes,' and repeats, 'river estuary'.

He checks: 'All word, Somali, English?'

We say yes, it's like a dictionary, and yes, that will be useful. Not for us though, it seems. He grins and marches off with it. We're disappointed. Someone has kindly sent it to us, and we'll probably never get to use it.

Saturday, 23 October

It's the first anniversary of our captivity, 365 long traumatic and depressing days since our idyllic cruising life turned into a nightmare in the dark of night. Rachel has another head cold. Double reason to be miserable. We listen to our favourite Saturday-morning Voice of America programmes and catch a news item mentioning us. The Somali information minister is calling for our release, saying our captivity is a shame on all of Somalia. The BBC broadcasts a report too. We are the longest-serving pirate hostages. Maybe we'll get a medal.

The gangsters say nothing to us about the milestone, though we suspect their hopes will be raised. Buggas has been very laid-back recently. He presides over such bountiful *chad* sessions each afternoon that they keep forgetting to give us supper.

By the end of October the mood of the gang has become

decidedly tetchy. Buggas yells a lot, either at the men or at his phone, which he swings wildly at arm's length while conversing. The others are petulant, picking on us. When we try to ignore Ali Yeri's requests for 'news', he stands over us teasing, 'Money, four million.' They mention 'Zimbabwe, money!' It's a reminder of how sick these people are. They're now hoping to get money from Save the Children! When they're like this, all we can do is sit it out or retreat into our dark room. The calming afternoon *chad* sessions are no more.

The seasonal climate change has started. The prevailing wind moves towards the north and we have rain showers, fairly short and light, most afternoons. There is no sign of any more bottled water. We ask every day, but the standard answer is an unconvincing '*baree*'. Eventually, Ali Yeri tells us to use the well water. We're sure there is no problem drinking the water from it. But why now? After all this time. Perhaps the money, or credit, has finally been exhausted. That could be a good sign. We add an item into the routine – boiling a kettle after breakfast each day. We decant it, after cooling, into the last of our empty water bottles.

The mosques are busy with their calls to prayer and sermons broadcast loud and clear. Is 1 November a special day? The village children are noisier than usual. We hear a whistle being blown and lots of shouting, as if they're having a football game. How we wish we knew what was going on, but it's futile trying to ask any of the gangsters. Sometimes we hear the sound of construction work – an unfamiliar sound – sawing and creaking, then a crash, repeated as several large trees are cut down just outside the compound.

Everyone is listless. There's little breeze so it's hot and sticky. Samata is as sullen as ever, walking around scowling, with a pistol in his hand, though he stays away from Paul. Sireet takes offence at me showing my legs, saying, '*Somali nag* [women], *maia . . .*' pointing at my khaki cotton three-quarter-length shorts. I'm not bothered, but I'm prompted to remind Buggas that the tailor has yet to return with my dress!

Wednesday, 3 November

The gangsters are in the back room playing dice, leaving a peaceful setting for our morning game of Scrabble. A mobile rings and the shouts begin. The next minute everyone is up, charging around the house and yard, grabbing their guns, preparing for action. A Toyota arrives and all four machine guns appear from the inner cupboard and the outer rooms. Hamoud and Senick each take one, wrapping the belts around their shoulders and waists. Buggas takes the other two out to the cars. Ali Yeri says there is a problem. Abbas comes over and says, 'Buggas. *Biu* [water].'

In the past, Buggas has often taken a bottle of water from us when he's going on a trip, but now we have none left. Abbas looks at us beseechingly and Fat Mohamed moves in to demand '*barballe* [bottle]'.

I say, 'No water. No bottle.' We have no spare bottles – just enough to keep our boiled drinking water in. We will NOT be inconvenienced by their stupid demands. The stand-off continues. Thinking it might suffice, I pick up an old water bottle we keep for washing our hair. Fat Mohamed grabs it. Paul doesn't want him to have it, so grabs it back. Fat Mohamed is incensed. He stands back, raises his gun, points it at Paul and cocks it. Abbas pushes through and seizes the gun while others drag Fat Mohamed away. They grab the bottle again, plus another half-full bottle, and rush off.

I'm stunned. How close was Paul to being shot? Shy Sireet just stands there and witters on about 'militia problem'. We take a deep breath and sit down, picking up the Scrabble tiles that have been scattered everywhere. We recreate our game and continue. Another day . . . another sign of how tense Paul is.

We don't hear any fighting and things go back to normal. There is no aftermath from our confrontation, no harangue from Buggas.

A day later, all seems quiet when we hear the sound of a car pulling up at the side of the house. There's a small hole in our window shutters from which we can glimpse a little of what's going on outside. Rachel spies a smart white Toyota parked nearby. We listen out for signs of special visitors and hear Fat Boy's distinctive laugh. This is the first time we have seen him, or any of the leaders other than Buggas, since we returned to Amaara. We hope it's a good omen. He holds a pow-wow on the patio, and afterwards everyone is making phone calls. Kindly Abbas says to us, 'International community,' as if it's significant.

Fierce argument erupts the next day, mostly between Fat Boy and the gangsters, sometimes with Buggas. Two older men, quite smartly dressed – one wears a tunic, trousers and glasses and carries a stick with luminous tape around it – appear in the afternoon. They have an air of authority, but they don't talk much. The mood amongst the gangsters is sullen and resentful. More turn up in the afternoon. Fat Boy holds another big gathering, followed by a lot of arguing on the sidelines and phoning. Abbas and HSB tell us, 'Three . . . prison.' Despite repetitions, we don't understand. Tension builds. There's a sense of waiting, of anticipation. Everyone is unsure, nervous.

We wake on Saturday to find a large, boisterous group in the yard. Sharif is sitting in Rachel's chair. When she approaches, he scowls and points his gun at her. He doesn't cock it; the threat is not real. We no longer fear guns being pointed at us. He's just reminding us who's boss before giving up the chair.

Afieri starts asking us about news. He keeps saying, 'Three British, *nin*, *budde* [boat], one *mort*.' After a long exchange we understand him to mean that three British have been attacked on a boat in the Indian Ocean, with one killed while two have escaped. Do they mean a yacht? There is no report

343

on the World Service. After dark there is yet another long, restrained pow-wow with Buggas and Fat Boy in the outer room. All is quiet afterwards.

Buggas and Fat Boy leave at first light the next day. HSB is speechless – something must be up! Ali Yeri gives us a short measure of stock for breakfast. He too is sullen. He comes into the hall, 'No money, you dead! *Baree*, you dead.' Can this be it? Have they finally been made to realise that they won't get rich from this venture?

For the next few days the gangsters are very pissed off. Buggas brings *chad* in the afternoon and sits in the yard, chewing it, with Afieri, HSB and Ali Yeri. All day long they taunt us, telling us again and again of the incident in which three British people were attacked. Now they say one man fought and was shot dead, while his wife and ten-year-old daughter were taken by al-Shabaab. Their boat ran aground. That's our best guess at interpretation.

They won't bring us hot water for tea. Paul demands some from Afieri, who comes over and squats by us, smiling. Then he says, 'Give money, one million five hundred.' We laugh and tell him the usual – no money, old people, no big ship. He tells us that al-Shabaab will take us tomorrow. They will kill us. '*Bim. Bim*,' he mimes shooting, pointing at Paul, then he makes a decapitating gesture at Rachel.

'He lies,' says Buggas, who is sitting on the step. We're surprised at Buggas's intervention, as it's the first time he's spoken to us in days. He remains calm and not unfriendly. We sense he is keeping an eye on things – but Afieri won't let up. 'Where *midi*?' he demands. He wants the knife. We point to where it has been all day, sitting in a bowl. Afieri insists Paul finds it, so Paul picks it up, shows it to him and drops it again. Buggas is smiling as he says, 'He has no eyes.' HSB joins in the chorus of 'You. Al-Shabaab. *Mort*'. Buggas points at HSB: 'This man *ari* [goat].' The men are quiet – for once the *chad* isn't making them laugh.

Afieri is the one most enraged. He probably has the most to lose if we are right and they have finally realised there are no millions of dollars. Being part of the attack group, he would expect a bigger share. According to Ali Yeri, he's already had his Toyota as a reward and has crashed it!

In the morning the gang are subdued – yesterday's *chad* has had its effect. After breakfast Buggas has a pow-wow for an hour. Again it is muted. Remarkably there is no argument. Paul hears the number 600 mentioned.

Afieri continues to be in a foul mood, muttering 'al-Shabaab' whenever we're near and shouting at us. We hope his behaviour is a sign they are giving up. In the afternoon Abdullah and Ali Ad turn up and join in more heavy discussions with Buggas on the patio. Ali Ad keeps glancing over at us. We hear mention of 'Zimbabwe' a couple of times.

Wednesday, 10 November

Abbas asks, *'Kam malmod* [how many days]?'

'Sadeh bocol yr sideeten,' Paul replies, writing '380' in the dust.

Abbas thinks, then writes '390' in the dust. *'Sadeh bocol yr segashen* free,' he says, making a flying gesture with his hands.

Three hundred and ninety – after ten days we will be free? Can we truly start to believe? Abbas is always well meaning. But this isn't him trying to cheer us up. This is him giving us information. There must be something in it. With the mood change, the finishing of the water, the visit from Fat Boy, surely there are too many signs for it not to be true? Tentatively, we start to believe.

Ali Yeri and HSB pester us for news. They won't take no for an answer. Every couple of hours they taunt us. Before lunch they become aggressive, crowding us in the hall. Another man comes up behind them. He is armed with an AK-47, but he is not one of the gang. He is a little older, better dressed and quiet. His presence unnerves Ali and HSB. They slink away. The stranger gestures to Paul, with five fingers spread on one hand. What can he mean? He goes away, crosses the yard and stands by the wall, in sight of the patio and hall. He is keeping an eye on us. Whenever one of the gangsters approaches now, he is not far away, watching, but he doesn't speak to them.

On Friday morning Ali Yeri goes out. When he returns, he comes over to us full of boyish energy and says, 'Four *malmod* you free. All *nin* free' – indicating the gang with a sweep of his arms. He continues, 'Buggas speak Mohamed Aden.'

He is serious. We're used to his mood swings. He has got over the melancholy, the disappointment. He's stopped goading us about millions. He will be glad to see the back of us, but what next? Perhaps he will go to fight with al-Shabaab. Probably not – he is a thinker, not stupid.

We talk it through. First Abbas, now Ali Yeri, both somehow believable; and the stranger with his hand of five. Is there such a thing as sceptical optimism? If so, we embrace it.

Buggas comes to see us in the afternoon: his first approach since bringing the last parcel. He chooses a moment when there is no one close. From his body language it looks as if he is psyching himself up. 'You go,' he says hesitantly. 'After three days, week, Sunday, Monday, you go airport. Somali family give 200. You go London.' Then he waddles off.

We are astonished. Is this the news we've been longing for? He seems so calm. We'd expected him to be angry. We certainly didn't expect any 'polite' notice. We assumed we'd be bundled into a Toyota, taken on another long journey and dumped in a remote location where our rescuers would find us. We must take it easy, go on as if 'normal' and avoid confrontations. If it really is true, and their hopes of big payouts have been shattered, we can expect resentment, at the very least.

Saturday, 13 November

I'm awake in the early hours, sick with diarrhoea. As soon as it's light I go to get water from the well. The yard is full of gangsters, but they're friendly. Sharif says, '*Sadambe* London.' Abdullah and Ali Ad concur. Surprisingly, everyone is buoyed up.

After breakfast there is a quiet pow-wow in the back room. The stranger who had on Thursday given us the 'five' sign is there with Buggas. The assembled gangsters listen to him attentively.

When the gangsters drift away they seem happy – at least not angry or sullen. Sayid, Hassan and Abbas come over to us, smiling as they say, 'You free *baree.*' They hide any disappointment well; are they relieved, looking forward to resuming their normal lives? Afieri, HSB, Ali Yeri, Sayid and Abbas all ask to come to London with us!

Rachel's tummy problems have not abated – hardly surprising given the turmoil in our minds. But we concentrate on our daily game of Scrabble. It is our 151st game in Somalia, and yesterday Rachel crept ahead by 15 points in the current rubber – still a long way from the 500-point lead necessary to win.

Halfway through the game, Sharif comes and tells us to pack, gesticulating with his AK-47. He hassles us to bring our bags onto the patio. HSB and Ali Yeri watch as we put them down. 'Books,' they say, pointing at the bags and miming opening them. They still won't touch our things. It's as if they are under strict instructions not to – though some of them are happy to help themselves if we leave things lying around! What do they want books for? These three can't read Somali, never mind English. We humour them, passing a novel to Sharif. He riffles the pages and hands it back, shaking his head. 'Books! Books!' he says, losing patience. Paul pulls out a plastic bag containing his handwritten summary timeline for John Gribben's book – a thick bundle – and three faces light up. Sharif snatches it away. They are looking for what we have written, for our diaries! Ali Yeri, in particular, has always taken a keen interest in our diary writing. We shuffle through our bags, trying not to disclose anything, handing over different books and getting them back when they find no handwriting. Their attention switches to Rachel. Sharif stands over her and insists she empty her bag. She cannot hide her diary any more. He takes it with glee, and her notebook, even her address book. Paul takes the chance to open his second bag and starts getting out clothes, diverting attention from the first bag. 'OK. OK,' is the response, so Paul stuffs as much as he can back into the first bag, burying his diary, our ship's papers and other documents. HSB grabs Rachel's purse – given back to her on the *Kota Wajar* – finding somewhere to hide it while the others are distracted. Sharif and Ali Yeri are content with what they've got and leave us to re-pack.

The search was very inept. Surely Buggas or others would have searched properly if the order was from above? We suspect it was Ali Yeri, who knows we keep diaries. He is scared of retribution and persuaded Sharif to take action. Rachel is disappointed about surrendering her diary and notes, but philosophical. It's all in her head. After all we've been through, she is determined not to let a little incident like this upset her. But what is going on? Will we leave today? Should we resume our game of Scrabble?

The gangsters are ready, hanging around like us, waiting and expectant. And there are two strangers. They stand apart, watching the gangsters – and us. It's almost as if they're on our side. When anyone else approaches, these two keep them under eagle-eyed scrutiny, as if to check we are OK. Another mystery.

Three hours later Mr F turns up. He saunters across the yard, smiling and offering his hand. We shake, out of politeness. 'You go. Now.' We ask about our boxes of household things. Should we bring them along? Mr F smiles. 'No need.' He picks up a bag.

> Senick comes over, smiling. He is encumbered with machine gun and ammo belt, but he makes light of it. He too offers me his hand. I am confused, conflicting emotions run riot. But he means well; he is genuine, has no guile. His naivety has often been such a welcome relief from the intensity and nastiness of many of our captors. I shake his hand, say goodbye. I am smiling too.

Senick regains control of his machine gun and points it at us, finger back on the trigger, selector set to semi-automatic. He swings it towards the gate. It's time to leave. At gunpoint, we walk through the yard and out.

Three Toyotas are parked a short distance away, alongside a row of houses. The gangsters are milling around. As we get in, village children of all ages are standing close by, watching the activity, gawping at us, interested to see what, or whom, all the fuss has been about. Our bags are put in the back of the car, but it takes a while to get organised. Buggas is moving around, barking orders. The other cars manoeuvre; gangsters argue about who goes with whom. After three whole months inside, we are finally leaving the 'big home'.

But for where?

Passage to freedom

Saturday, 13 November continued

Buggas jumps in through the tailgate of our car. He slouches on the bags, clutching a bunch of *chad*. Someone passes him a machine gun. The back window stays down. He arranges himself so that he can point the machine gun out in chief gangster pose and shouts to the gawping crowd as we pull out of Amaara. Our driver is Hurday, an aloof character, not a day-to-day gangster. Senick sits in the front, with his machine gun. Sandwiched into the back with us are Deli, Hassan and five AK-47s. The men are heavily armed, but there are no Land Rover escorts, just two other Toyotas crammed with gangsters; they're not expecting a fight. Somali music plays loudly on the radio; everyone is chatty – except us.

We drive westward, freedom beckoning. Buggas asks Rachel how she's feeling and then for her phone number in England. After a sharp intake of breath, Rachel reminds him she no longer has a number; Buggas has taken everything. He replies, 'You London. Give money for hotel Amaara.' He wants us to send him money for our board and lodgings! Pirate humour again? We say nothing, exasperated.

For five uncomfortable hours we sit tight. These could be the most dangerous few days of our ordeal.

We follow a now familiar route but eventually divert northwards, perhaps to avoid the larger villages. It's unbearably squashed with four of us on the back seat. The drivers make frequent stops for debate, accompanied by long, heated mobile phone discussions; they're unsure of directions. Finally, it's time for dusk prayers, and we're allowed out. Rachel lies on the ground to rest her aching back. We re-start, and there are now only three of us in the back. Someone has registered our discomfort. Buggas has gone too. It must be even more crowded in another car.

From time to time the convoy changes – a car leaves, another one joins. Two more Toyotas join us, so we are now six cars. As we converge, we realise that Fat Boy, the Commander and Omar are here. Maybe they have driven out from Adaado to wish us goodbye?

Eight p.m. We stop in an area of low bush and scrubland. Hurday drives on a hundred yards beyond the other vehicles. The gangsters spread around. We wait. Now, above all, we must be patient. We're allowed out to straighten up and stretch. The gangsters form small groups and sit, smoking and talking, not far from us. The top brass are gathered around the other cars. There is no sign of a camp being made. No food or drink on offer. We don't want anything – only freedom.

Hurday returns. We must get in the car and sleep. One of us can move into the front passenger seat, which reclines. Three men sit ten paces away on watch. Paul takes out his lenses and gets in the front. Rachel curls up on the back seat. It's hard to relax. We went through all this in June and can't help feeling jittery. Could this be another of their cruel tricks? We keep our negative thoughts to ourselves. Privately we are both alert to the slightest sound. Time passes.

Clunk!

Hurday locks our car doors with the remote key. Fear rises . . . Why would he do that?

It's OK – we can still open the door from the inside.

We wait . . . And doze fitfully.

Three a.m. I become aware of a man standing on my side of the car, only three or four paces away. There's something odd in his demeanour. Or is my state of heightened nerves letting me make something of nothing? I try to doze again.

First light, about 5.30 a.m. Translator Ali appears by our car. He's here too! Surely a good sign. He asks if we have all our possessions. Paul tells him the gangsters have taken Rachel's diaries. Rachel chips in to say that Buggas has her jewellery. Ali just strokes his chin and wanders off. Some hope, but worth a try! We're stiff and want to stretch our aching limbs. Tentatively we open a door and ask to go to the toilet. Hurday gestures towards a bush not far away. We walk gingerly through the scrub – Rachel leading a contact lens-less Paul – and find a bush big enough to squat behind. Business done, we move a few yards and crouch down together while Paul puts in his lenses.

The sky lightens by the second . . .

A stranger approaches on foot, followed by two others with guns. He's wearing a flak jacket and baseball cap and waving what looks like a British passport. 'I am Kadiye,' he says. 'I am British, from East London. *I have come to take you home.*' We shake his hand. We hug. There are tears in my eyes. I look at his passport – Dahir Abdullahi Kadiye – but there is no need to check. My senses are screaming that this is genuine. This man is our rescuer, my Number One Superhero.

Is this for real? Where did he come from all of a sudden? I look at him wide-eyed. Who is this smartly dressed man, showing us his British passport? He says he's a friend of Stephen's. I manage a meek 'yes' in reply. When he hugs us, I'm even more dumbfounded by this extraordinary behaviour: so warm, so kind, so compassionate. This is a very special man indeed.

The morning is now bright. A white Toyota edges close. 'My car,' says Dahir. 'My men,' he indicates the two armed Somalis with him, also smartly dressed. He asks about our belongings. We point towards Hurday's Toyota and say we have five bags. They've been with us this long; we don't want to lose them now. Dahir organises the transfer, talking in Somali to his guards, then in English to us. He hands Rachel his phone to speak to Stephen while they're loading up our bags. Stephen confirms that Dahir is a friend and it's OK to go with him! The call is short: the line isn't good and Dahir is keen to move on. We won't see Stephen until we reach England, but Helen, Paul's niece, is in Nairobi. Stephen warns of intense media attention and to avoid giving interviews. Presumably, he wants to fill us in on what has happened first. That makes sense. It's all beginning to fall into place.

Dahir leads us to his car, an upmarket Toyota like Ali's, and introduces us to a journalist, who starts filming and asking questions. So much for avoiding the media! We sidle into the comfortable back seat. Dahir and a driver get in – and we're off! Two other cars of Dahir's, bristling with guards, escort us. We drive past the gangsters' Toyotas and head away to the west. They follow us, driving in echelon, for 30 or 40 yards then converge on the track. Dahir explains that they will stay with us, as protection, until we are closer to Adaado, where Mohamed Aden's troops have control.

In between phone calls, Dahir says he's taking us into Adaado, where we'll meet Mohamed Aden and then fly to Nairobi. Who is this amazing man, Dahir? What has prompted him to put himself in harm's way to rescue us? He tells us how he and his family arrived in Britain from Somalia as refugees in 1997 and how his son Yusuf came home from school last spring and pleaded, 'Dad, can't we do something to help these people?' Dahir has been here for six months trying to get us out and has trained up a militia especially for this operation. He seems an unlikely military man, at least not the loud, muscular type. Then again, he's very organised and reassuring, despite talking non-stop. We so want to believe he can get us out of here.

We make our way through the scrub, slowing down at the rocky bits, sometimes stopping for a short while, then moving forward again. After about ten minutes, Dahir is looking out of the window. He points to where our gangsters are now parked, just off the road, watching us go by. Finally we are left – three cars, driven by the good guys, on our way to freedom.

We don't look back at what we're leaving behind: our attackers, captors and tormentors of the last 388 days. Good riddance . . . we hope! Can we genuinely believe we are free now?

Dahir phones Yusuf and passes us the handset. An enthusiastic youngster tells us how happy he is to speak to us. He's so proud of his father.

We stop again. We're in the middle of nowhere, just scrubland, and no sign of Adaado. Some of the men get out and walk around as if checking for something. Dahir is making lots of phone calls. For us, it's a moment of heightened concern. No doubt Dahir is being careful not to frighten us, but we know there are risks. We hold each other tightly, apprehensive but certain that we are in good hands. Then we move on again.

At last we see the outskirts of Adaado. As we approach, Dahir tells us more about his security arrangements. He says Mohamed Aden has a militia of 60 men, but there is always a chance that the loyalty of some may waver. So Dahir has one of his own armed men with each of Aden's men. He also has small groups of men in strategic positions around a 20-mile circumference from Adaado, ready to alert him. The risks are huge. Another local gang could have a go at capturing us; al-Shabaab or Ahlu Sunna Wal Jama'a may see an opportunity to make mayhem; or a splinter group of our original gang of kidnappers might attempt a further attack. For the time being we will be at a very high risk of re-capture, injury or even death.

Dahir calmly runs through the plan with us. We will have a medical check, followed by a shower, breakfast with Mohamed Aden and then a short meeting with local elders. Afterwards, we will be taken to the airport and out of Somalia. He keeps telling us we mustn't worry, we are now free. We're happy to go along with his plan. What else can we do? We know that we're not yet safe, but we're so close, and we'll cooperate with whatever face-saving exercises the local elders require.

Adaado is not the metropolis of multi-storey buildings we had imagined, just the usual clusters of single-storey huts and stone/blockwork buildings, though more extensive than any towns we have seen before. We reach a tarmac road – the first we've seen in over a year. A few minutes later we come to a large, walled compound on the left, a pair of blue gates swings open, and we drive in. The gates slam shut as we come to a halt outside a substantial rendered block building, with a big official emblem next to the entrance. 'Republic of Somalia Himan & Heeb Regional Authority' is written in a circle around an image of a spiky tree with two Somali flags projecting from its foliage. We have reached the next stage.

A short, chubby man in his late 30s, wearing Western dress of trousers and a blue striped shirt, baseball cap and designer sunglasses, grasps us firmly by the hand as we get out of the car. 'Ah'm Mohamed Aden, welcome to Himan and Heeb,' he says, in perfect American. He's not at all like the 'elder' we expected.

There are many people milling around, armed with cameras if not guns. After a few introductions, we're taken inside the administration building and shown into a small side-room, with our bags. It's confusing, with many people coming and going, asking us questions, but it feels good to sit down in a proper building, a normal room with furniture and lighting.

The next few hours are a blur. Dr Hangul, who examined us in January near Amaara, is here. He didn't know what state we might be in and is relieved not to have to do more than get out his stethoscope and blood-pressure monitor. After examining us he concludes we are in surprisingly good condition, though we're both dehydrated with rather high blood pressure. With a grin he prescribes rest, knowing there will be precious little of that today. He explains that he is based at the Medina hospital in Mogadishu and has been working towards our release for some time with Dahir and another man who is arranging the plane.

Mohamed Aden presents us with clean clothes: a traditional Somali dress and shawl for Rachel, shirt and *ma'awiis* for Paul. We take turns in the shower and change before breakfast. The bathroom is a wonder: large and airy, with a wide-open window, a blue curtain billowing in the breeze. Washing is by the usual method – a jug dipped into a big barrel of water – but there is an unfamiliar bit of kit under the window. A Western WC!

Once we are dressed in our new Somali outfits, we sit down to breakfast in the main room. Mohamed Aden sits on one side of a large table, properly laid with knives and forks, plates and a bowl of lovely fresh bread rolls. He invites us to tuck into omelette and fried eggs, with tomatoes and flatbread. 'The nearest I could get to an English breakfast,' he says. Dahir is busy outside, checking on the security; a few Somali journalists hover, wanting to take photos and ask questions. We recognise Mohamed Dahir who interviewed us in July. Hungry and desperate to eat, we keep being interrupted by requests to speak to the media. A female caller from Al Jazeera on Mohamed Aden's phone asks Rachel to hang on indefinitely for their next 'live' show. Rachel politely declines, preferring to eat her breakfast! Paul is called away to talk to the World Service and then Voice of America. Another caller insists on telling Rachel she has a bag of toiletries for her. We simply want to do justice to our freedom breakfast!

In between phone calls and snatched bites of breakfast, Mohamed Aden explains more about the meeting with elders. Soon we'll go next door, where they are assembling. There will be speeches, but we won't have to do anything he reassures us. Then we'll have a rest before the plane arrives. We're looking forward to that. After a sleepless night, all this attention is exhausting.

Dahir comes in briefly to tell us we can't fly straight to Kenya; we must go to Mogadishu to meet the prime minister and members of the TFG. No problem. So long as we're on our way home, we're happy. Paul is excited by the thought of seeing Mogadishu, a place we've heard mentioned so often on the World Service news. Rachel's keen to meet the prime minister and hear what he has to say.

We adjourn to a separate building, a crowded meeting hall. The front rows of seats are filled with men of all ages, mostly dressed in traditional gear. The local elders? A small group of women sit together at the back. The top table is covered in decorative bags, woven baskets and leather pots. Five or six men are at the table, including Mohamed Aden on one end. We sit next to him, and he promises to translate.

Short speeches follow. The elders are effusive and apologetic, expressing their deep sorrow and regret about what has happened to us and insisting that the gangsters are not representative of their community, their culture or their faith. Another man, from the Somali diaspora in the USA, rails against the international community for not doing enough to help. He clearly has an axe to grind! Some other elders come to the front. Their body language shouts 'I'm not comfortable with this'. Mohamed Aden translates: 'We wish we could have helped, but we were not powerful enough.' Oh yes? But you managed to get Frans Barnard out.

It's our turn to speak! Wearily, we stand up. There is no sense in being anything but polite. We just want to be allowed to go home to our family, so we accept their apologies gracefully. We certainly don't hold these people fully responsible for our ordeal. Perhaps some good can come out of what happened to us. Maybe it will help galvanise action to solve the complex problem that is Somalia. We promise we don't think all Somalis are bad. We're genuinely thankful to those who've contributed to making today possible.

A woman comes to the front and presents us with some of the craftwork on display: a woven handbag, two woven saddlebags and a lidded container that smells of goat. We accept these small examples of local enterprise graciously.

As we leave, I ask Mohamed Aden to introduce me to the women, who are sitting at the back. They smile at my greeting, and one of them chastises me for not wearing the traditional scarf over my head. She rearranges it to cover my hair and we laugh together. Oh, that this was another time, another place . . . I don't think these are inherently bad people, but sadly their sons are easily led astray.

We walk back into the sunshine for yet more photography. It's strange being the centre of attention, albeit friendly. At last we can have a rest for an hour before going to the airport. Next stop Mogadishu. The capital of Somalia might be one of the most dangerous places in the world, but we don't feel frightened. For the first time in 388 days the end is in sight. We might as well enjoy the process. We get out of our traditional dress and lie down, but it's impossible to rest. Instead we re-pack our bags. Do we want to carry all these books back to the UK? How about donating some to Mohamed Aden for the local school? Amongst others, he gets *A Tale of Two Cities* and *Huckleberry Finn*.

Finally it's time to go. We climb eagerly into a Toyota with Mohamed Aden, driven by a burly, smartly dressed Somali. Mohamed Aden's militia are definitely a cut above those we've been used to. There are no armed men in the car, but we pull out of the gates into a convoy of more than fifteen Toyotas and three or four Technicals. Is this the real danger time?

We count ten cars ahead, while two or three kick up a cloud of dust each side in echelon formation as we race along the thin tarmac road towards the airport. We pass the Adaado orphanage, a big low building with a bright-blue roof. A gaily painted sign reads 'Kafaalo Schools'. Is this an example of what Mohamed Aden's governorship is achieving?

It's a mere ten minutes' drive south to the airstrip. As we veer off the tarmac for the last mile we see a car – not one of ours – being shouldered aside by one of Mohamed Aden's pick-ups.

We lurch to a halt where a row of small stones marks the taxiing area. The minute airstrip building is off to our left, two more Technicals with big guns parked close by. With impeccable timing, a small twin-engine plane, 5Y-RJA, taxis towards us, turning and coming to a halt 50 yards away. This is it! Escape at last! We look at one another, close to tears. It's beginning to sink in. We really are leaving this place that has stolen almost 13 months of our lives.

We hurriedly shake hands with Mohamed Aden, while Dahir urges us towards the steps that are coming down from the plane. A tall, tanned, European man with dark hair, neat beard and moustache jumps down and introduces himself with a handshake as Dom. In jeans, desert boots and a short-sleeved shirt, he has an aura that tells you he knows how to look after himself, the sort of man you'd want on your side in a fight. He *is* on our side. But there's no time for pleasantries – he ushers us up the steps with our four bags in his hands. Dahir is already on board.

By the time Dom has thrust our bags in through the door there is a crush at the bottom of the steps. A Somali man, determined to gatecrash the flight, hurtles up the steps and rams his big case halfway through the doorway. He's no match for Dom. The case is hurled back on the dirt, and the burly Somali man joins it.

Steps coming up, Dom shouts to the pilots, 'GO, GO, GO.' Door latched, Dom crouches behind us as we pick up speed and take off. We are still at risk from big guns and rocket-propelled grenades . . . but not for long . . .

Up in the air, our relief is indescribable. We look at one another again, sharing a brief moment of euphoria. We've just taken another big step in the direction of freedom. Then we are distracted. It's not a time for tears. Everyone is happy, wanting to talk to us, to tell us things. We have no time to think or reflect.

On the plane, we feel like VIPs. With eight of us on board – two pilots, Dahir, Ahmad and Hussein from the TFG, and Dom – there is a further round of introductions. Everyone is eager to talk and tell us about their role in our release. It's so strange being treated as equals after so long as pawns. Dom – Paul's Superhero Number Two, another man who has boldly risked his life to save ours – takes on the air-hostess role, serving tea and fresh croissants. We sit back into our seats and enjoy the moment.

Dom explains that he is a security consultant and has been working alongside Dahir and Dr Hangul to secure our release. He tells us there is no charge for the plane; in fact, the owner has kept it available for ten days, idle and reserved for our extraction – another kind and generous act. Dom is in charge of the logistics and security, from Adaado to Nairobi. He confirms the prime minister of Somalia's TFG wishes to meet us at Mogadishu airport.

As we approach Mogadishu, we see the sea for the first time in over a year. What a wonderful sight! A deep oceanic blue expanse, with sunlit white breakers on the shore.

Coming in to land, we see first the port and then the war-torn city. After months of being cooped-up inland, cut off from the world, it is an exhilarating feeling to be up in the air, arriving at a new destination from seaward. I think briefly about my last glimpse of *Lynn Rival*.

Our landing is a perfect, gentle touchdown onto a concrete runway. Through the tiny window, we see a heavy presence of uniformed troops from the African Union force. One smiling soldier comes up the steps to greet us. As I get up to walk out, he tells me to wear something on my head. I don't have time to ask why before Dom grabs a red baseball cap and sticks it on me! We're escorted to a waiting Armoured Personnel Carrier, followed by the rest of our planeload. Another APC is nearby, full of media people.

Dom is concerned that we don't waste time now that we have to travel into the city centre to meet the PM – it is too dangerous for the PM to come to the airport! He says we have to get to Nairobi before dusk. Two Ugandan soldiers stand between us, on ammo tins so they can operate the heavy machine guns mounted on the roof. The thick-glass windows are marked with bullet damage, but no holes . . . yet. As we move through the city, we observe the war-scarred landmarks among signs of everyday business. The parliament building, damaged by shelling, reminds me of demolition work in the UK. On the other side of the road, undamaged, clean and white, is the main mosque. After some twisting and turning through checkpoints we arrive at the presidential palace, Villa Somalia.

Hussein keeps up a running commentary on the sights. I'm doing my best to take note of everything we're being told, but so much has happened since dawn, we're in danger of sensory overload! I don't want to forget a thing or fail to appreciate a single second of this gripping experience.

Despite the devastation in Mogadishu, we see shops open and people going about their business as usual. We wonder at how ordinary Somali people live in these conditions.

We're impressed by the friendly and cheerful AMISOM troops. This last year has made me realise how lucky we are to be born in a country with good security and how we take it for granted. These troops are at the sharp end, putting their lives on the line for others, and getting little thanks for it.

Villa Somalia is a small haven in the midst of so much destruction. The buildings are not grand, but intact, and the first well-furnished place we've been in for over a year. The prime minister greets us warmly. He says all the things you'd expect: how sorry he is about our ordeal, that they were doing as much as they could to help us and they are so glad we are free. We meet and shake hands and have photographs taken with the deputy prime minister, the minister of information, the former minister of information, the chief of staff, the Mayor of Mogadishu, the leader of the house . . . They want to hold a press conference, so we agree to answer a few questions.

It's our first real intimation that the whole world and his dog may be interested in Mr and Mrs Ordinary of Tunbridge Wells. There are statements by the prime minister and other dignitaries, to which we respond, expressing our relief and gratitude. Paul says that he's impressed by the airport bus!

Dom calls time, leads us out through the scrum, and we board the APC for the return trip to our plane. Paul has his camera ready and with one hand takes a few pictures as the APC hurtles wildly down the airport road, swerving between the bright red-and-white concrete barriers, the gunners hanging on to their weapons. As we career across a main road junction, Hussein shouts out, 'Kilometre 4 – the most dangerous place in Mogadishu.' Phew! Into the airport. We can breathe again. There's the plane, engines running. We jump out and re-start our escape. There's just time for a few words of thanks to the AMISOM troops.

> As we approach the plane steps, I look back at the airport building. Hussein is next to me. 'Any chance of an exit stamp?' I wonder aloud. 'No problem,' he says, taking my passport and marching off towards the building. By the time he comes back, I have told Rachel, who is rather covetous of the stamp, so Hussein is despatched again with her passport. Finally, we're aboard and safely airborne, hoping to reach Nairobi within three hours, before dark.

Another round of Dom's tea and pastries perks us up. Everyone is relieved that it all went as planned. Dahir tells us the Somali diaspora are arranging a gathering at Heathrow and want to know when we'll be returning. We've no idea what plans will be made for us. Of course we would like to join in his triumphant return, but it's hard to think that far ahead. We don't know what our family have arranged.

> After an hour, we cross the Somali–Kenya border. Now
> we are safe; free, safe and together.

Dom is on the phone again, in discussion with the Kenyan authorities and FCO staff, planning how to avoid the media. Isn't this all a bit OTT? Surely there can't be that much interest? It seems so unlikely that we will be the focus of an army of reporters and camera crews. Dom tells us that we're expected to land at Wilson Airport, the one used by charter planes. As we near Nairobi, he pulls some strings and we land at the military airport. We disembark alone, leaving Dom and the others to fly on to Wilson.

We are soon in the hands of the British High Commissioner, the Defence Attaché and High Commission staff. Another set of names and faces to remember! In response to their warm welcome, we rather desperately respond: where are the toilets? They've been primed and we're escorted – upstairs! – another first – to what seem like palatial facilities: WC cubicles with toilet paper, basins with running hot and cold water, soap, towels and a mirror.

> Emerging back into the cool Nairobi night air, I realise
> that I do now feel free – and safe. The frantic process of
> our release is finally over.

On our way, Rob Macaire, the High Commissioner, tells us about our options. We can stay in Nairobi as long as we like; we can go home as soon as we are ready. Of course we want to get back home as soon as possible. During the short journey, plans are made over the secure communication system on how best to avoid the press pack. Having dodged them at the airport, we now have to run the gauntlet at the Residence. It's dark, but as we enter the compound we see the media a short distance away, watching the wrong gate!

Helen, my niece, is waiting inside – she's her usual blonde, bouncy and very loving self, wearing a bright-red sweatshirt. We hug. Rob introduces his wife, Alice, who invites us to stay as their guests for as long as we need. We're shown into a spacious drawing room and left where we can chat privately with Helen. We hug her tight again then she sits us down, either side of her. There's something she must tell us.

It's the news I have feared; my father died in July. It's not unexpected – he was 99 and a bit. But it's still sad. I ask Helen how her mother, my sister Jill, is faring. Helen is positive. Of course Jill will have coped, but I begin to realise how hard it must have been. And it awakens my hatred of Buggas. That man made my father's last eight months hell.

Helen is our first proper contact with family, and with reality. Now I can begin to think about getting back to normal – and believe it can be achieved. When Helen gives us the news of Paul's father, tears fill my eyes. I can't help but feel sad that he died without knowing we would live. Then I pull myself together, knowing that Pa wouldn't have wanted us to mope. He would have been so happy to know we are free and want us to get on with rebuilding our lives.

The doctor comes next. A visual inspection, a few questions and we're declared 'OK'. Helen shows us our room. It's an enormous suite, with a massive bed, thick mattress and lovely linen, a luxurious bathroom with proper plumbing and a sitting room. We have many welcome gifts. The BHC staff have shopped for clothing and toiletries. Helen has brought more – even some of our stuff from *Lynn Rival*, including a pair of trainers. At last Rachel can wear something other than the trusty, tatty pair of flip-flops commandeered from Paul! We want for nothing.

As the evening wears on, it's even harder to take it all in, especially the news about *Lynn Rival*. She's all taken care of – by Helen and our insurers – and is under wraps at Bucklers Hard. Dare we hope to be able to restore her and go cruising again? It's too soon to know.

We freshen up and go downstairs to do the photo-op wave for the media – a moment Paul's father would have so loved to have witnessed. We take a quick look at the TV news. The main channels are wall-to-wall Paul and Rachel. It adds to the unreality. Us, the lead item on global news bulletins! Is this all a dream?

We make brief phone calls to the rest of the family, too tired and emotional to say much more than, 'We're fine. Don't worry. We're OK.' We just want to see them now, to hug them, to know that they are all really, really OK. We join Rob and his family for a supper of our choice: bangers and mash, avocado salad, fried bananas and pineapple. Paul has his first beer. We talk and talk and talk. It's so wonderful to be surrounded by loving, caring people, but we're now exhausted and running on empty.

Another round of treats follows: a long soak in the bath, then into a lovely bed with soft pillows and crisp linen. To think, 30 hours ago we were in the house in Amaara . . .

> I wake early from a disturbed sleep after our first night of freedom. It's all too much to take in. The subconscious mind is suspicious. It's been let down before. But this time our release is real. I reach out and touch Rachel. Yes, it's real. I have a good cry. Grief. Then I'll be OK. As I get up, Rachel tells me I attacked the table lamp in the night – I can't remember a bit of it! Rachel has a resurgence of tummy problems, so I go down for a full English breakfast and leave her to rest.
>
> When I go downstairs, Paul, Rob and Helen are watching the TV. I'm flabbergasted to see that we're still the main news, along with the release of Aung San Suu Kyi. To see ourselves on TV continues to be a weird experience.

Then I have a long phone call to Stephen. He is so happy he seems almost hysterical. We're also receiving many messages of support from all over the world. It's all so heartening – and so bewildering. I had no idea that so many people would be affected, that they would care so much about what happened to us.

We spend the day relaxing, being cosseted by everyone. The prime minister, David Cameron, phones. He's pleasant and asks me to let him know if there's anything he can do to help. It's a bit late, I think! The BHC helps us issue a statement to the media about my father, requesting space. Rob and Alice, and their daughters and dogs, make us so welcome that it's tempting to stay, but we want to get back to our family in the UK, so we agree with Jim (our FCO minder) that we'll fly tomorrow. I start thinking about practicalities. How can we get mobile? Will our car start? Will any of our bank accounts be operable? Jim is arranging a family reunion at a secure location near Heathrow where we'll be able to stay for a couple of days, then we'll have to learn how to make decisions again!

The next morning I wade through a hearty breakfast. Helen goes out to buy us some coats for our arrival in London. We have no winter clothes and will feel the cold after so long in the tropics.

Soon it's time to say our farewells. We have been so well looked after. I would love to stay longer. Who knows if we'll ever be able to come back? At the airport we're treated like VIPs and taken straight to the plane. Sitting on the tarmac someone deals with our passports and other mundane details – surely a once-in-a-lifetime experience! We are waved off by various High Commission and government officials. By accident or design, the two of us, plus Helen and Jim, have an entire Business Class cabin to ourselves.

Appropriately, my first sip of alcohol for over a year is

a glass of champagne. I must be careful not to overdo it after so long on detox! Finally my tummy has settled down and I enjoy my airline meals all the more – especially the cream tea!

Our touchdown at Heathrow is delayed by fog, dampening our emotional arrival back on British soil. Circling over London we hear of a royal engagement. Hooray! How kind of Prince William and Kate Middleton to replace us in the headlines.

We walk off the plane and transit through the VIP lounge in a matter of minutes before being whisked away. We just do as we're told, like good hostages. We're now fixated on getting back into the real world, being with our family and friends again.

Our family – or rather families – are not what you would call 'close'. We keep in touch to varying degrees, but we are not on each other's doorsteps all the time. We have a healthy respect for one another and can go for weeks, months or even years without phoning! Now they're all here, and we're so happy to see them looking fine, if a little older. There's so much to catch up on. Each has had his or her own experiences, and part to play, during our captivity. We want to know about what's been happening in their lives.

During our stay at the 'safe house', we have a short consultation with a Navy psychiatrist who declares us no less sane than we ever were!

It's a relief to find we've all kept our sense of humour. It's not long before Stephen is telling pirate jokes and everyone is laughing at our tales of gangster antics. We are so lucky to have them all. Our ordeal has taken over their lives, and they have had to deal with the consequences. They've worked together marvellously as a team, doing their best for us and supporting each other.

Paul and I are awakening from our passive roles as hostages at different paces. We're used to being independent, and it's difficult being in this position, reliant on others for information. Paul desperately wants his life back, but there is so much to sort out: our affairs, his father's affairs and *Lynn Rival*. I'm more relaxed and enjoy being pampered. We'll have some difficult decisions to make, and I don't want to rush them.

Amongst the papers given to us are press cuttings: a quick look through confirms the extent of our public exposure. I'm fascinated and daunted. I'm sad when reminded that our lives will never be the same again. What has happened to us is so momentous we will always be 'Paul and Rachel Chandler, ex-hostages'. We'll just have to make the most of it!

The ransom issue weighs heavily on my mind. We're told firmly not to worry about it. More than anything else, our family want us to get on with our lives again and will do what they can to make that possible. It's hard to take in. We half expected them to forbid us to ever go sailing again – though they do joke about buying us an autopilot hardwired so we just keep going round and round the Isle of Wight! Now we can start dreaming about the possibility of restoring *Lynn Rival*. Why not? It's the life we chose.

After two nights in the safe house, we move on, taking our first drive in daylight through the English countryside. Little by little, we learn to be normal again.

Over the next few days we're re-introduced to the delights of shopping, of choosing what to eat and where to go. It's very strange and unfamiliar. We pick up the pieces of life in the UK and find out what has been going on here. I'm excited about our newfound freedom, while trying to focus on the practicalities. There is much to do before we can regain control of our lives and recover in peace. It's hard work, but there is a bonus . . . a reunion with poor old *Lynn Rival* – patiently waiting for us to reclaim her.

It's time for the moment that we never dared to hope for . . .

Lynn Rival

27 November 2010

On a bright autumnal day – 13 months after our capture, a fortnight after our release – we're driving to the Agamemnon Boatyard at Bucklers Hard in the heart of the New Forest. It seems incredible. *Lynn Rival* is safe. While we were being kept in covert locations in the Somali bush, hidden from view, imprisoned by callous ransom-seekers, she too was concealed, shrouded under a tarpaulin in the safe confines of a boatyard associated with Nelson's heroics at Trafalgar. Her location is the best-kept secret on the south coast.

'It's not about the bike,' was how Lance Armstrong famously titled a memoir about his journey back to life from near-terminal illness. For us, it *is* about the boat. As we posted on our cruising blog:

> After a long enforced interlude, we have now 'ticked off'
> Somalia and will soon resume normal service . . .
> Thanks to everyone who has sent emails; we will respond
> to you all soon. We hope to be reunited with *Lynn Rival*
> before long. Special thanks to the Navy for making that
> possible!

And here we are, with the prospect of reunion so close. For us, she's more than a sailing boat. She's our home and our life, providing not just shelter and a means of travel but challenge and adventure. We think of her with the affection one might have for an old friend. She can be demanding in her needs, but so long as we look after her, she provides us with limitless

369

opportunities to achieve that rare thing – contentment.

The last time we saw *Lynn Rival* – when we thought it was *the* last time we would see her – she was bobbing, battered and ransacked, like a toy next to the commercial bulk of the *Kota Wajar*. That last glance down at her, looking forlorn yet noble even in her abandonment, remains seared as a poignant memory. *Lynn Rival* embodies so much happiness. As she was cut adrift, we assumed she would be scuttled to prevent her posing a hazard to shipping. We had seen the warship in the distance but reasoned that large ships can't tow a 38-foot yacht. The thought of her being sunk deliberately and slowly spiralling down to the ocean bed was devastating.

As we progress towards our reunion, we can hardly wait . . . but at the same time we wonder what that first glimpse will be like? What state will she be in? Are we strong enough to cope with the emotional impact of revisiting the scene of our nightmarish ordeal? Is she still 'our' *Lynn Rival* or is she now contaminated, violated by Buggas and his gang's brutality?

Helen is accompanying us for this watershed moment, and it's comforting to have her by our side. We're physically and emotionally exhausted from our ordeal and, since release, living in a cocoon of love and support. After 388 days of hell, we are overwhelmed by people's warmth, their generosity of spirit and all the good news. Of course, it started while we were in Somalia with Superheroes One and Two – as Paul calls them – the men who risked their lives to enable our release. Then we learnt that the Royal Navy brought back *Lynn Rival* and our insurers had transported her to the boatyard, where skilled craftsmen can now help restore her. Our family have looked after our affairs; letting agents have kept our small flat in order. Practicalities aside, we're touched by how many ordinary people are willing us to rebuild our lives. As a cruising couple, we're used to our own company. We love sitting in a busy yacht club, people-watching over a beer or a cup of tea, but we're not used to being the centre of attention. We are surprised and delighted when strangers come up and simply say, 'Welcome home.' As hostages, we've not been treated as human beings ... and we've come back to all this goodwill and compassion. It is a wonderful experience – one that few will ever have – of human nature at its very best.

Our family are protective, anticipating our concerns and gently steering us towards an acceptance that we can regain our lives. They are insistent that the ransom the family raised is not something we are expected to repay in the short term. We aren't going to have to sell off *Lynn Rival*. When we clap eyes on her, we can envisage sailing her again.

Helen leads us into the familiar atmosphere of a working boatyard, and there she is. We feel sheer joy to see her sitting solidly up on wooden props – though strange to see her stripped of mast and rigging. Paul, ever practical, checks her out with his engineer's eye and is relieved to see she is only superficially damaged. Rachel needs to get up the ladder, look her over and go down below deck.

> As I go down the steps and glance around the saloon, there's a tiny, chilling sense that they haven't quite gone ... small flashbacks of memory ... of gangsters sprawling in the saloon, rooting through lockers, loose Scrabble tiles on the floor, grease and rice spilled all over the galley, books and papers strewn ... The feeling passes. I know I'm not fit enough yet, but I feel a surge of energy: I can't wait to get my overalls on and start clearing up! It will take a lot of work to exorcise the ghosts: cleaning, testing and restoring what equipment is left, sourcing and installing replacement kit, general refurbishment. Regular maintenance and improvement are part of her life, and part of ours with her. Until she's shipshape, our 'home' and our cruising life are in limbo, but I'm happy that she will be ours again.
>
> I'm quietly over the moon. Without *Lynn Rival*, our recovery would be much more difficult. She would have been just a bittersweet memory.

The reunion is emotional, but for me not in the way one might think. It's a relief to see that she is not structurally damaged, that all she needs is a lot of TLC. She's bruised and battered, she's been abandoned but never forgotten. Her rigging was unceremoniously cut so she could be plucked from the ocean. Her equipment is wrecked or missing, presumed stolen by brigands. We find a bullet hole right through the boom, but there are no major gashes or holes, just a multitude of scratches on her topsides – and those can be sorted.

When we stripped our small flat, sold most of our belongings and put the rest in storage in order to embark on our cruising life, I felt very keenly – more so than Rachel – the fact that we no longer had a bricks-and-mortar home. *Lynn Rival* was our home . . . and she was taken from us.

But today we can rebuild our home and life. Starting now.

19 December 2010

Blog entry from Owner/Skipper Rachel and Paul Chandler:

A very Happy Christmas to all those who supported us throughout our excursion to Somalia. The kindness of the many well-wishers who have been in touch is both inspiring and uplifting.

We're looking forward to a busy 2011, getting ourselves and *Lynn Rival* back into shape.

Behind the scenes

Distress, search and rescue – a missed opportunity?

We can now cast more light on the events of the first week after the attack, having undertaken some research since our return. Although there is some surmise in the following, the timings and details together give overwhelming support.

It was a surprise to learn, soon after returning to the UK, that our EPIRB had actually been detected and the position of our distress was known. The chain of events that we expected to follow activation of our EPIRB is summarised below:

- The EPIRB sends a distress signal in short bursts, every 50 seconds or so.
- The signal is picked up by a GEOSAR (Geostationary Earth Orbit Search And Rescue) satellite and relayed to earth.
- Within a few minutes, an alert with details of the EPIRB (but not the position) is passed via the UK MCC (Mission Control Centre) at RAF Kinloss to the MRCC (Maritime Rescue Coordination Centre) at Falmouth. *Lynn Rival*'s details and our UK contacts are now known by the authorities.
- Within the next two hours (the average is about forty-five minutes), the signal is picked up by a LEOSAR (Low Earth Orbit Search And Rescue) satellite, which, using Doppler shift measurement, establishes the position of the EPIRB to within about 5 km. This information is issued to both Falmouth, as above, and to the Seychelles coastguard (via the Indian MCC in Bangalore).

- The Seychelles coastguard takes over coordination of search and rescue.
- An EGC (Enhanced Group Call) to all vessels in the area, sent over the Inmarsat satellite communications system.
- Aircraft and coastguard vessel search of the area. (After all, we were less than 60 miles from Mahé.)

As we saw and heard no sign of any vessels or aircraft until the evening of our fifth day under hostile control, we assumed that the twenty minutes for which the EPIRB had been on was insufficient for the position information to be obtained.

What actually occurred was (times are local, four hours ahead of GMT):

- The EPIRB worked and at 0305 (i.e. 35 minutes after the attack) the alert was received at Falmouth.
- By 0355 Falmouth knew the position of *Lynn Rival* to within 5 km. Seychelles assumed search-and-rescue coordination.
- Falmouth checked with our UK contacts and the Seychelles authorities and established that *Lynn Rival* had indeed left Port Victoria the previous morning.
- At 0620, Falmouth noted that Seychelles had not requested an EGC and arranged it themselves.
- At 1331, Seychelles search aircraft reported nothing seen.
- At 1338, Falmouth pointed out to Seychelles that they had sent their plane to the wrong position (ten miles in error). Seychelles reported no further air-based action.
- At 2230, a Seychelles naval vessel was 'expected' to reach the distress position.

So, the EPIRB worked and despite it being on for only a short time the authorities knew our position within an hour and a half of the attack. A search plane was sent to the area eleven hours after the attack, seven and a half hours after dawn. Unfortunately, by then we had motored perhaps 18 miles towards Somalia. Together with the Seychelles error of ten miles, that probably put us out of visual range. If only they had sent the plane soon after dawn, or even if they had revisited to the correct position, surely we would have been found? Of course, it may have made no difference to our ordeal. But the Navy would have had five extra days to mount an enforcement operation: perhaps sufficient time to come up with a plan that would have been successful.

We do not generally expect or rely on outside assistance, as we often sail in areas where SAR facilities are less developed. It is ironic that we were so, so close to a modern port, with access to air and marine resources, yet the system appears to have failed. Had we had a 'normal' accident – perhaps a fire, or striking a submerged container – it could well have been a matter of life or death. The staff at Falmouth did all they could; they did their very best to help us, but at such long range their input was limited.

In this instance, we were alone, missing, presumed lost at sea? For five days. There is an alternative explanation. Perhaps the UK authorities did accept that we had been seized. Maybe they requested that the SAR operation be curtailed so that plans could be developed while lulling the pirates into a false sense of security.

On Tuesday, 27 October 2009 (day five), shortly after the time the seven men left *Lynn Rival*, seven Somali pirates in two skiffs attacked a French trawler, the *Cap Saint Vincent*, and were repulsed by French soldiers on the trawler. According to EUNAVFOR (European Union Naval Force Somalia) reports, they were found by the helicopter from the Spanish warship *ESPS Canarias*, and apprehended by the German warship *FGS Karlsruhe*. The seven are now on trial in Mombasa. There is a possibility that they may also be tried for their part in the attack on *Lynn Rival*.

Just before dusk the same day, we were overflown by a helicopter. As soon as it was heard, Buggas and his two cronies joined us below deck and stayed out of sight. A photograph, which was widely published at the time, shows *Lynn Rival*, making way under sail and engine, taken from above and with no people visible. This is confirmed in an EUNAVFOR press release to have been taken from the military helicopter of *ESPS Canarias*. Captions generally indicated that *Lynn Rival* had been found adrift in that state. That is incorrect. We were at the time below decks, under the guns of three of our attackers.

Why did the Navy not mount an operation? At the time, we hoped and hoped that they would. We believed then and believe now that such operations should be considered as law enforcement, not rescue operations, and that the risk to our lives should not outweigh the benefits of sending a clear message: '*We will not tolerate this activity.*'

It is evident that the rules of engagement of the anti-piracy task forces in the western Indian Ocean are inappropriate. Detention of captured pirates and their trial in Europe is expensive and is likely to result in a stay in a comfortable jail followed by asylum upon release – an outcome the pirates may consider a success. The problem is escalating – attacks are becoming more violent and ransom payments increasing – but while the financial cost of piracy is borne by insurers and ship owners, and the human cost is not seen by Western governments as great, the absence of resolve to deal with the problem is understandable.

At the time, there was considerable coverage in the media, much of it critical of the Royal Navy. This included reports that RFA *Wave Knight*, while closely watching our transfer to the *Kota Wajar* and the abandonment of *Lynn Rival*, was carrying a detachment of Royal Marines, but they were not deployed. Given that our government sees an operation in such circumstances as 'hostage rescue' rather than law enforcement, it is inevitable that in the absence of a suitably trained special-forces team no action was taken.

It was also reported that *HMS Cumberland* arrived at the scene too late to become involved, an SBS squadron having been delayed in transit to the area. The press reports suggest that there was the political will to take action and that a special-forces operation was authorised. Was the window of opportunity just too short? From the time our situation was confirmed to our transfer to the *Kota Wajar*, only 29 hours elapsed. To launch a hostage rescue mission in the middle of the ocean, some 4,000 miles away from home, is something few nations could contemplate. To do it within such a short time unfortunately proved impossible. We believe that our professionals in the Royal Navy did their very best.

What can the government do?

Our case was evidently discussed at high level within government. At an early stage, the Foreign and Commonwealth Office (FCO) took the lead role. Our case was handled as a counter-terrorism matter, rather than as a criminal kidnapping. This meant our family did not have the full benefit of police expertise on kidnapping, as would ordinarily be the case in a criminal matter.

We realise that, once we were within Somalia, the government could do little directly to help us, but they could and should have done more to support our close family members. We were disappointed to learn that the assistance from the FCO was, if anything, negative. The support and advice to our siblings, who were always likely to be on the receiving end of begging phone calls, was distressingly inadequate. The FCO's efforts to keep our family informed were derisory. We have not been made aware of anything helpful being done 'behind the scenes'.

After our release, we received excellent support from the FCO, both in Nairobi and London, up to the point where we were ready to face the outside world. We have cooperated fully with all official requests for debriefing and sincerely hope that lessons will be learned.

Ransom

There has been much media interest in who paid what to whom. Our family have confirmed that $440,000 was air-dropped to the gang on 17 June 2010. They have declined to give us details about who contributed to the sum – choosing to encourage our return to normal life and insisting firmly that there is no expectation of repayment. We respect their desire for privacy and for a return to their own normal lives.

It is likely that more money changed hands at the time of our release. Press speculation as to sources for this last payment includes the Somali Transitional Federal Government and the Somali diaspora. In a report by BBC Security Correspondent Frank Gardner on 15 November 2010, Prime Minister David Cameron was quoted making clear no UK aid money had been diverted to help pay ransom: 'The Government has a policy on ransom payment, which is: we don't do them.'

As we have written, two days before our release Buggas mentioned $200,000 'from my family', which we presume to mean clan – and therefore, perhaps, a sum put forward by (pirate?) elders to resolve the matter and secure our release. We have been unable to cast any further light on this.

Irrespective of whether any money was paid for our eventual release, we are grateful to all who played a part in achieving our freedom.

Chaos, children and superheroes – how our freedom was gained

Chaos theory explains how the fluttering of a butterfly's wings in the mountains of the Andes can trigger a chain of events leading to thunderstorms in Britain. Incongruous as it may seem, in truth it was a call from a young boy in East London to his adored father, then in Brussels recovering from minor surgery, which started the process that led to our release.

In the spring of 2010, Yusuf Kadiye asked his father to help – he was too ashamed of his countrymen to play football with his mates. Dahir flew straight to Nairobi, to see what he could do.

It was always apparent to us that the gulf between the gang's expectations and the amount of money that could be raised was unbridgeable. There needed to be pressure from the elders of the clan, sufficient to overcome the reluctance of Buggas to accept a lower sum and loss of face. The longer things went on, the harder it became for Buggas to concede defeat – he had already spent a lot of money guarding us and would be seen as a complete failure by his gangsters and peers alike.

Buggas and his men are of the Suleiman branch of the Habar-Gedir, a sub-clan of the Hawiye. Dahir is also Suleiman; he had been a successful businessman in central Somalia before the collapse of governance, and his family are still much respected in the Himan and Heeb area, where Buggas operated. So Dahir, working completely under cover, started to awaken old ties and friendships. For six months, based first in Nairobi, then in Mogadishu, he built a network of contacts and informers, often the parents and grandparents of the young pirates and gangsters. His cover story was the establishment of a trading business. Our family knew nothing.

As his plan progressed, Dahir worked with Dr Hangul, also Suleiman, who is well respected and enjoys a certain freedom of movement in central Somalia. Finally, Dom joined the triumvirate, providing the essential security and logistics know-how for the extraction. It was vital to maintain secrecy until near the end; in Britain, the only person who knew what was going on was Liban, Dahir's elder son. Only on 5 November, nine days before our release, did Dahir make contact with Stephen.

The rest, as they say, is history. Yusuf and Liban can hold their heads high and be very proud of their father.

Postscript

2011: The ex-hostage learning curve

At first, the euphoria of our release kept us going. We were physically unfit from so little activity and went to the gym to recover our lost muscles. Everything was strange – sometimes exciting, occasionally annoying – with so many explanations required to sort out our personal affairs. We soon left behind our simple life as hostages, where all we had had to do was stay alive. Eventually we got back in control of our lives but few people understood that we wouldn't feel normal again until we resumed cruising on *Lynn Rival*. The interest in us – and wariness of some because of what we've been through – has become part of our lives. When we got down to writing the book after six months of freedom and cosseting by our family, we had to dig deep at times, but the process allowed us to share our experiences. It was not until later in the year, when invited to appear before a parliamentary select committee, that we felt the authorities were interested in learning lessons from our case.

Our goal was always to restore *Lynn Rival* and return to our cruising life as soon as possible. She was battered, bruised and ransacked but structurally sound. After a long process of preparing estimates for damage and missing items, we reached a settlement with our insurers. We then brought *Lynn Rival* overland to a Dartmouth boatyard and started work. As practical boat owners we have done as much of the refurbishment ourselves as possible. It was therapeutic as well as economic! We relaunched in September 2012 and are heading for the south Atlantic.

For us the last two years have been filled with happiness. Life isn't fair and what happened to us was horrific but not a day goes by without us thinking how lucky we are to have been born in a peaceful and secure country.

Organisations and areas referred to

Ahlu Sunna Wal Jama'a: association of Islamic militias opposed to al-Shabaab's terrorism

Al-Shabaab: Islamist terrorist group fighting the TFG, et al.

AMISOM: African Union 'peace-keeping' force in Somalia, supporting the TFG

Habar-Gedir: sub-clan of Hawiye

Hawiye: one of the four large Somali clans

Himan and Heeb: administrative region of central Somalia – capital Adaado

Puntland: semi-autonomous region of north-east Somalia

Somaliland: independent (but unrecognised) region to the north-west of Somalia

Suleiman: sub-sub clan of Habar-Gedir

TFG: the UN-recognised Transitional Federal Government of Somalia

Acknowledgements

We are grateful to everyone who encouraged us in this endeavour and especially those who provided material, including Stephen Collett for transcripts of phone calls, Dr Hangul for the recovery of Rachel's diary and Ed Campbell for video footage and transcripts.

Thanks also to our agents, David Luxton and Rebecca Winfield, for their input, and to those who assisted us in the writing and editing, including The Lamb at Hindon for their hospitality.

Above all we've appreciated the help and guidance of Sarah. While the story is all ours, she is responsible for setting the scene and weaving together our separate accounts in a very short time. Her gentle probing and prompting on the many difficult emotional issues has helped us explain these as fully as possible. And without her professional approach in arbitrating between our different styles and approaches to storytelling we would still be squabbling over the first hundred pages.

Paul and Rachel Chandler

This book has been an intense writing project with a tight deadline, and I must thank Brian and Disie Johnson for inviting me to start my part of the process in the peaceful beauty of Fonte Pitacchio. Thanks, too, to the London Library for its air of industriousness and to Gill Ross for a desk and some quiet space down the road from home.

A meeting with Dahir Abdullahi Kadiye and his son Liban provided new insights and background detail into Paul and

Rachel's eventual release. Many thanks for their time and salutary perspective on life in the failed state of Somalia. Stephen Collett, too, gave me some indication of his role as negotiator on behalf of the family.

Thanks to Bill Campbell for his support and to Ailsa Bathgate for so meticulously going through the manuscript. David Luxton and Rebecca Winfield have been unstinting in their encouragement and jovial hospitality along the way, as well as being valuable sounding boards in the matter of 'voices' as they read the manuscript. Anthony Gardner must be hailed as a brilliant and sensitive reader who helped us judiciously trim our second draft. I am grateful for valuable feedback from Patrick and Elizabeth Edworthy. Finally, mythanks to Isabella, Alexander and Emily for their patience, and to Rory both for urging a perfectionist approach to the business of writing and for doing more than his fair share of dog walks.

Sarah Edworthy

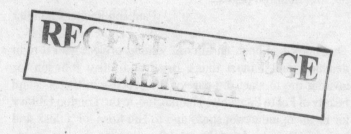